the Path of Truth

Volume I

SUNDAY SCHOOL AND DISCIPLESHIP MINISTRIES

The Path of Truth
Published by
Mesoamerica Region Discipleship Ministries

Cover design: Samuel Marroquin
Interior Design: Samuel Marroquin and Jerson Chupina

Translated into English from Spanish by:
Dr. Dorothy Bullon
Yadira Morales

ISBN: 978-1-63580-015-9

Table of Contents

Presentation

The Path of Truth has been for many years the book that has helped us in the preparation of Sunday School classes for youth and adults. In this edition, through the four quarters, students will learn about: how we got the Bible and generalities of it; basic themes of our Christian faith; taking care of our body as the Holy Spirit's temple; and a challenging quarter studying men and women who traveled in obedience to a call from God.

Today we're introducing a renewed book. Generally, it's said that a person listening to a presentation retains 80% during the first twelve minutes of class, but only 20% during the remaining time. The lecture approach promotes mental passivity even of the best students.

For that reason, we've put our efforts into developing a more dynamic and interactive book. In the middle of the lessons are included some questions you can use to make the class more participatory. And at the end of each lesson you'll find an additional activity that can be used during the lesson at a time of your choosing. As the teacher, you must find ways to involve your students in the learning process. You must not waste any opportunity to make them think, to respond to the received information and to share their own experiences and concerns.

All this will be beneficial, because they'll not only have those truths obtained by their own exposure to those truths, but they can also learn from the ideas and applications of their fellow students. At the same time, they'll be using more of their senses and mental functions to learn. As their leader in teaching of God's Word, you must involve your students in the learning process. This will force you to create activities that require them to think about the subject, to react to the information presented to them during class, and make it an experience of their Christian life.

As result of this process, they can incorporate into their lives the received truths, implement them, and share them with others. These truths, when staying in their hearts and becoming a part of their daily lives, will help them be a living example of Christ among us.

God continue to bless you.

Patricia Picavea
Editor of Departmental Publications

Recommendations

Being a Sunday School teacher is a privilege that God gives us. It's also a great responsibility. The privilege comes of have been taught first, and the responsibility is to teach others what we have received (Matthew 28:20). If we understand well the dynamics of discipleship, the responsibility won't scare us, but we'll enjoy the privilege and we'll train constantly to form Christ in others.

We encourage you to study each lesson carefully and in advance. That way, you'll have a better grasp of each topic and with contributions from other people, without any doubt, it will be a time of spiritual growth. Below are some suggestions:

Preparation of the Lesson:

1. Pray to the Lord asking him for the wisdom and discernment to understand the scriptures you'll study, applying them to your life first. Also, pray, asking that your students will be receptive to the teaching of God´s Word.

2. Prepare a place without distractions for studying the lesson, where you have a table or a desk. It's important to have some tools like paper, pens, pencils, eraser, etc.

3. Besides the book, The Path of Truth, have an English dictionary, a Bible dictionary and some good Bible commentaries.

4. Read the lesson of the Path of Truth as often as necessary at the beginning of the week. This will help you to prepare the materials you'll need for the class, and to be attentive to news and other information that you could include in the lesson that you're preparing.

5. Look at the Bible and read each passage indicated.

6. Read the purpose of the lesson to know where to direct to your students.

7. Write on a sheet of paper the name of the lesson and the points that will be developed. Then, type the title of the first point and develop your own summary as you study the lesson. Write and highlight biblical quotations that will be read during class.

8. Write the meaning of unknown words, so you can better understand the lesson, and you can explain to people who will ask you about them.

9. Make comparative tables to analyze and compare the study points. For example, if the topic of the lesson is: Purpose of the Gospel, you can draw a picture like this:

Gospel	Author: Name and Important Facts	Date Written	Receiver(s)	Purpose

10. Read the section "Resources." There you'll find several aids you can consider using. Among them are:
    - "Additional Information": This information does not necessarily need to be shared with the class, but can serve to increase your knowledge and understanding of the lesson.
    - "Definition of Terms": There you'll find the definition of some important words.
    - "Additional activity": You'll find dynamic, brief questionnaires, case studies or other ideas that you can use to present the topic.

11. If you research on the Internet, take care that information pages are reliable. Remember that the Internet is an open space where everyone can upload the information they want. Unfortunately, not all the information that is there is accurate and reliable.

12. Prepare lessons in the most dynamic and participatory way as possible. This is a very special time where sharing experiences will help enrich the learning process. By doing so, people are more interested in class; people will remember more of that which they have participated in or what they did together; and they'll appreciate being heard and participating.

Lesson Presentation:

1. Arrive early to your class. It's important that you be there when the first person arrives.
2. Position the chairs in a half circle, circle, groups, etc. This will help the group feel more comfortable in participating.
3. Prior to the lesson, welcome your students. This allows you to create a pleasant learning environment. Take interest in people and pray for those in need.
4. Begin the class with prayer, asking the Lord to help all of you understand His Word and obey and apply the truths to your lives.
5. Write the lesson title and text to memorize on the board. Read the text several times with your students to memorize it. Once you start the lesson, write the main points of the lesson at one end of the board. This will allow you to view the sequence of points that you'll teach.
6. Make the introduction as attractive as you can. Try to vary it in each class.
7. Explain in order the development of the subject. Write the title of point I and begin to explain. Use the board as a teaching resource to annotate keywords, etc. When you finish point I, write the title of point II and so on.
8. You can divide your class into working groups to answer questions or discuss the point. This will allow everyone to participate. Don't force anyone to participate, but make sure everyone knows you like and appreciate the contribution of each of them. On the other hand, don't let one person dominate the discussion. In a friendly way, help the class to listen to the opinions of others.
9. Spend a few minutes discussing how to apply the biblical truths to our daily life.
10. Read the conclusion and motivate your students to study at home during the week, following the biblical texts of the lesson. Invite them to attend next Sunday. Encourage them to invite others to the Sunday School class. Finish the class with prayer

Other Suggestions:

1. Goals and Awards: You can offer a simple prize for students during each quarter if 1) they learn all the memory verses and say it to the class, and 2) attend each class on time, 3) etc...
2. Certificate: If you wish, you can give a certificate with the name of the students who were faithful in attendance and not absent more than one or two classes in the quarter. This may give the idea that their learning is progressing and can motivate others to attend faithfully.
3. Review Lesson: In each quarter, lesson 13 is for review. This will allow you to give an overview of the subject of the quarter.
4. During the second quarter, "What do we believe?" you'll find lesson number 18, "Atonement, grace and regret", that you can use on Palm Sunday and the lesson number 25, "The Resurrection, Judgment, and Destiny" that you can use on Easter Sunday. Check the calendar and change the order of lessons so that these lessons will be taught on those special days of Holy Week.
5. During the fourth quarter, "Travels with Purpose," you'll find lesson number 46, "The Journey That Preserved Our Lives." This lesson can be used for Christmas time.
6. Enjoy the class and let your class enjoy it also. Trust in the Lord and pray that every word reaches the hearts of your students.

Learning About Our Bible

Preparation and Preservation of the Bible
Languages and Translations of the Bible
Overview of the Old Testament
The Pentateuch
The Historical Books
The Poetic and Wisdom Books
The Major and Minor Prophets
Overview of the New Testament
The Gospels and Acts
The Epistles of Paul
The Universal Letters
Revelation
The Book of Books

The Writing and Preservation of the Bible

Lesson 1

Eduardo Aparicio (USA)

> **Memory Verse:** "Heaven and earth will pass away, but my words will never pass away." Matthew 24:35.
>
> **Lesson Goal:** That students understand that the Bible was written by many authors inspired by the Holy Spirit of God and preserved by him through the years.

Introduction

In Matthew 24:35 (Mark 13:31; Luke 21:33), Jesus Christ tells us, "Heaven and earth will pass away, but my words shall not pass" And so it is. God spoke and then the sacred authors wrote that divine word. Despite the time that elapsed, the Word of God remains today and will remain until the Lord's return.

The word "Bible" comes from the Greek "Biblion," meaning collection or library. So the book that Christians call "Bible" is really the grouping of 66 books; 39 of them are the Old Testament and 27 are the New Testament.

The 66 books were written over the course of hundreds of years (approximately 1,500) by more than twenty authors inspired by God. Most of them didn't meet personally. However, all the books show us one God who is teaching his way of relating to human beings and his plan of salvation for humanity. In this lesson, we'll learn relevant aspects of the history of how the Bible was written and how it came to us.

I. The Bible: A collection of books inspired by God

The apostle Paul told Timothy, "All Scripture is inspired by God and profitable for teaching, for reproof, for correction, for instruction in righteousness ..." (2 Timothy 3:16).

We understand that inspiration is the special capacity that the Holy Spirit gave the holy authors to receive the truth of God, put it in writing, and communicate it to others without error. Thanks to this participation of the Holy Spirit, we can say that the Bible is the Word of God.

A. The Bible - how it was written?

The Bible as written word began with the work of Moses, who is credited with having written the first five books of our holy scriptures.

With the passage of time, the Lord raised up other servants such as Joshua, David, Solomon, Ezra, Nehemiah, Isaiah, Jeremiah, Zechariah, Malachi, among others, who in the stories of the Old Testaments put into writing the religious experiences of Israel before the time of Christ.

They showed their faith in the one God, creator of the universe, who revealed himself and led his people with his covenants, laws, and promises. This people was unified by faith in the true God amid times of difficulties, disgrace, victories, and prosperity, strengthening their faith by being continually challenged with the demands of holiness, justice and brotherhood. These men wrote the history of Israel in light of their faith, the teachings of the prophets, the wise teachers, individual and community prayers, and reflections of inspired poets.

After the first coming of our Lord Jesus Christ, his disciples and believers committed themselves to passing on the historical truth of that coming, and put into writing his life, passion, resurrection and departure to heaven, and the announcement of his second coming.

Luke and Paul, who didn't have the privilege of walking with the Master during his ministry, but had a personal experience of conversion, were inspired to record the first steps of the Christian church. They also wrote about the implications of the revelation in Christ for those who came from "darkness to the marvelous light" either as practitioners of Judaism or "pagan Gentiles" who were far away from knowing God's will.

Of course, those Christians had no idea that their writings would be considered sacred. Over time, Christianity, through a process that lasted centuries, was bearing witness to the divine inspiration of the stories, letters and visions of Mark, Matthew, John, Luke, Paul, Peter and Judas.

B. The Bible - how did it come to us?

How is it that we can now read the Bible printed on paper or in electronic format? We know that the invention of printing was done nearly fourteen centuries after the first coming of Jesus, and that computers have been around for about the last thirty years.

On the other hand, we also know that the sacred writers couldn't speak or read English. So, how is it that we have God's Word in our language? What was the process that took place so that we can say that our English Bible is the inspired Word of God? The answers to these questions have to do with the love for God and His Word by those who at the time participated in the process of copying and translation of the Scriptures. Men and women who were willing to give a life of discipline and commitment to preserve the form and content of the original writings.

On the one hand, we're indebted to the Jewish community for the preservation of the writings of the Old Testament. We must also thank the Lord for the work done by those who had the responsibility of translating the writings of the New Testament from Greek into other languages.

II. The Bible: The result of hard and conscientious work

We don't have the original manuscripts of the sacred authors of the Old and New Testaments. Why? The materials upon which the Word of God was written eventually disintegrated.

Before the invention of printing and modern paper, the most common writing materials, and also the most expensive, were papyrus and parchment.

Papyrus: It was a water plant. Through a special process, the plant was crushed and rolled together and dried, forming a kind of paper.

Parchment: This was tanned and polished animal skins. It was tougher than papyrus and was also easier to write on.

Both of these were materials that required special care, since moisture and mold were bitter enemies. Divine providence made it that weather conditions were favorable for the preservation of many of the scrolls. Also, the work of those in charge of preserving the sacred writings made possible that the scriptures were preserved from generation to generation.

Aside from the physical aspects, it's also the fidelity of copying letter by letter to produce new documents. For example, in biblical times there was a profession of "amanuensis". These were members of the priestly class who copied the Word of God from an old roll of papyrus or parchment to a new papyrus or parchment scroll.

(At this point, if you wish you can share the rules followed by the clerks to do their job and copy the Bible from the supplementary information section.)

Archaeological discoveries (in 1947 and 2005) in the caves of Qumran of fragments of scrolls written between 250 B.C. and 66 A.D. have demonstrated the accuracy of the work of the copy clerks, since no significant differences were found between those texts and what we read in our Bibles today.

So in this process we see another of the ministries of the Holy Spirit. He not only inspired the sacred authors to write the Word faithfully, but he also inspired scribes to copy exactly the message that God gave his people.

For that reason, we affirm that the copies that the scribes made are reliable or credible.

Conclusion

The Bible is a collection of 66 books written by men inspired by the Holy Spirit, whose teachings and promises never pass away. We must live according to God's original purpose and what it teaches us.

Resources

Additional information

The rules that scribes (amanuenses) followed in order to do their job and copy the Bible were:

1. Before copying, they had to bathe and put on special clothes. They used papyrus rolls that were only prepared by Jews. And if they had to use parchment, they could only use leather from ceremonial clean animals.
2. The ink had to be black. They prepared the ink from a secret recipe.
3. As they worked, they had to keep silent. They didn't write anything from memory. Their responsibility was to copy the message of the Word of God as it was in the original document.
4. The distance between a point and the next should not be more than the thickness of a hair. They are written in columns, and each line or row of the column had to fit 30 letters. Each column must not have less than 48 nor more than 60 lines.
5. When writing the name "Yahweh" (Jehovah) they had to change pen and ink, because Yahweh is the sacred name of God. Some historians say they also had to wash their hands.
6. Nothing should interrupt the amanuensis while copying the name of Yahweh.

They had to be very careful so that the copied text had the same number of letters as the original document. If they had more or less letters than the original, the parchment or papyrus was burned.

Definition of Terms

* **Papiro:** Water bush, grown in swamps and ponds (Job 8:11 Isaiah 35:7) throughout ancient Egypt ... had its roots in the mud, its thick, triangular cane was 6cm around, and it stood between 3 and 6 meters tall. The roots were food for the poor. From the fiber of the cane were made sandals, dresses, baskets (Exodus 2:3) and even boats (Isaiah 18:2a).

   From 3000 B.C., a papyrus paper was produced in Egypt from a special process. After the bark was detached, the interior fibers were cut into strips of 32 to 36 cm long and they were put side by side on a base of hardwood. Other strips overlapped transversely, and then pressure was put on the strips, as well as water and starch. Once dried, polished and softened, these white sheets of papyrus lasted quite awhile. They were treated with oil, and they yellowed over time. About twenty sheets of papyrus glued together formed a long strip that could be rolled into a scroll. (Illustrated Dictionary of the Bible, USA: 1983 Caribbean, p.485).

* **Parchment:** (derived from the name of Pergamum, an ancient city whose kings encouraged the making of this material in which texts were written). It was more durable and expensive than papyrus material, and it has been around since 300 B.C. The preference was to make them from the processed skins of calves, sheep or goats, but skins from adult cows and pigs were also used.

   The skins were subjected to a bath in lime that took off the hair. They were then washed and scraped, and finally stretched and covered with white lead (basic lead carbonate used for paints). The final color was white, but could be dyed with saffron or purple paint (Illustrated Bible Dictionary, Caribbean, p.504).

Additional activity

Dynamic: Making a Story

Objective: Explain in a practical way that the extraordinary thing about the Bible is that it was written by different people, at different times and yet keeps a singular logic and sequence.

Time: No more than 10 minutes.

Activity: Have the class sit in a circle. Then you tell the beginning of the story, "Mary ran". They must continue to build on the story that they'll make up. Each person must add a word or two, no more, that is related to what was said before. Once all have finished, ask if it was easy to make up a story working as a group that way, and if they imagined that it would end the way it did.

Languages and Translations of the Bible

Eduardo Aparicio (USA)

Memory Verse: "They read from the Book of the Law of God, making it clear and giving the meaning so that the people understood what was being read." Nehemiah 8:8

Lesson Goal: That students understand the care of the Holy Spirit for God's Word to be translated into other languages and thus get the gospel to the ends of the earth.

Introduction

Bring to class magazines, books or Bibles written in three or four different languages. Give materials to the students as they come to class and have them read the material. If they don't know these languages, ask them: "what should we do to understand these materials that are written in different languages?" No doubt the answer will be that they need a translator or interpreter.

Explain to them that this is what happened to God's people in the time of Ezra when they found the Law or God's Word in the rubble. The people gathered to hear the reading of the law that was written in Hebrew, but they didn't understand because almost everyone spoke Aramaic. For that reason, Ezra appointed interpreters, and God's Word says, "... They read from the Book of the Law of God, making it clear and giving the meaning so that the people understood what was being read." (Nehemiah 8: 8).

To understand the Bible message, which was originally written in Aramaic, Hebrew and Greek, many servants of God translated it into different languages, including English. Thanks to their work, we can read and understand in our language the message of salvation that God has for us today.

Bible is a Greek word that means "collection or library." As we saw in the previous class, it contains many books written at different times and by different people. We could say that it's like a small library contained in a single book. Besides being one of the most read books in the history of humanity, it's been translated into 2303 languages and dialects. It's the book that keeps faith alive for Jews and Christians in different parts of the world.

Take some time to talk with the class about: What the Bible is for them?

I. The Original Languages of the Scripture

The Bible was written in three languages: The Old Testament in Hebrew and Aramaic and the New Testament in Greek.

A. Aramaic

Aramaic (from the Hebrew, Aramí, that means ¨land of Aram¨) it's a Semitic language with a history of at least three thousand years. Some sections of Old Testament were written in Aramaic; by example: Jeremiah 10:11; Daniel 2: 4-7: 28; Ezra 4: 8-6: 18; 7: 12-26.

Furthermore, through biblical evidence, we know that Aramaic was the language of the Assyrian diplomacy (2 Kings 18:26, Isaiah 36:11).

In the New Testament we find a few words and phrases in Aramaic; such as "Talitha koum" (Mark 5:41); Ephphatha (Mark 7:34); Eli, Eli, lema sabachthani? (Matthew 27:46); Abba (Mark 14:36). It was probably the language spoken by Jesus.

B. Hebrew

The Old Testament was written in Hebrew. Originally this term was used to designate the persons who belonged to God's people, but it was used later to refer to language of the people. The Jews called the Hebrew language, "the language of Canaan" (Isaiah 19:18) or "the language of Judah" (Isaiah 36:11).

The Hebrew alphabet consists of 22 consonants. The vowel sounds were not written because they understood when they saw the word. It was not until the year 800 A.D. that the school of Masoretes (Jews who replaced the scribes in the responsibility of making reliable copies of the Holy Scriptures), developed a system to indicate vowel sounds.

C. Greek

Just as Hebrew is the language in which Old Testament was written, Greek is the language of New Testament. Alexander the Great, king of Macedonia, promoted throughout the Roman

Empire the use of Greek. In this way, the language became the means of communication commercially, culturally and in literature throughout the Roman Empire, including Palestine. It's for this reason, that the writers of New Testament wrote the teachings of Jesus Christ in Greek.

II. Translations and Versions of the Scriptures

What is a version? According to the dictionary, version is a translation.

God didn't want the salvation message to be proclaimed only in Aramaic, Hebrew and Greek. His purpose was to have his message of liberty to be known throughout the world and proclaimed in every language. For this to be fulfilled it was and is necessary to translate the Bible into all the languages of the world.

A. First Translation of the Old Testament

The Septuagint (LXX) or seventies version, was the first translation of the Old Testament into Greek. Why? The Jews who were scattered throughout the known world of that time, lived in countries and cultures where Greek was the common language. For them and for future generations, it was easier to think, speak and read Greek. It was therefore natural that they would prefer to read the Bible in their common language.

B. The Bible's Latin translations

1. The Old Latin. It includes all Latin versions of the Old and New Testaments. It's likely that in the late second century AD they translated the Septuagint (Old Testament) into Latin. Years later

the New Testament was translated into Latin directly from Greek.

2. The Vulgate. By 200 AD several Latin versions of the Bible circulated. It was in 383 AD that Eusebius Hieronymus, now known as Jerome, reviewed all of the commonly used Latin versions of Bible and the result of that work is known as the "Vulgate" or common version.

C. How Do the Teachings of this Lesson Help My Life?

In Mark 13:31 Jesus said, "Heaven and earth will pass away, but my words will never pass away." That means that nothing will stop God's Word from being known throughout the world.

Now that we know how the Bible came to us, we should read it with renewed interest, so we have a spiritual revival within us, and also so that we can share it with our friends and neighbors so they can know the message of salvation, like it was in the days of Nehemiah 8:1-9.

If many have given their lives to translate and proclaim God's Word, what is stopping us from talking with our family about the message of salvation?

Conclusion

In our world, there are men and women who have fought, suffered and sometimes given their lives so that God's Word could be heard. That is part of the history of this book we have and read at home and in church: The Bible.

Resources

Additional Information:

Interesting facts about the Bible:

1. In the year 600 AD, the Roman Catholic Church made a decree that the Bible was to be read only in Latin.

2. In 1454 John Gutenberg invented the printing press, and the Bible was the first book printed.

3. The original texts (Hebrew, Aramaic and Greek) from the Old and New Testament were not divided into chapters and verses. Over time, certain divisions were introduced, but were strange, complicated and none of them were universally recognized. In 1206, at the University of Paris, professor and cardinal Stephen Langton, divided the whole Bible in roughly equal chapters. His system of division was used because of its clarity. However, it was not until 1555 that Robert Estienne indicated the "verses" in the margin. In 1565, Theodore de Beze introduced the indication of the

verses within the text itself. The division into "chapters-verses" of "Langton-Estienne" was officially recognized.

Definition of terms:

Septuagint: This name comes from the legend of Aristeas, according to which 72 Jews prepared the translation in 72 days. But the Septuagint is the result of a much slower process. The Pentateuch was translated in 250 B.C. and gradually the other books were completed in 150 BC (Illustrated Bible Dictionary, Caribbean editorial, p.655).

Supplementary Activity

Reflection for Class

Read with students Nehemiah 8:1-9. Then ask, what were the reactions of people in the reading of the Law of Moses? (They listened attentively (vv.3 and 5). They understood (v.8).)

It is important when we go to the Scriptures, to listen and pay attention so that we better understand this special book.

Overview of the Old Testament

Eduardo Aparicio (USA)

Lesson 3

> **Memory Verse:** "We also have the prophetic message as something completely reliable, and you will do well to pay attention to it ..." 2 Peter 1:19a.
>
> **Lesson Goal:** That student learns generalities of the Old Testament and its message for the church today.

Introduction

Begin by asking the following questions to get an idea of how much the class knows about the subject.

- What is the Old Testament?
- How was it created?
- How did it get to us today?
- How were the first events preserved?

I. Formation of Old Testament

The formation of Old Testament has two periods: the oral and the written.

Oral Period: At first, there was no paper, and the Jews had not developed an alphabet, but they, like most Eastern cultures, kept their records in the collective memory. The Jewish people, didn't have a written language, but they were storytellers. They held on to their history by telling stories from generation to generation. Today it's thought that songs were remembered the most in the hearts of the people, and that they are the original stories that were best preserves in the memories of the people.

Written Period: Books began to be written between 1200 and 900 BC. Possibly during the reign of King David writing was given greater importance and gradually the old stories/songs were written on scrolls. At first, several individuals wrote and circulated separate scrolls. Around the year 300 B.C. a collection of manuscripts was found, which we know today as the Pentateuch, these make up the first five books of the Bible.

Around the year 200 B.C. a second collection was created which would come to be called "the prophets". And finally "the writings" appeared in which all historical books, poetic literature, and minor prophets were included.

By the time of Jesus, the Jews considered these 24 books divine and today they make up the Jewish Canon. Without much evidence, it's said that at the end of the first century B.C., the Jews gathered in Jamnia (Jewish school of that time), and in what some call the Council of Jamnia, they ratified the 24 books. In content, they are the 39 books of the Old Testament that we have today, but they were organized differently.

It was not a quick and easy process, but it was a great work that lasted about 1300 years, until it was unified and formed into what we now know as the Old Testament.

II. The Term Old Testament

A. How long has the term "Old Testament" been known?

Professor Merril F. Unger says the following: "The terms 'Old Testament' and 'New Testament' have been used since the end of the second century to distinguish the Hebrew Scriptures from the Christian scriptures.

The formal collection of Christian writings made in the second half of the second century was called the 'New Testament" (New Bible Handbook, USA: 2002 Unilit, p.9). From then on, the Hebrew Scriptures were called the 'Old Testament'. The use of the term testament refers to covenant, hence Old Testament means the old covenant that God made with the people of Israel.

B. Titles Given to OT in the New Testament.

In the time of Jesus, the Old Testament was the only book recognized as sacred and inspired by the Holy Spirit and some of the titles given to it include:

1. Our Lord Jesus Christ and his disciples called it "the Scriptures" (Matthew 21:42; Mark 14:49; Luke 24:32; John 5:39; Acts 18:24; Romans 15: 4). "The law of Moses, the Prophets and the Psalms" (Luke 24:44).

2. The apostle Paul spoke of the Old Testament

as "the Holy Scriptures" (2 Timothy 3:15; Romans 1: 2).

3. Other titles include: "The law or the Prophets" (Matthew 5:17; 11:13; Acts 13:15). The shortest title: "the Law" (John 10:34; 12:34; 15:25; 1 Corinthians 14:21).

III. The Order of O.T. books

Two divisions of the O.T. are known: The Hebrew Canon is divided into three sections and the Christian Old Testament is divided into 5 sections.

A. Jewish Division

The Law, The Prophets and The Writings.

1. The Law (Torah) is the first five books: Genesis, Exodus, Leviticus, Numbers and Deuteronomy.

2. The Prophets (Nebhiim). The prophets before the captivity: Joshua, Judges, I & II Samuel, I & II Kings. The post-captivity prophets: Isaiah, Jeremiah, Ezekiel, and the 12 minor prophets (because they are shorter books): Hosea, Joel, Amos, Obadiah, Jonah, Micah, Nahum, Habakkuk, Zephaniah, Haggai, Zechariah and Malachi.

3. The Writings (Ketubhin). Job, Psalms, Proverbs, Song of Songs, Ruth, Lamentations, Ecclesiastes, Esther, Daniel, Ezra and Nehemiah (as one book), I & II Chronicles.

B. Christian Division

The Christian community has determined to divide the Old Testament into five parts, traditionally the divisions have been taught as follows:

1. The Pentateuch: The first five books of Bible: Genesis, Exodus, Leviticus, Numbers and Deuteronomy.

2. Historical Books: These books begin with the entry of Israel into the Promised Land narrated by the book of Joshua and the next books: Judges, Ruth, I & II Samuel, I & II Kings, I & II Chronicles, Ezra, Nehemiah and Esther.

3. Wisdom and Poetry Books: These books describe and illustrate the poetry, wisdom and worship of the people of Israel. They are: Job, Psalms, Proverbs, Ecclesiastes and Song of Songs.

4. Major Prophets: These books have been so called, not because of their theological content, but by the extension of the oracle. These books are: Isaiah, Jeremiah, Lamentations, Ezekiel & Daniel.

5. Minor Prophets: We have in this division twelve prophets, these books complete the 39 books of the Old Testament: Hosea, Joel, Amos, Obadiah, Jonah, Micah, Nahum, Habakkuk, Zephaniah, Haggai, Zechariah and Malachi.

IV. The Message of the O.T.

What is the message of the Old Testament? Does it's message have any relevance to us who are part of the church of Christ? First, we'll summarize the message of the Old Testament according to the thematic division. Second, we'll see the relevance of the message for us today.

A. Summary of the O.T.'s Message

1. *The Pentateuch:* It tells us that Jehovah is the only Creator of the heavens, earth and all living things (Genesis 1-2). Man disobeyed and that brought enormous consequences for man-kind, it highlights man's sin and God's mercy, a God who forgives and saves. Jehovah is the only holy God who deserves worship and obedience.

   He chose a people, Israel to manifest through them all his glory, care, grace and salvation to all mankind.

2. *Historical Books:* These books reveal a God who fulfills the promises he makes to his people, who works in human situations, fulfilling His redemptive purpose. They contain fascinating stories and messages.

3. *The Wisdom and Poetic Books:* They present a perspective of evil and the integrity of a man who followed God in the book of Job. The book of Psalms is known as the hymnal of the Israelites. Proverbs presents an excerpt from the popular wisdom of Israelite scholars. Ecclesiastes warns us that if we do not put God first, all is in vane. And finally, the Song of Songs, is a message that shows the love of a couple, conjugal love that does not escape what God instituted in the Garden of Eden.

4. *Major and Minor Prophets:* They describe morally critical periods, a spiritual decline in all spheres. But they also present men called by God to denounce the social evils, injustices, sin and God's judgment. These prophets also warned the people of their condition and what was going to happen as a result of their behavior, they acted as watchmen for the people of Israel. The Old Testament ends with the Israelites returning back in their homeland after a period of captivity.

B. The Relevance of the OT's Message for Today:

Of course, the message of the Old Testament is relevant to us today. The reasons are:

1. Paul said in 2 Timothy 3:16: "All Scripture is inspired by God". When Paul says this he is referring to the Old Testament, regarding it as God's Word.

2. In the first chapter of his second letter, the Apostle Peter says, "For prophecy never had its origin in the human will, but prophets, though human, spoke from God as they were carried along by the Holy Spirit." (v.21). That is, the Old Testament is God's message for all people of all times and places.

3. The entire Old Testament, points to God's redemptive plan with humanity being reflected through a people. A clear message to understand our mission today as a church: be God's instruments for the salvation of mankind.

4. Christ, the promised Messiah, is the fulfillment of the promises that Jehovah gave to His people throughout the Old Testament (Matthew 12:15-21; 13:34-35; 21:4-5; Luke 1:31-33; 79).

5. Jesus repeatedly quoted the Old Testament as an authority for human activity (Matthew 19: 4-5; 16-22; 23: 2-3). This shows us that the principles of life established by God are still valid.

6. The Old Testament shows us God's faithfulness to his people in spite of their infidelity. It shows us a God who is faithful to his covenant, fulfilling promises and fulfilling his purpose with mankind.

Conclusion

Throughout the Old Testament we see God's hand creating, guiding and caring for his people while he weaves his redemptive plan for mankind. Today, we who were reached by God and have been made part of his people, are responsible for reaching all nations with His message.

Resources

Additional Information

"Apart from any theory about the inspiration of the books of the Bible or how they came to have their present form, or how much the text has been modified by editors and copyists; apart from the question of how should be understood literally and/or figuratively, or how much is historical and poetic; if we assume that the Bible is simply what it appears to be and we study the books to know it's content, we will find that there is a unity of thought which suggests that just one mind inspired the writing and formation of the whole series of books; which bears the stamp of its author, and it is, in a unique and distinctive sense, God's Word" (Bible's Manual Compendium, Henry H. Halley, p.22).

There are Four Canons of the Bible

The Jewish Canon: Only accepts 24 books of the Old Testament (In content they are the 39 of the evangelical canon). They don't accept any book of the New Testament.

The Protestant Canon: Accepts 39 books of the Old Testament and 27 of the New. Total: 66 books.

The Catholic and Orthodox Canon: Accepts 46 books of the Old Testament (the Jewish canon 39 and 7 Deuterocanonical) and the 27 books of the New Testament. Total: 73.

Definition of terms

• *Canon:* The word "canon" comes from the Greek language and corresponds to the expression "a straight rod that is useful to hold something right." For us, it's like a rule of faith to determine if something is true or false.

Supplementary activity

Dynamic: Memorizing books.

Materials: Paper posters with the names of the 39 books of the Old Testament.

Time: Five minutes

Development: Before class, stick the posters with all the names of the Old Testament books on the classroom wall (grouped with the Christian division that is presented in the lesson). Take some time during the class for the students to repeat several times the names of the books.

Leave the posters on the classroom wall and during the next several Sundays, have your students study the names of the different books. Take some time each week for the students to memorize them. It will be easier if you learn them by the Christian divisions.

The Pentateuch

Leonel de León (Guatemala)

> **Memory Verse:** "Your commands are always with me and make me wiser than my enemies" Psalms 119:98.
>
> **Lesson Goal:** That the students discover that in the Pentateuch God revealed His purpose for humanity and not just for one nation.

Introduction

Start the class by having the students answer these basic questions:

1. What's the meaning of "Pentateuch"?
2. Who wrote these books?
3. Can you name the contents of each book?
4. Can someone tell us what Abraham meant when he told the rich man in Luke 16:29: "They have Moses and the prophets, let them listen to them...?

Thank those who participated, and let them know that they are an important part of the lesson by their contribution.

I. Basic Info About the Pentateuch

Pentateuch is the name by which the first five books of the Bible are known. Initially these books were a single unit, (Genesis, Exodus, Leviticus, Numbers and Deuteronomy). The name Pentateuch was assigned 300 years BC by a group of scholars called the "seventy" or Septuagint. They decided to divide the book into five volumes because it was too large to handle as one book. So they decided to divide it this way and assign a name to each of them.

The authorship of these books is attributed to Moses, called by many Bible scholars as "the great lawgiver" because he received from God the laws that would govern his people. (Read Exodus 17:14; 24: 4; 34:27; Numbers 33: 1-2; Deuteronomy 31:24; Matthew 4: 4; Romans 10: 5). Although the last chapter of Deuteronomy 34 was obviously not written by Moses, but some scholars attribute it to Joshua.

II. What Does the Pentateuch Contain?

Contents of the five books of the Pentateuch and the truths they teach us are:

A. Genesis

This is the beginning of everything, including God's redeemer plan. "Genesis provides a fitting introduction to the Bible. It's a book of beginnings: The physical universe, plants, animals and human life ... Genesis traces the beginning of God's redemptive work for humanity. After Adam and Eve sinned, redemption became absolutely necessary. In Genesis 3:15, the reader realizes that the Redeemer would come from 'the seed of the woman'. The line of descendants goes through to Shem's family (Genesis 9: 26-27), and then to Abraham's family (Genesis 12: 3). The Messiah's line continued along Isaac's line, and then Jacob's line" (Study Bible: LBLA USA:. 2003 Editorial The Lockman Foundation).

Something remarkable is that out of the eight most important Scriptural covenants, four are found in Genesis: Edenic, Adamic, Noah and Abraham.

An important truth in the first book of the Bible is that we and the world are God's creation, according to his intention and made for fellowship with Him.

B. Exodus

The emphasis of Exodus is on the life and early ministry of Moses and his role as legislator and deliverer of the Hebrew people. "The book of Exodus describes how the Israelites came to be under the covenant of the Mosaic Law. It tells about how God gave the law, as well as the contents of the tabernacle and the provisions for worship in the tabernacle during the years in the desert. This book helps Christians remember that God's salvation not only liberates from sin's slavery, but also allows them to know His will and to experience His presence in everyday life" (Study Bible: LBLA USA. 2003, Editorial: The Lockman Foundation).

A truth that we can highlight in Exodus is that as human beings, we tend to complain and be dissatisfied even when God works in our favor. Therefore, we must be alert and look for the fullness of the Spirit in our lives to trust God despite the circumstances. The law's delivery to the people helps us to understand an important truth in our relationship with God, i.e., we must follow God according to His commandments and not ours. In them, we'll find joy and satisfaction.

C. Leviticus

Its main feature is the establishment of values, beliefs and foundation of faith in the Lord. It's in this book where God manifests the difference between the Egyptians and His people. It was necessary that his people learn to live as a free people, with initiative to form the great nation that God promised Abraham.

"The divine model of Leviticus is not limited to the religious life of Israel. All aspects of the life of the Israelites would be led by God. Leviticus constantly emphasizes God's holiness and man's need to respond with holiness in every aspect of their daily lives "(Study Bible: LBLA USA: 2003 Editorial: The Lockman Foundation). Leviticus helps us understand the worship that pleases God. A truth that we must always remember is that God is holy, so our worship of Him must be to live apart from sin and dedicate ourselves to God.

D. Numbers

As its name implies, Numbers emphasizes the two surveys, one to count those who left Egypt and the other, roughly 39 years later, to tell everyone who could go out for war (Numbers 26:2). The book describes God's plan for the conquest of the Promised Land, the sending of the 12 spies into Canaan to see spy out the land and the enemy, the report of those spies, the rebellion of God's people against Moses and God, and the life of the Israelites during their 40 year in the desert because of their rebellion.

One of the truths taught by the book of Numbers is that we must obey God and put our trust in Him, despite how difficult the situation may seem.

E. Deuteronomy

Deuteronomy is translated from the original Greek as "Second Law," or more appropriately as "repetition of the law". It's characterized by a series of sermons and instructions of Moses to the Hebrew people in their formation as a nation. A generation of people with a slave mentality and dependency had died, and a new generation with a very specific mission was forming. Therefore, repetition of the law had great importance in this historic moment of the people of Israel.

"The book of Deuteronomy is written in the form of a treaty between a king and his typical vassal state of the second millennium BC. It calls on Israel to remember who God is and what He has done, the lost faith of the older generation and their pilgrimage of forty years and then death in the desert. They left Egypt behind, but they never knew the Promised Land. Now on the riverside of the Jordan River, Moses prepares the children of that generation, devoid of faith, to take possession of the land. After a brief history lesson in which the great deeds of God for his people are stressed, Moses reviews the law. Then he reaffirms the covenant, the contract between God and his people" (Bible daily living USA: 1996 Editorial Caribe, page 228). Many are the truths that we find in Deuteronomy, but one that stands out is that "... God is God, he is the faithful God, keeping his covenant of love to a thousand generations of those who love him and keep his commands..." (Deuteronomy 7: 9).

III. God's Law for My Daily Living

The whole Bible, including the Pentateuch, remains valid for our lives today. Jesus and the disciples spoke of these books as Holy Scripture, on which they based their arguments and principles for living a life pleasing to God. Today, these books continue having the same validity for our lives as God's sons and daughters. Certainly, the laws have been summarized and fulfilled by Jesus Christ in two great truths: "Love the Lord your God with all your heart and with all your soul, and with all your strength and with all your mind; and, Love your neighbor as yourself" (Luke 10:27).

The psalmist in Psalm 119: 97-105 says that he loves the law. The reason is very interesting. It not only helps us in our daily lives, but it also helps us to learn to relate to others and to please God. The law is perfect, because there it says, "Your commands make me wiser than my enemies ..." (v. 98). To live for God based on his will reflected in his Word, makes a big difference. It makes us wise, knowledgeable and outstanding. "True wisdom is beyond accumulated knowledge. It is the application of that knowledge to daily life. Smart or experienced people are not necessarily wise. We're wise when we follow what God has taught us "(Bible daily living USA: 1996 Editorial Caribe, p.824).

We now understand better why God set for "his people", his holy nation, a different law to all the pagan peoples around. God's people make a difference when they live in God's plan.

The Psalmist reflects that it is God who teaches him (v.102). God's Word bring us closer to his heart and it makes us dependent on his grace for daily living. This brings as a result pleasure in the Lord's sweet law, and hated of the bitterness of sin (vv.103-104).

Then in verse 105, the psalmist mentions two very important words, lamp and light.

They really are not synonymous, but one is the object that produces the light that illuminates our way. This is something like walking in the dark; suddenly I find myself stuck in the mud. The light helps me see where I stand and I realize that I need to get out. When I make the decision to get out, the lamp shows me the way, it illuminates the way out and helps me to see so I won't fall into the puddle and mud where I was.

Conclusion

Allow students to make the conclusion. Are the Pentateuch's truths active in my life today? Name two applicable truths.

Resources

Additional Information

The Pentateuch represents the basis of God's thought, and it's where God is known to man as being the fair redeemer after man's fall.

The books of the Pentateuch were first named by the first words of the Hebrew original book. Genesis 1:1 Bereshit (in the beginning); Exodus 1:1, Shemot (names); Leviticus 1:1 Wayiqra (and He called); Numbers 1:1, Bemidbar (in the desert), and Deuteronomy 1:1, Debarim (words).

Then they put the names that are now known, and in some cases, they have to do with the content of the book. Genesis (Principle); Exodus (out); Leviticus, because the tribe of Levi; Numbers, because the two censuses of Israel, and Deuteronomy, by repetition of the law, which was written for second time (deu = second and nomos = law) (Illustrated Bible Dictionary, USA: 1983, Editorial Caribe, pp.162, 220,250,376,456).

Definition of Terms

Pentateuch: The Greek name means "five cases" (Penta = five, teuch= vessels or containers) which were the boxes or vessels where the scrolls were kept so they wouldn't deteriorate. Today the most common definition is "the five scrolls or Moses' books." The Hebrews also assigned the name "Torah" which in its limited way means "Law." But its broad meaning is "Lead, direct, teach or instruct" (Deuteronomy 31:9).

Additional Activities

Memory task:

The Ten Commandments are the essential basis of the Pentateuch; therefore, encourage your students to memorize it as they are in Exodus 20: 1-17. Give them an opportunity to use a marker to underline each of them, and ask someone to remind the class during the week to memorize the Commandments.

If you as the teacher memorize them and say them, it will be more powerful and challenging for your students.

Dynamic: "Applying"

Materials: Paper and pencil

Objective: That every student learns how the Pentateuch refers to each area of the human being.

Time: No more than seven minutes.

Development: Allow your students to make five circles on a sheet. In each circle, ask them to write the five most important areas of the human being: physical, intellectual, emotional, spiritual, and social. Then ask everyone to discover how the Pentateuch refers to each of these areas.

For example: The physical area: Genesis when God made man from the dust and from his side he made the women. Intellectual: "he made him to his image and likeness". Social: he gave man laws to live in community and so on.

The Historical Books

Joel Castro (Spain)

Memory Verse: "Keep this Book of the Law always on your lips; meditate on it day and night, so that you may be careful to do everything written in it. Then you will be prosperous and successful" Joshua 1:8.

Lesson Goal: That the student learns to recognize the divisions of historical books of the Bible and their spiritual wealth.

Introduction

The historical books cover a period of about a thousand years. They date from Canaan's conquest (about 1400 BC) to the walls' reconstruction and the temple in Jerusalem after the captivity (approximately 400 BC).

The historical books, in addition to their historical accounts, are also very rich in spirituality and counseling. They are the framework on which the Old Testament rests. Through them we can see the history of Israel and God's prophecies.

I. Overview of Each Book

A. Joshua

Its very name tells who the author is, although the last part of the book (24:29-33) was not written by Joshua. Some commentators claim that they were probably Aaron's sons. Joshua in Hebrew means "Jehovah is salvation" and in Greek means "Jesus". Numbers 13:16 tells us that the original name of Joshua was Hoshea, and Moses changed it. This book chronicles how the people of Israel took the Promised Land.

B. Judges

It begins about two decades later. After the people of Israel took possession of Canaan's land, they began to turn away from God, and as a result suffered the siege of border enemies, especially of the Philistines. That's when judges appeared (leaders that God chose and trained to release or to save the people from enemies). According to the Jewish Talmud, the author of this book was Samuel. It covers a period of approximately 300 years.

C. Ruth

The Book of Ruth is from the time of the Judges. While some Bible scholars differ on the author of Ruth, the Jewish Talmud attributed the authorship to Samuel.

This book is very important in the Old Testament because through it, we meet Ruth and Boaz, who was the great-grandfather of David. With him began the royal lineage that ended in our Lord Jesus.

D. First and Second Samuel

"In the Hebrew text, the two books of Samuel were one. The Greek Old Testament regarded the books of Samuel and Kings as a single historical work ..." (New Bible Commentary, XXI Century; p.318). The author is unknown. It emphasizes that it was Samuel who began to write it, but there were other writers. In 2 Samuel 1:18, Jaser is named. In this book, we read of the hierarchical change in leadership from judges to kings. Samuel was the last judge.

E. First and Second Kings

The author of this historical section is unknown, although it's known that there was only one, because the style the same. The author was helped by other sources, such as the Chronicles of the Kings of Israel, which is different than the books of First and Second Chronicles we have in the Bible.

The history of 1 and 2 Kings includes about 400 years; from the last days of David (971 BC) to the 37th year of the Babylonian captivity (561 BC). They were turbulent years due to the political instability that existed.

F. First and Second Chronicles

Chronic means "events", "Annals", "memories". Therefore, the author of Chronicles wanted to show the line of God's people from the beginning. Although it seems to be a summary of the previous two historical sections, these two books give us more information. Chronicles begins from the time of Adam until Cyrus' decree that provides for the Jew's return to Judah from captivity. According to Jewish tradition, Chronicles was written by Ezra, after the return from captivity.

G. Ezra and Nehemiah

According to scholars, these books were written in the same period, approximately 480 and 430 BC when the captives returned to Jerusalem. Ezra and Nehemiah were the authors of these historical books. Both intervened and helped in the possession of lands in the deserted Israel. On the one hand, the priest and scribe Ezra led the people to not abandon God's law; and Governor Nehemiah led the people to rebuild the walls of the Temple of Jerusalem.

H. Esther

The date of the events of this book is during the time of Ezra. The book of Ezra tells what happened in Jerusalem, and the events of Esther that happened in a province (Susa) of Persia west of Jerusalem. As to the book's author, Charles F. Pfeiifer suggests: "Although Josephus believed that Mordecai had written the book, it seems that the passage of 10:2-3 excludes this possibility. However, the author must have been a Jew who lived in Persia at the time of the events narrated, and who had access to the official history of the kings of Media and Persia (Esther 2:23; 9:20, 10:2) "(Charles F. Pfeiifer, Moody Bible Commentary. 1996, Kregel).

II. Spiritual Wealth of Historical Books

The writers of the books were, undoubtedly, inspired by God. They speak to us today that we're his church. God needs committed leaders, and in these books, we find specific characteristics that identified every leader that God raised up.

A. Joshua and Esther: Courage (Joshua 1:6, 8:3; 10:25; 23:10; Esther 4:16)

Courage is a vital ingredient to be conquerors like Joshua. Today, the Lord Jesus calls us to conquer our neighborhoods with the sword of the gospel of salvation. Esther is also a living example of courage.

B. Gideon: God's presence (6: 34; 7: 15)

Only the presence of God will give us good results, no matter our skills. Gideon conquered because God's Spirit was with Him. Today, thanks to the Holy Spirit's presence in our lives, we're more than conquerors (Romans 8:37).

C. Ruth: Love (1:16-18)

Ruth is the best example of love. God rewarded her love for her mother-in-law by giving her a new life with someone who loved God, and gave her the great honor of being a part of David's genealogy and of our Lord Jesus's genealogy. God will reward our love for our neighbor in ways that we cannot even imagine.

D. Samuel: Obedience (1 Samuel 3:10)

Obedience is the key to the power of God being shown in our lives. Obedience is not easy, but must be learned in us as Jesus did (Philippians 2: 8). We can say that the Christian life is summarized in one word, "Obedience." If we say that we walk by faith, it's because we obey God, trusting in his promises.

E. Solomon: Wisdom (1 Kings 3:27)

In the book of Kings, we find Solomon's story, a man who was known for the wisdom that God gave him. We must not hesitate to ask God to make us wise to accomplish the mission that He asks of us.

F. Elijah: Faith (1 Kings 17:22; 18:6-38)

Faith is necessary to believe in an almighty God. God wants to do great deeds through us. He only expects us to trust completely in him.

G. Ezra: Integrity (7:10)

If we want to be used by God, we must be pure instruments. In other words, to have integrity. Any responsibility that we have demands integrity. Integrity is demonstrated in the study and practice of God's Word.

Conclusion

God still is the same. Today, holding God's hand; is our chance to write the history. What will your story be?

Resources

Additional Information

Curiosities of the historical books

- Joshua: "The day lasted more than 24 hours because the sun stood still" (10:12-14).
- Judges: "Jephthah had to sacrifice his only daughter because he made that promise if he got the victory" (11: 30-40).
- Ruth: "A shoe or a sandal was testimony of the purchase or renounces of a right in favor of another" (4: 7-8).
- Samuel: "Twice the statue of Ashrod (Philistines' god) ended prostrate before Lord's ark" (5: 3-4).
- 1 Kings: "Solomon was not only the wisest of all time; also he was the richest (10: 14-25). He also composed three thousand proverbs, one thousand and five songs (4:32); and he had 700 queens and 300 concubines"
- 2 Kings: "When Elijah was taken into heaven, fifty men, with the consent of Elisha, searched for him for three days in the mountains and valleys" (2:16-18). Also, there was a child who sneezed seven times and then was resurrected (4:35); and Naaman dipped himself seven times in the Jordan and was healed of leprosy (5:14).
- 1 Chronicles: "David had 26 sons, besides the sons of the concubines; and Tamar is named as the only daughter" (3:1-9).
- 2 Chronicles: "Jehoshaphat is named as the only king who defeated three enemy armies without using armor ... they won only by chanting" (20:20-25).
- Ezra: "With the slogan "to please God," many had to depart from their foreign wives" (c.10).
- Nehemiah: "We see the story of a butler who become one of the greatest rulers, administrators and architects" (chapters 1-3).
- Esther: "In Susa was held the first beauty pageant, and Esther won. And with his choice the king helped a good cause: helping the Jews" (Chapters 1-10).

Definition of Terms

Chronicals: In the Hebrew canon, Chronicles was one book called "facts of days". In the Septuagint (LXX), it was divided into two parts called "Omitted Things" because it was believed that it contained the "omitted" history of the other historical books (Illustrated Dictionary of the Bible, USA: 1983 Caribbean, p.138).

Kings: In the Hebrew canon, these books are only one and are called "Kings". It was in the LXX where the division was done in two books and these were called "3 and 4 Kings". In the LXX 1 and 2 Samuel were called "1 and 2 Kings" (Illustrated Bible Dictionary, USA: 1983 Caribbean, p.556).

Supplementary activity

Name: Fixation

Make posters of approximately 12 x 4 inches (30 x 10 cm). Type out the name of each book before hand, and then paste the names on the board as you talk about of each of them. This will help your students to remember the historical books.

Introductory Activities

You can use one of the following activities as an introduction to the topic.

What Book are We Talking About?

Name some of the curiosities of every book that is in the supplementary information. This will help them think about how much they know, or don't know, about these books.

The Correct Order

Materials: Rectangular cards of approximately 5 x 2.5 inches (12 x 6 cm), with the names of the 12 historical books written on them. In other identical cards, enter the number of chapters of each book. You should have as many sets of cards as the number of groups formed in the class.

Objective: To know more about the history books.

Time: Five minutes maximum.

Activity: Divide the class into two or three groups of four people. Give each group two sets of cards (one with the names of the books and the other with the number of chapters) and ask each group to put in order every book correctly with the corresponding chapters. Give them 2 minutes to complete the activity. Be sure to mix up the cards beforehand.

1. Joshua - 24,	2. Judges - 21,
3. Ruth - 4	4. 1 Samuel - 31
5. 2 Samuel - 24	6. 1 Kings - 22
7. 2 Kings - 25	8. 1 Chronicles - 29
9. 2 Chronicles - 36	10. Ezra - 10
11. Nehemiah - 13	12. Esther - 10

Variation: Instead of number of chapters, you can use a key verse of each book or the outstanding characteristic of the main character, historical period, etc.

The Poetic and Wisdom Books

Lesson 6

Pedro Julio Fernández (Canada)

> **Memory Verse:** "To God belong wisdom and power; counsel and understanding are his". Job 12:13
>
> **Lesson Goal:** That students learn the generalities and content of the books of poetic and wisdom books.

Introduction

They are a collection of five books that are grouped as poetic and wisdom books by their content and nature. These books are: Job, Psalms, Proverbs, Ecclesiastes and Song of Songs. They include the life experiences of God's people and individuals in particular. The topics range from human suffering to the highest descriptions of love by a couple to wise counsel of how we can live better.

To introduce these books, you can ask someone in the class to read with expression parts of these books. For example: Job 12: 13-16a; Psalm 3: 1-3; Proverbs 6: 16-19; Ecclesiastes 5: 1-7 and Solomon 8: 6-7.

I. Overview

Poetic and wisdom books cover all the activities of life, from birth to death. Here are some generalities of these books.

A. Job

It is not known exactly who wrote the book of Job. Some scholars say that it was Job, others that it was Moses, and others that it was Solomon. As to the date it was written, it is equally difficult to specify. It was probably written around the time of Solomon (950 BC). Its central theme is hope in the midst of human suffering. This book shows that trust in God is the key to understanding and getting through a situation of extreme pain. Wisdom in life becomes a powerful testimony for not attributing evil actions towards God's children to Him. Through Job, we learn that we can be fair, sinless, and respectful of God and still pass through difficult times.

Job's book is considered the oldest in the Bible, although the content of the book of Genesis refers to the time of the origins of all things. Moses as writer of Genesis is more recent than Job. Job was a God-fearing and righteous patriarch (Job 31). His experience is a reliable source of encouragement for those who suffer while doing good.

B. Psalms

Psalms is a collection of psalms written by different authors, the main one being King David, who wrote the most - 73. Asaph wrote 12, Korah's sons wrote 9, Solomon wrote 2, and Heman alongside Korah's sons Ethan and Moses wrote one each. There are 51 anonymous psalms, though the New Testament attributed to David the authorship of two of them (Psalm 2 in Acts 4:25 and Psalm 95 in Hebrews 4:7). Being a collection, it doesn't have a fixed date when the Psalms were written. It's estimated that they were written from 1440 to 586 BC. Because there are many, the Psalms have groupings, but prayer and praise stand out as main topics. Many of them are the result of victorious moments which the authors experienced. Experiences and intimacy with God produced beautiful psalms that exalt God in days that began with anguish, but ended in peace. For example, Psalm 30 recognizes that there are moments that anguish has a temporary dominance, but God's favor lasts a lifetime.

C. Proverbs

Solomon was one of the main writers of Proverbs, though Agur and Lemuel contributed some final parts. It contains an abundance of moral and spiritual education for all. There is an urgent call to seek wisdom. It states that wisdom exceeds the value of gemstones and money. It says that those who possess wisdom will avoid the road to hell and live the life that pleases God. It's thought that Solomon compiled some of these proverbs during his reign (971-931 BC). It's very probable that in later times, the collection we have today (Proverbs 25:1) was completed.

D. Ecclesiastes

The author of Ecclesiastes, also called the Preacher, expresses the vain human reasoning and simple way to live life. The predominant word is "vanity," stating that even the good is short and temporary. It also emphasizes that eagerness and anxiety have tiredness and fatigue as their reward. Ecclesiastes expresses clearly the benefits of doing well, giving to the needy, and fearing God at all times. Some say that Ecclesiastes is a testament of Solomon's conversion, who by the influence of his wives, turned away for a while from the Lord's ways. The authorship of the book is given to Solomon, and many agree that was from the end of his reign (971-931 BC).

E. Song of Songs

The Song of Songs is also attributed to Solomon, and probably written early in his reign. Through poetry, a loving relationship between a man and a woman is described. This kind of love is presented here as in no other book of the Bible. Some have criticized it by its sensual and even erotic language.

Song of Songs presents an unequaled romanticism. It honors the marriage union and enjoyment of sex in the context of marriage.

II. The Content

These books contain practical ideas, powerful examples, high-level testimonies that teach us to live, popular sayings, and wise counsel. Here are some examples:

Job 23:3-4: "If only I knew where to find him; if only I could go to his dwelling! I would state my case before him, and fill my mouth with arguments". People who need God must know where to look, and go to his throne to find help in time. Desperate situations can upset us and even confuse the way, but by coming to God, we have a ray of hope.

We are confident that we can talk with God, who is attentive to my prayer and is a fair counselor, Father, Prince of Peace and much more.

Psalm 103:1 "Praise the Lord, oh my soul; all my inmost being, praise his holy name." David established a firm commitment to praise and bless God for all the good that he did for him. Can you identify God's benefits for your life? Worship is a lifestyle; it's a way to live life, always doing what pleases God.

Proverbs 1: 7: "The fear of the Lord is the beginning of knowledge," and then it defines the "fear of the Lord" as hating evil. (Proverbs 3:7 and 8:13) Everything begins with the fear of God,

with the reverent acknowledgment that God is power and authority, and that his laws are just and true. It's not synonymous with fear, but power, love and self-control to hate evil and to do good. According to Genesis 39:9, Joseph was wise because he feared God. Nehemiah was also fearful of God as he lead the people, as we read in Nehemiah 5:15.

They had the opportunity to hate evil and keep the good and they did it because, as Proverbs 1:33 says, "Whoever listens to me will live in safety and be at ease, without fear of harm."

Ecclesiastes 12:13 says: "Now all has been heard; here is the conclusion of the matter: Fear God and keep his commandments; for this is the whole duty of man." Solomon puts things in black and white. If we consider the time that Ecclesiastes was written, we appreciate these words even more, because the speaker is a man of much experience, success and wisdom.

Song of Songs 8:6 "... For love is as strong as death." We have a loving God who shared this attribute with man. In Eden's Garden, He put in man the capacity to love romantically.

The love described in the Song contains passion as a result of a decision. It's about a firm love which doesn't decrease based on time or circumstances (see 1 Corinthians 13:4-8); a love that is priceless and not selfish; a love that is freely given to make the other person happy.

III. The message

As God's Word, these books are useful for living our lives according to God's will. Poetic and wisdom books instruct, correct and teach the reader to practice the truths written in them.

In Job, we find God telling us that He is our witness in any situation, and we can worship Him for what we have and what we don't have. (Job 1:21-22) The psalms encourage us to pray, sing and live grateful to God at all times (Psalm 34), in days of trouble (Psalm 3 and 4) or in days of blessing (Psalm 103).

In Proverbs, wisdom in the form of useful counsel guides those who fear God to receive instruction and increase knowledge (Proverbs 1). It's an explanation of how we can get wisdom and knowledge of God to know how to live, avoiding danger and the snares of the enemy.

Ecclesiastes is a literary gem by which God speaks to us today to live the simple life - eating, drinking, doing well, fearing God and working with purpose (Ecclesiastes 3).

In Song of Songs, God speaks to us through the love of a man and a woman. "God created sex and intimacy, and it's all holy and good when it's enjoyed within the bonds of marriage. Married people honor God when they love and enjoy each other" (Bible of the daily living. USA: 1996 Editorial Caribbean, p.901).

Conclusion

We conclude with the words of the apostle Paul, "For everything that was written in the past was written to teach us, so that we, through endurance and the encouragement of the Scriptures, might have hope" (Romans 15:4).

Resources

Additional Information

Quotes of poetic and wisdom books of the New Testament. Many of the authors of poetic and wisdom books are mentioned in some portions of the New Testament. In Luke 24:44, Jesus divided the Old Testament into three parts: Moses' Law, the Prophets and the Psalms. David and the book of Psalms are quoted, either as author or as book, in Matthew 22: 42-45.

Solomon as writer of Proverbs, Ecclesiastes and Song of Songs is mentioned directly by Jesus when he compared him to the beauty of the lilies, (Luke 12:27) and with the visit that the Queen of the South made to hear the Wisdom of Solomon (Luke 11:31-31). In 1 Peter 3:10-12 is mentioned Psalm 34:12-16. James quoted Job 5:11.

Peter quoted at least twice the book of Proverbs: 1 Peter 5:5 he quoted Proverbs 3:34 and in 2 Peter 2:22 he quoted Proverbs 26:11. Song of Songs is one of the eight books of the Old Testament not mentioned in the New Testament.

Definition of Terms

Wisdom: "Wisdom literature in the Old Testament shows the clear perception and experience of the Jewish people to reflect on God's creation and man's place in it. Wisdom is more than knowledge or intelligence. It's the ability of mind to understand and the ability of heart to rejoice with the inner meaning, coherence, beauty and permanent principles on which existence is established. Wisdom is the ability given by God to deal intelligently with the varied experiences of the road, which is a blessing for all involved "(Beacon Theological Dictionary, USA: 1995, CNP, p.609).

Supplementary activity

Activity: **Memorization**

Materials: Blackboard, markers, chalk

Objective: To memorize the poetic books

Time: No more than five minutes

Development: Write the names of the five poetic and wisdom books on the board. Read it with the students several times. Then read it, but every time you read it, erase a name until there are none left.

Activity: **Bible Review**

Materials: Bibles.

Objective: To review the books of the Bible that has been studied so far.

Time: No more than 5 minutes.

Development: Students must close their Bibles. You'll say a verse that is located in the 22 books studied (from Genesis to Song of Songs). The person who finds it first must stand up and read it.

Variation: You can start reading and people in the class must find the passage, stand up and continue reading. Be sure to cover your Bible so students won't see where you open and read.

Major and Minor Prophets

Loysbel Pérez (Cuba)

Memory Verse: "The grass withers and the flowers fall, but the word of our God endures forever" Isaiah 40:8.

Lesson Goal: That the students can learn the essential aspects of the Major and Minor Prophets and apply their messages to everyday life.

Introduction

The Major and Minor prophets describe a period that has been called the period of prophetism in Israel; they make up a series of 17 books. A distinction has been made between the Major and Minor prophets according to their length. To reach successful conclusions about these books, we must first examine everything concerning the prophet and prophecy in the times that these servants of God were ministering.

These books cover a period from the eighth century B.C. until a period after the exile. You can show the class some pictures where the names of the 17 books appear.

I. Current Understanding of the Jewish Prophet and Prophecy

Today in popular ecclesiastical vocabulary, it's common that a prophet is seen to be someone who foretells the future, and prophecy is seen to be the words and writings of such prophets. Although these definitions contain some truth, they don't represent the biblical sense that we have in these books.

A. Who is a Prophet?

A prophet in the Jewish context is not a soothsayer, but a man called by God to guide the people of his time. The Greek word prophétés basically means someone who speaks on behalf of God. Many authors agree that a prophet is someone who proclaims, rather than someone who predicts. But both meanings are implicit in the word, and can be found in what the prophets said and did.

The term most commonly used in the Old Testament for prophet is nabi, which does not refer to the way in which the message is received, but makes a strong emphasis on the proclamation. The other terms used for prophet is "seer", but its use is not common.

The prophet was convinced that God had called him to communicate God´s message, even though what he had to say was unpopular, and he had to have faultless moral conduct.

B. Prophecy Today

We find in the biblical text that two elements are present in prophecy; the word addressed to the contemporary situation and prediction. Isaiah 7:14 represents a clear example of this where the oracle refers to a particular situation which was happening at the time of Isaiah, and at the same time it points to the birth of Christ.

Today we have distanced ourselves a bit from the Old Testament concepts related to the topic. The modern prophet is often seen as someone superior within congregations, and this prophet, when giving his prophecies, puts more emphasis on how he received the message rather than in the solidity of the words expressed. In many cases, what the "prophet" says does not match with the way he lives his life. Generally, these prophecies given are not against sin or moral ills affecting congregations, but are prophecies for the prosperity for the leaders with well-defined intentions.

Not everything is bad, and today God continues to raise prophets who actually communicate God's truth, but unfortunately, they are in the minority. Although from the etymological sense of the word, any person who communicates God's truth is a prophet.

Allow your students to recount experiences that they have had with modern day "prophets". Encourage them to give their opinion about all of this.

II. General Aspects of the Major Prophets

A. Isaiah is one of the largest books of the Old Testament. There are many different positions about who was the author. Some scholars suggest Isaiah as the only author of the book, while others see two different authors. The message of the book combines judgment and deliverance, despair and hope. Isaiah presents God as the Holy One of Israel, and deploys a new way of looking at holiness using the word impure, especially touching on the moral aspect of the human being. There are also many messianic passages.

B. Jeremiah: God put in his mouth the judgment that would befall the nation because of their sin. Jeremiah is the author of the book. The book's message is centered on the sovereignty of God and the confidence that the prophet had in God, despite the message he had received.

C. Lamentations: The book highlights one of the most terrible periods faced by the people of Israel. The prophet is touched to see his nation ravaged, the temple destroyed, his countrymen being taken to a foreign country, hence the five laments or dirges. Lamentations is presented as an anonymous work, although it's usually understood that Jeremiah was the author (2 Chronicles 35:25).

D. Ezekiel: The text of this book reflects the context of captivity or exile. It was written by the prophet Ezekiel. It contains a lot of symbols and visions, and is a distinctly eschatological book. His prophecy was centered in the hope of return and restoration of the nation.

E. Daniel: Daniel is another book that contains apocalyptic elements. It declares that the superiority of the kingdom of God over the nations would be established. There is considerable acceptance of the authorship of Daniel.

III. General Aspects of the Minor Prophets

A. Hosea: Hosea belongs to the prophets before the exile. He was a prophet who lived in the flesh the unfaithfulness of Israel to God, and felt the Lord's broken heart. Hosea spoke out against the moral problems of the people because of the lack of knowledge of the Lord, and the corrupt priests who ignored the righteousness and justice of God.

B. Joel: Like most of the books of the Old Testament, it is quite difficult to determine the date when it was written. Joel begins his book by announcing judgment, and appealing to the mercy of God. The book contains one of the most remarkable messages, mentioned explicitly in the New Testament in Acts, with the prophecy of the outpouring of the Holy Spirit, and ends with the promise of the liberation of the people.

C. Amos: Amos has been seen as the prophet of the poor. There was widespread corruption at all levels, justice was being bought, idolatry had proliferated and the presence of God was not present in the sanctuaries. It's for this situation that the prophecy of Amos is about justice.

D. Obadiah: We know very little about Obadiah except that he was one of the minor prophets. He developed a prophecy of judgment against Edom because of the evil that nation had committed, due to a conflict that had its roots in the relationship between Jacob and Esau, and continued within their descendants and peoples.

E. Jonah: He describes what happens to a prophet who ignores the call of God, and a sinful nation that obtains favor of the LORD. The book reveals the universality of salvation; God's dealings are not only with Israel.

F. Micah: Micah was a farmer, of a totally different social status than Isaiah, but the message and convictions are very similar. Most scholars accept that this book represents Micah's genuine oracles. In his prophecy, messages of judgment and hope are intertwined.

G. Nahum: The capital of the great nation of Assyria was being destroyed by Babylon. Nahum describes with virtuosity the entrance of the armies into Nineveh. His message focuses on the justice of God.

H. Habakkuk: There is no certain information of the life of the prophet and the date he wrote. The prophet couldn't bear Judah`s sinful situation and his message focuses on asking for God's judgment.

I. Zephaniah: Zephaniah broke with the prophetic silence which had reigned for half a century in Judah during the violent and corrupt government of Manasseh. Zephaniah's writings speak out emphatically against the prophetic silence of the people God had called to preach against the evil deeds of Manasseh.

J. Haggai: Haggai is one of the postexilic prophets. By this time, Persia, led by Cyrus, had conquered Babylon. Cyrus allowed all exiles to return to their home countries and even financed the rebuilding of the temple of Jerusalem. The Israelites had before them a big job to do.

K. Zacharias: Regarding the authorship of the book, there are different criteria. Some hold that there were multiple authors. Among the topics covered are fasting and the promise of the restoration of Israel.

L. Malachi: Malachi is outraged because the people were not fulfilling God's commands. In his prophecy, there is strong condemnation against these evils. He finishes with eschatological words of the implementation of a reign of justice.

IV. Messages of These Books for the Church Today

1. A prophet is someone who not only predicts the future, but is moved by the Lord to condemn sin without fear.

2. In Isaiah, we have a holy God who demands holiness of our lives.

3. In Jeremiah, we can learn that God calls us today to fulfill His purposes, and that we'll not always see the expected results.

4. Lamentations shows us that although the mercy of God is great, He does not tolerate sin, and this has consequences.

5. Ezekiel shows us that despite the difficult times through which the church can pass, God is not inactive, and He is doing great things.

6. In Joel, we can learn that God continues to pour his Spirit out today.

7. Micah teaches us that although there may be moral, financial and social calamity all around us, we can look up to the God of heaven.

8. The lesson of Jonah is that we should not resist the call of God.

9. Obadiah tells us that God does not overlook those who abuse their children.

God works in ways which we cannot imagine to give the best to his people.

Conclusion

The same God, who called these men to fulfill the prophetic ministry, calls us to minister His Word as prophets of this century. Today, it's up to us to live a life of holiness, condemn sin and proclaim hope in Jesus Christ.

Resources

Additional Information

Prophecy is a window that God opens to his people through his servants the prophets. Through it one can see God's redemptive purpose. Prophecy gives us a greater understanding of what God has done for his people, with His people and through the people in the past, and a clearer understanding of His purpose for the present. Although prophecy does not satisfy the insatiable demands for specific details about the future, it gives us a clear sense of where God is leading humanity, and the consequent obligations that fall upon His people (Various authors. Panorama del Antiguo Testamento (Panorama of the Old Testament). Buenos Aires: 1995. Nueva Creación, p. 300, translated from Spanish).

Definition of Terms

Oracle: oral proclamation on behalf of God.

Additional activity

Group Dynamics: "Who remembers most?"

Objective: See if they remember the lesson and strengthen some learning

Time: No more than eight minutes.

Activity: Divide the class into two teams. The teacher names a minor prophet and the group who first gives some correct information about the book wins. The group who answers correctly more times will win.

Overview of the New Testament

Lesson 8

Eduardo Aparicio (USA)

Memory Verse: "In the past God spoke to our ancestors through the prophets at many times and in various ways, but in these last days he has spoken to us by his Son, . . . " Hebrews 1:1-2a.

Lesson Goal: That the Students can get a panoramic view of the New Testament.

Introduction

When we talk about generalities of the New Testament, there is much information to be learned, such as:

A. The New Testament is a unique library of 27 books of different literary genres. For example, there are gospels, epistles or letters written to churches and people like Timothy, Titus and Philemon. We also have theological documents like the Letter to the Romans, and the book of Revelation that belongs to the genre of apocalyptic literature.

B. The New Testament was written over the course of nearly 100 years, and it's likely that most of the authors knew each other. For example, Luke and Paul were companions in evangelistic tours.

The common characteristic of these authors is that everyone, without exception, loved the Lord Jesus Christ and was committed to the proclamation of the gospel of salvation.

I. The Inter Testamental Period

This is the period of 400 years that runs from the ministry of the prophet Malachi, the last prophet of the Old Testament, to the ministry of John the Baptist. Although the Bible does not describe the historical processes that took place during these 400 years, it's important to know the characteristics of those times.

A. The Silence of God

One of the characteristics of the inter testamental period was what theologians call the "silence of God". Why? This was because there were no prophets to preach the Word of God between the end of Malachi's ministry until the arrival of John the Baptist.

B. Preparation for the Preaching of the Gospel

Although there was no prophet in Judah, however, the conditions were being prepared for the advance of the gospel. How?

1. Thanks to Alexander the Great, Greek became a world language (IV century B.C.). Greek culture and language broke boundaries, because all the inhabitants of the known world of that time spoke Greek.

2. The Roman Empire united everyone politically and administratively. The Romans built beautiful cities, and wide roads that connected major cities, and at sea had the best merchant fleets

All of this allowed the gospel message to permeate the whole empire quickly, even as far as Spain.

II. The Origins of the New Testament

A. The Oral Sources

John the Baptist, Jesus Christ and the apostles preached the message of the kingdom of God (Matthew 3:1-2, 4:17; Luke 3:18; 8:1; Acts 5:42; 8:4-5; 12; 9:20; 13:4-5; 1 Corinthians 1:17) and emphasized, especially to the Jewish people that Jesus was the promised Messiah.

As far as we know, Jesus didn't write his teachings but spoke a lot to the people. At the same time, he chose twelve disciples and others to proclaim the good news of salvation. Naturally, at first this transmission was primarily oral in character (Luke 9:1-2). After the resurrection, Jesus again spoke to his disciples, told them to be his witnesses to the people and to teach them (Matthew 28:16-20; Acts 1:1 to 3.8).

A great emphasis was placed on the fulfillment of the task of giving testimony and the great value of conserving the traditions (Acts 2:32, 3:15, 5:32, 10:36-43, 13:31, 22:15, Galatians 1:9, 1 Corinthians 11:23,24). That oral message continued for several years until they saw the imperative need of putting the gospel message into writing.

B. Written Sources

In the 60-70 A.D., a series of crises which warned the church took place, especially the martyrdom of several apostles. With the disappearance of many witnesses, it became necessary to write down the traditions, even though the Jews preferred oral transmission. Obviously, with the permission of the church in Jerusalem, John Mark wrote the sacred traditions in Rome (65-70 AD), and thus was born a new literary genre: the Gospel, whose purpose was to convince the reader that Jesus is the Messiah and Son of God.

In the following years (71-75), the Gospels of Matthew and Luke, using Mark's gospel as an outline, were written. According to tradition, it was the apostle John who wrote the last of the four Gospels. Years later, the church recognized the writings of the Gospels and Acts and the Epistles and Revelation (New Testament) as the word of God, inspired by the Holy Spirit.

III. John the Baptist, the Forerunner of Christ

The Jews were waiting for the promise of God, the Messiah, because they were sure that he was the only one who would deliver them from Roman oppression.

A. John prepared the way for Jesus

The appearance of John the Baptist was the first sign to forewarn the Jewish people that a new stage of divine revelation was coming (Mark 1:1-8). For the people, it was refreshing to hear again the voice of God through a prophet, "a voice of one calling in the wilderness, 'Prepare the way for the Lord, make straight paths for him'" (Mark 1:3). They had no doubt that this was a message they were waiting for (Matthew 3:1-6).

B. John announced the arrival of the Messiah

The Jews were expecting the Messiah, and imagined that he would come as a great soldier, on a beautiful horse with his sword in his hand, to free his people from the Roman Empire. But to their surprise, the Messiah came as a child born in a manger, and most of them didn't believe in him, but John the Baptist did (John 1:23-27). When he saw Jesus, he said, "Look the Lamb of God, who takes away the sin of the world!" (John 1:29).

C. John preached about the kingdom of God

John announced that the kingdom of God was at hand, and if they wanted to be part of the Kingdom, they had to repent.

IV. The Church is Born

After Jesus' three years of ministry, he was crucified to give us salvation and freedom. That was the greatest proof of the love of God toward us.

A. The Resurrection of Jesus Christ

Christ, through his resurrection, showed that death was conquered and only in Him can we have eternal life. Furthermore, the Bible says that his resurrection was the first fruits of all those who had died (Matthew 28:1-10; Mark 16:1-8; Luke 24:1-12; John 20:1-10; 1 Corinthians 15:20-21).

B. The arrival of the Holy Spirit

Christ promised his disciples that when he returned to his Father, he would send the Comforter. And so it was. The Holy Spirit came at Pentecost and empowered the apostles and others to be witnesses of Jesus Christ and preach his gospel (Acts 2:1-4). Immediately afterwards, Peter first preached to the Jews (Acts 2:14-40). "Those who accepted his message were baptized, and about three thousand were added to their number that day.

"They devoted themselves to the apostles' teaching and to fellowship, to the breaking of bread and to prayer" (Acts 2:41-42). The life of the early Christians is described in Acts 2:43-47 "And the Lord added to their number daily those who were being saved" (v. 47b). This was a church that was growing.

V. The Books of the New Testament

They are classified as follows:

A. The Gospels

The gospels are the first four books of the New Testament in its canonical order, bearing the names of Matthew, Mark, Luke and John, and contain the "good news" of Jesus Christ (the gospel).

B. The Acts of the Apostles

Acts is the fifth book of the New Testament canon, and is the second book written by Luke telling the story of the origins of Christianity, as a continuation of his gospel. It's the first written history of the church, and also gives us the historical framework for the Pauline epistles.

C. The Epistles or Letters

Twenty-one of the books of the New Testament are epistles; thirteen were written by Paul, and eight are universal or general epistles attributed to various apostles.

1. The Pauline Epistles: They were written by the apostle Paul and are classified as:

   - Great Epistles: Romans, 1 & 2 Corinthians, Galatians, 1 & 2 Thessalonians.
   - Prison Epistles: Ephesians, Philippians, Colossians and Philemon.
   - Pastoral Epistles: 1 & 2 Timothy and Titus.

2. Universal Epistles: They were written by different apostles and are: Hebrews, James, 1 & 2 Peter, 1, 2 & 3 John, and Jude.

D. The Book of Revelation

After all the other books, John wrote Revelation to the persecuted church.

Conclusion

The New Testament is a library of 27 books inspired by God, in order to reveal the redemptive plan that God has for all human beings.

Resources

Additional information

The English word Bible is from the Latin biblia, but comes ultimately from Koine Greek "ta biblia", "the books." It is the name given to the collection of writings that the Christian church considers divinely inspired. The Bible is divided into two parts: the Old Testament, written before Jesus Christ, and the New Testament, which refers to the life of our Lord and the work of the church in the first decades after the Resurrection. Almost the entire Old Testament was originally written in Hebrew, although some portions are in Aramaic, the language which became common among the Jews a few centuries B.C. The entire New Testament was originally written in Greek, which was the common language of commerce and communication of the time of Jesus Christ.

Definition of Terms

Pentecost was the second of the three great Jewish annual festivals; the others were the Passover and the Feast of Tabernacles (Exodus 23:14-16; Leviticus 23:15-21; Deuteronomy 16:1-17). It was held seven weeks or fifty days after the Passover. Every male Jew had to appear before the Lord on the day of Pentecost to present an offering of gratitude for the harvest and to remember the liberation from Egypt.

Forerunner: a person that precedes the coming or development of someone or something else.

Prophet: The Hebrew word nabi, translated "prophet" probably derives from a root meaning "to announce" or "proclaim". The Old Testament applied this term to a variety of people. In the New Testament, the Greek word profétes applies especially to the prophets of the Old Testament, but occasionally it's used for Jesus, John the Baptist and certain people in the church.

Additional Activity to do at the Beginning of the Class

Bring to the Sunday school class several very different books. Then distribute them among students for them to look at. Then ask: What do these books have in common? Do you know these authors? Do they match the topics they wrote?

After hearing the responses of students, start with the introduction of the lesson.

The Gospels and the Book of Acts

Lesson 9

Eduardo Aparicio (USA)

Memory Verse: "But you will receive power when the Holy Spirit comes on you; and you will be my witnesses in Jerusalem, and in all Judea and Samaria, and to the ends of the earth" Acts 1:8.

Lesson Goal: That the students learn the general message of the Gospels and the book of Acts.

Introduction

The first-century Christians had no New Testament as we know it today, but they did have the Old Testament or Septuagint (which was a translation of the Old Testament into Greek). Today each of us has a Bible or New Testament, and through these we can learn about Christ, the Holy Spirit and the beginning of the church.

I. Important Facts About the Gospels and the Acts of the Apostles

A. The four Gospels

1. Matthew, Mark, Luke and John are the first four books of the New Testament; but, according to historians of the Bible, the Gospels were not the first documents to be written by the sacred authors, but rather the letters or epistles were written before them.

2. On the other hand, it's interesting to note that Matthew was not the first gospel to be written but Mark, around the year 65-70 A.D., although many believe that Mark was written earlier, perhaps by 50 A.D. The Gospels of Matthew, Luke and John were written somewhere between the years 60-90 A.D.

B. The Acts of the Apostles

After Luke wrote his gospel (60 A.D.), he found it necessary to write what happened to the message of the gospel after Jesus' resurrection and ascension to heaven. That is why we have the book of Acts of the Apostles or the history of the early church.

II. Characteristics, Authors and Message of the Four Gospels

A. Characteristics and Authors of the Gospels

1. The Gospel According to St. Matthew

   • *Characteristic:* It shows Jesus as the promised Messiah and King of the Jews (Matthew 1:21-23).

   • *Author:* Matthew, also called Levi (Matthew 9:9), is the author of the first gospel. It was written roughly between the years 60-70 A.D., so that the Jewish people would know that Christ was the promised Messiah.

2. The Gospel according to Mark

   • *Characteristic:* it's the shortest of the four Gospels (16 chapters). It shows Jesus as the suffering servant of God who came to serve and give his life as a ransom for many (10:45).

   • *Author:* it's very likely that it was written by John Mark, the young man who may have been present when Jesus was arrested (14:51-52; Acts 12:12).

3. The Gospel according to Luke

   • *Characteristic:* it's the most complete account of the life, ministry, death and resurrection of Christ. Luke shows Jesus Christ as the Son of Man (9:44; 21:27; Daniel 7:13).

   • *Author:* Luke was a doctor according to Paul (Colossians 4:14). Luke is the only Gentile author of the New Testament.

4. The Gospel according to John

- *Characteristic:* John shows Jesus Christ as the Son of God, so that readers would believe in him and have eternal life in his name.

- *Author:* John, the disciple whom Jesus loved, testified "to these things and ...wrote them down (21:24).

B. What is the message of the Gospels?

The word "Gospel" means good news, and that is what Matthew, Mark, Luke and John have told us in writing, the good news that God has for his people and for us today. But what is this good news?

1. God the Father became incarnate in His Son Jesus Christ (John 1:1, 14), the promised Messiah, and came to this world to preach the gospel of the Kingdom of God (Matthew 3:17; 4:23), serve and give his life as a ransom for many (Mark 10:45). In other words, he came to save us from our sins (Luke 1:69).

2. To be saved, we must believe in Him. That means we must repent of our sins (Mark 1:15; Luke 13:3) and receive Him as our Lord and Savior.

3. After we're saved, we become children of God (John 1:12-13), and our mission is to proclaim to others what Christ has done for us to save us from our sins (Matthew 28:19-20). John 3:16 is the verse that sums up the message of the Gospels.

C. Is the message of the Gospels relevant for us today?

Of course it's relevant for the following reasons:

1. We also need the salvation that God offers through Christ. "Salvation is found in no one else, for there is no other name under heaven given to mankind by which we must be saved" (Acts 4:12).

2. Thanks to this salvation we're children of God (John 1:12-13). This salvation allows us to walk with God and have daily communion with Him through Christ.

3. We have the ministry of announcing to others the message of the gospel of salvation, beginning in our home, our neighborhood and around the world (Matthew 28:18-20).

III. The Message of the Book of the Acts of the Apostles

A. Characteristics of the Book of Acts.

1. It's the second volume written by Luke; the first volume is his gospel. It tells of the growth of the Christian church from the coming of the Holy Spirit at Pentecost, until the time when Paul preached the gospel unhindered in Rome for two years (28:30-31).

2. What Luke wants to emphasize in this book is that the church grew not by its own power, strength or courage, but by the power of the Holy Spirit

B. Message of the Book of Acts

It is clearly explained in Acts 1:8 that what Christ wants of us is to be his witnesses, starting at home and reaching out to the ends of the earth. So that this task or mission could be a reality, he sent us the Holy Spirit so that with his help we might preach with authority and power.

C. How Does the Message of Acts Help the Church Today?

There are three main points:

1. Christ died, rose from the dead and ascended to heaven, but will return to reign with us (1:9-11).

2. Our mission is to preach the salvation of Christ, but we cannot do this alone. The fullness and power of the Holy Spirit is essential in our lives and in the church (2:1-13).

3. The message of Christ is for all, both Jews and Gentiles; God makes no distinctions (28:28)

Conclusion

The message of the Gospels and the Acts of the Apostles confirms that the promise of salvation from God announced by the prophets has its fulfillment in Jesus Christ, the Son of God.

Resources

Additional information

Definition of Terms

Difference between "the Gospel" and "the Gospels":

The "Gospel" (from the Greek euaggelion = good news) is the message of God to men, the good news of salvation for a world lost in sin. It's the joyful proclamation of the redemptive activity of God in Christ Jesus to save mankind from the slavery of sin.

It is the story that tells us what God has done to save sinners, through the incarnation, earthly pilgrimage, the mighty deeds, sufferings, death and resurrection of his only Son.

The second use of the word "gospel" refers to one of the four books that present authoritatively that good news. **"The Gospels"**, then, are the first books of the New Testament, which bear the names of Matthew, Mark, Luke and John, and contain the gospel of Jesus Christ.

The oral and written Gospel: Matthew was an eyewitness, as was also John. According to all the ancient writings, Mark received his information from an eyewitness, Peter.

Luke also received his information from eyewitnesses; He spent some time in Caesarea and Jerusalem (Acts 21:8) Therefore, he must have had many opportunities to do careful research.

Meanwhile, eyewitnesses had received their information from none other than Jesus Christ himself. He was the one who spoke the beautiful words of life, and illustrated his words by his own earthly pilgrimage, death, resurrection and ascension.

His disciples, each with a slightly different purpose and a different style, proclaimed the same message to the world.

Acts: The book of Acts has a unique place in the New Testament. It's a logical link between the Gospels and the Epistles. One would have great difficulty reading and understanding Paul's letters without the background provided by Acts. The Book of Acts also gives us the historical framework for the Pauline epistles (except the pastoral epistles). It's the first written history of the church, but only covers a period of 30 years (or 62 A.D. 30-61) (Comentario Bíblico Beacon, USA:1991, CNP, p.257 tr. Spanish).

Apostle: The word "apostle" comes from the Greek word apostolos. "An apostle is a messenger, envoy, delegate, one commissioned by another to represent him in some way, especially a man sent out by Jesus Christ Himself to preach the Gospel; an apostle" (Strong's Concordance). The apostles were, in the first place, the twelve that Jesus Christ chose to be especially his constant companions as well as the initial proclaimers of God's kingdom (Matthew 10:1-8; Mark 3:14; Acts 1:26)

Church: The New Testament word for "church" is ekklesia which means "the called out ones" (Baker's Evangelical Dictionary of Biblical Theology).

Messiah (The anointed one): The Greek translation of the Hebrew word "messiah" is "Christ". The Messiah had a divine charge to establish on earth the Kingdom of God, foretold by the Jewish prophets. Christians recognize Jesus as the Messiah.

Additional activity

Before concluding the class, ask your students the following questions. They can respond orally or by writing on a slip of paper:

1. Why is it important to know the date and the authors of the Gospels and the Acts of the Apostles? a) That way we know that they are historical and not fictitious documents. b) Since the sacred writers knew Jesus Christ, we know that the Gospels and the Acts of the Apostles are firsthand accounts.

2. After knowing what the message of the Gospels is, do you believe in God the Father and His Son Jesus Christ, and have you received him as Lord and Savior? YES - NO. If not why not?

3. Which is the key verse of the Acts of the Apostles?

4. Have you received the Holy Spirit and are you a witness of Christ? YES - NO. If negative explain why not.

5. What is the new teaching(s) you have learned in this lesson, and how does it (they) apply to your life?

Epistles of Paul

Grisel Blaya (Cuba)

Lesson 10

> **Memory Verse:** "So then, brothers and sisters, stand firm and hold fast to the teachings we passed on to you, whether by word of mouth or by letter." 2 Thessalonians 2:15
>
> **Lesson Goal:** That students will be able to appreciate Paul's epistles, see the relevance for their lives of their content, and recognize the validity of his message.

Introduction

Of the 27 books that make up the New Testament, 13 are Pauline epistles. Paul's letters contain rich history, shed light on some of the social, philosophical and religious contradictions of the time, and show the vision and conclusions of the church around them. In addition, they provide an overview of the development of theological thought of the early church, as well as those first Judaizing and Gnostic heresies that the apostle condemned repeatedly in each of his letters.

I. General Characteristics of the Epistles of Paul

A. Paul and the Churches

Paul was set apart by the Holy Spirit (Acts 13:2), thus beginning a long missionary career. Three missionary journeys are attributed to Paul, as well as the trip to Rome. During his travels, he incessantly preached the gospel. On these trips, Paul and his companions founded several churches, to which Paul returned confirming the faith of those who believed.

B. Paul and the Epistles

The epistles were powerful tools used by the apostle to look after the work when he was away. In them we can observe some of the peculiarities of the writing of the time. It was customary to use a scribe (amanuensis) to whom he would have dictated the letter. Then the author would put a greeting in his own hand as a sign of approval. Paul also used a secretary (Romans 16:22; 1 Corinthians 16:21; Colossians 4:18; 2 Thessalonians 3:17). A letter written in the author's own hand was of great importance, as we can see in Paul's letter to the Galatians 6:11-18 and in his letter to Philemon 1:19.

II. Specific Characteristics of the Epistles of Paul

A. Main Divisions

The Pauline epistles can be classified according to their content and status of the author, as follows:

1. The great letters (Romans, 1 & 2 Corinthians, Galatians and 1 & 2 Thessalonians). They are so called because of their dense doctrinal content and the depth of thought that characterizes them. They were written in the middle of Paul's missionary activity.

2. The Prison Epistles (Ephesians, Philippians, Colossians and Philemon). They are so called because Paul was a prisoner when he wrote them. In them we can find deep revelations about the church and the apostle's tireless struggle against heresies. They also show how Paul, in the midst of such a difficult situation, continued to be joyful.

3. The Pastoral Epistles (1 & 2 Timothy and Titus). These are letters written to Timothy and Titus, who were carrying out a pastoral work. They contain numerous tips for ministry.

B. Main topics of the letters

• **Romans:** The structure of this epistle suggests that it can be considered to be a doctrinal treatise. Of all Paul´s epistles, it is the least personal. He appears to be debating with someone who opposes him and occasionally asks questions. The letter to the Romans is the most extensive and profound in its thinking. Its vocabulary is rich in theological terms, such as sin, anger, death, law, justice, salvation, redemption, justification, circumcised and uncircumcised, Jew and Gentile, faith and hope.

- *1 Corinthians* is written as a reproof of the chaotic spiritual state that this congregation was experiencing. The following is a list of some of the problems: lawsuits among Christians which had been brought before secular courts, excesses in the Lord's Supper, doubts about the resurrection, use of spiritual gifts, among others. The apostle sought to teach about proper Christian practice, seeking to restore the communion, order and holiness of the church.

- *2 Corinthians:* There is no doubt that this letter is Paul's most personal letter; even if it's a little difficult to follow his thoughts, his feelings can be easily captured. All this occurred because some Corinthians had misread the intentions of Paul's first letter and questioned his authority. The apostle writes this time in order to assure them that he loves them. At the same time, he defends his apostolic authority, and encourages them to complete a collection for the poor Christians in Jerusalem.

- *Galatians:* The hard work for the spiritual development of the churches of Galatia was interrupted by the teachings of Judaizing teachers. They demanded the fulfillment of the Mosaic Law as a requirement for salvation emphasizing circumcision.

- *Ephesians:* Paul makes an important statement about the equality between Jews and Gentiles in the body of Christ. The theme of the unity of the church in matters of faith is discussed and considerable attention is given to the purpose and will of God. This letter bears some resemblance to Colossians since Paul speaks in both of the signs and requirements of new life in Christ.

- *Philippians:* With 2 Corinthians and Philemon, the Letter to the Philippians is one of Paul's most personal ones. He uses the personal pronoun about a hundred times. He warns against Judaizing and against the idea of attaining perfection by works (3:2). Paul's main purpose is to thank the Philippians for the gifts they have sent him. Although the nature of the letter is not ethical or doctrinal, teaching and moral precepts are interwoven in it.

- *Colossians:* This church was not evangelized by Paul but by Epaphras, his secretary. Apparently there had been some religious syncretism in the church, an amalgam of Christianity, Judaism and Gnosticism. Paul proceeds to fight the gnostic-Judaizing heresy by exalting the person of Christ and underlining the nature of the new life in Him. The theme of the letter is the supremacy of Christ in contrast with human philosophies and superficial ritualism.

- *1 Thessalonians:* This is an epistle to exhort and comfort the believers in Thessalonica who were suffering persecution for the gospel. It presents a defense to Jewish opposition. The main theme revolves around the Second Coming of Christ.

- *2 Thessalonians:* Paul learned that some Christians misunderstood his teaching about the second coming of Christ, and had left their jobs. So the apostle corrects these errors and exhorts believers to return to work. The main theme of the letter is the second coming of Christ and His meeting with believers, just retribution that God will give to the oppressors, the emergence of apostasy, and the opposition of the man of sin.

- *1 Timothy:* After some time, the apostle decided to send a letter to advise and encourage his young disciple. Paul challenges Timothy to maintain spiritual health amid the typical moral corruption of Greco-Roman culture. Some heresies were appearing which were threatening the unity of the church.

- *2 Timothy:* The apostle Paul was imprisoned in Rome waiting for his death when he wrote this letter. It's a letter full of advice about the character of the minister, and it can be said that it's a kind of spiritual testament.

- *Titus:* Shortly after having left Titus on the island of Crete, the apostle wrote this letter to him to give him the necessary instructions to help him in the difficult task entrusted to him. He reminds him of his mission and exhorts him to continue his work: to rebuke false teachers and establish local leaders.

- *Philemon:* The main purpose of tis short letter was to intercede with Philemon for his slave Onesimus, who had escaped and accepted the gospel with Paul. This letter deals with the problem of slavery. The apostle does not directly attack slavery, or recommend rebelling against or defying the law and order. The main theme of the epistle is reconciliation.

III. Validity and Application of the Epistles of Paul

A. Reasons for its Validity

Paul wrote in another time and context. However, his words become fresh to situations that arise in today's world.

B. Examples of Relevant Texts

Discuss with your class the application of the following texts to our current context

1. "Do not conform to the pattern of this world" (Romans 12:2).
   To conform to this world is a danger to every Christian who lives in this context that, offering you the means, invites you to conform to the current trends and philosophies that lead to destruction. Among other things, the modern believer risks conforming to materialism, disbelief or the false prosperity gospel which is being preached today.

2. "For the time will come when people won't put up with sound doctrine" (2 Timothy 4:3a). Over the years, truth can be distorted, so that all claim to have the truth, and many are far from it. The rest of the verse indicates one of the causes of this deviation: "Instead, to suit their own desires, they'll gather around them a great number of teachers to say what their itching ears want to hear (4:3b).

3. "Their destiny is destruction, their god is their stomach, and their glory is in their shame. Their mind is set on earthly things" (Philippians 3:18-19). This is a danger: the desire to satisfy above all their human needs. Taking the case of our appetite for food as an example, if we just live to eat, we're making our stomachs a sort of god.

4. "Now there is in store for me the crown of righteousness, which the Lord, the righteous Judge, will award to me on that day—and not only to me, but also to all who have longed for his appearing" (2 Timothy 4:8).
   In these times, science and technology has provided us with more and more pleasures, which make us more comfortable. The Christian should always bear in mind that nothing that he/she has on earth is worthy to be clung to. More than anything in the world, the church must expect and love the coming of Jesus Christ.

Conclusion

Because the message of Paul's letters is always relevant, we need to come to it with open hearts, ready to apply each of his teachings in our own lives. Our aim as Christians is to be transformed and become more and more like Christ.

Resources

Additional information
New Testament Epistles:

"A written communication; a term inclusive of all forms of written correspondence, personal and official, in vogue from an early antiquity. As applied to the twenty-one letters, which constitute well-nigh one-half of the New Testament, the word "epistle" has come to have chiefly a technical and exclusive meaning. It refers, in common usage, to the communications addressed by five (possibly six) New Testament writers to individual or collective churches, or to single persons or groups of Christian disciples. Thirteen of these letters were written by Paul; three by John; two by Peter; one each by James and Jude; one--the epistle to the Hebrews--by an unknown writer". (http://www.biblestudytools.com/dictionary/epistle/).

In the New Testament the epistle reaches its peak as a vehicle of revelation and even becomes a new literary genre. The epistles have a place in the canon because they have proven their inspirational power in the churches. Each responds to specific needs. They were read in worship and almost since their composition were accepted as God's Word (1 Thessalonians 2:13; 1 Peter 1:12; 2 Peter 3:15).

"Saint Paul, the Apostle, original name Saul of Tarsus (born c. 4 BC), in Tarsus in Cilicia [now in Turkey]—died in Rome 62–64 AD. He was one of the leaders of the first generation of Christians, often considered to be the second most important person in the history of Christianity. In his own day, although he was a major figure within the very small Christian movement, he also had many enemies and detractors, and his contemporaries probably didn't accord him as much respect as they gave Peter and James. Paul was compelled to struggle, therefore, to establish his own worth and authority. His surviving letters, however, have had enormous influence on subsequent Christianity and secure his place as one of the greatest religious leaders of all time" (http://www.britannica.com/biography/Saint-Paul-the-Apostle).

Additional activity

Reproduce on separate sheets the information in point II: "Specific characteristics of the Pauline epistles". In the class, give each student a sheet to read the information on one of the letters. You can form groups to discuss the information and then each person can present to the class the central theme of their epistle and its main characteristics.

The Universal Letters

Ramiro Juárez (USA)

Memory Verse: "... fixing our eyes on Jesus, the pioneer and perfecter of faith. For the joy set before him he endured the cross, scorning its shame, and sat down at the right hand of the throne of God." Hebrews 12:2.

Lesson Goal: That the students understand that General Epistles are inspired by God and promote and protect the integrity of the gospel of Jesus Christ.

Introduction

Of the 27 books of the New Testament, 21 are epistles, of which 13 are known as Pauline epistles and eight as the Catholic or General Epistles attributed to various apostles and servants of Jesus Christ. The epistles have a place in the biblical canon because they have demonstrated their inspirational power in the churches. Each responds to specific needs and almost from the beginning were accepted as the Word of God (1 Peter 1:12; 2 Peter 3:15). Many letters were written with the help of secretaries who helped develop them.

I. Hebrews

A. Author, Place of Origin and Date

The letter to the Hebrews lacks the formal characteristics of a letter. It has an epistolary conclusion (13:22-25), but neither its author nor the intended recipient is mentioned, and Hebrews does not have the usual greetings and thanksgiving. It's rather a long sermon or several sermons joined together. The author calls it "word of exhortation" (13:22).

Scholars have suggested that this epistle was written by Paul, Barnabas, Apollos, Priscilla or Aquila, etc. but we're not sure who wrote it. Due to the style and thinking, almost all scholars reject the idea that Paul was the author. It has been shown that in language and concepts, Hebrews is similar to Luke. Therefore it can be concluded that the author was a Jewish-Christian from a Hellenist background who knew the Greek language very well and used the Septuagint for his Old Testament quotations.

Various locations such as Rome, Egypt, Ephesus, Antioch, have also been proposed but none has been adopted as final. We can say that it was written before the year 96 A.D., because Clement of Rome wrote his letter to the Corinthian church that year and included in his letter a number of quotations and allusions from the Letter to the Hebrews.

B. Purpose

The letter does not address a specific heresy. The recipients had worked with love for the Lord, even suffering persecution (6:10; 10:32-34), but were going through a period of weakness in faith, fear of suffering and lack of fidelity to the congregation (5:11; 10:25, 35; 12:3,12; 13:17).

The author describes masterfully the great salvation that they have, and warns his readers of the danger of apostasy if they don't persevere and maintain their hope in the efficacy and reality of salvation given by God in Jesus Christ. The readers were in danger of backsliding from the gospel they had received. Therefore, he urges them to "pay the most careful attention, therefore, to what" they have heard, so that they "do not drift away" (2:1).

The message of the letter is clear: keep the faith, obey the Word of God, stay strong, and look after their salvation in Jesus Christ. The author warns against the sin of unbelief that degenerates into apostasy.

II. The Epistle of James

A. Author, Recipients and Date

The author describes himself as "James, a servant of God and the Lord Jesus Christ" (1:1a). Because James, son of Zebedee, died too early to be the author the letter, the church attributed the epistle to James of Jerusalem, brother of the Lord (Matthew 13:55, Mark 6:3; Acts 15:13; Galatians 1:19). According to the historian Josephus, James was a bilingual Christian Jew who apparently resided continuously in Jerusalem, from Pentecost until his martyrdom 32 years later,

Moreover, some scholars attribute this epistle to another unknown James, based on the following factors: the almost complete lack of specifically Christian doctrines and the name of Jesus Christ (it appears only in 1:1; 2:1); the elegant and fine language that would indicate an author whose native language was perhaps Greek; and the delay that the epistle suffered to be accepted into the biblical Canon. However, James the brother of Jesus is largely accepted as the author of this epistle.

As to recipients, the letter simply says, "To the twelve tribes scattered among the nations" (1:1). It was written around the year 60 A.D., although others believe it was written later, between the years 70-110 A.D.

B. Purpose

"The purpose of the epistle is clearly practical and ethical. Doctrine is assumed more than enunciated. The thrust is for action and obedience. The law is to be lived. The ethical implications of the new faith need to be translated into practical realities if the believers are to advance along the way of holiness. The mood is exhortatory. The purpose is to correct faults, to instruct the wavering, to instill discipline, to rebuke backsliding, and to encourage genuine godliness throughout the redeemed fellowship, wherever believers could be found among the Jews who were scattered abroad" (https://www.biblicaltraining.org/library/epistle-james).

III. 1 & 2 Epistles of Peter

1. 1 Peter

A. Author, Recipients, Place of Origin and Date:

This general epistle begins with a salutation that contains the name of its author: "Peter, an apostle of Jesus Christ". Recipients: "to God's elect, exiles scattered throughout the provinces of Pontus, Galatia, Cappadocia, Asia and Bithynia" (1Peter 1:1).

Some have doubted that the apostle Peter is the author of the letter because the author's name was not used until the year 170 A.D., although this letter was known by the major Christian leaders in Asia Minor since 125 A.D. Other arguments against Petrine authorship are the excellence of the Greek used, hardly attributable to the Apostle Peter (Acts 4:13), and the similarity between the ideas of the epistle with Paul. However, considering the possible participation of Silas (5:12 implies Silas was both secretary and messenger) and the pooling of ideas because of Paul's undoubted influence throughout the missionary expansion. There is no reason to rule out Peter as the author of the epistle. One can assume that this letter was dictated by Peter shortly after the year 61 A.D. It's very likely that the letter was written from Rome.

B. Purpose:

The main purpose of the letter is to show Christians the magnitude of the grace they have received in their conversion.

2. 2 Peter

A. Author and Date:

This letter was also written by the apostle Peter at the end of his life and directed to the same readers of the first (3:1), about the year 64 A.D., possibly from Rome.

B. Purpose:

The main theme of 2 Peter is the defense of Christian hope against those who deny the Second Coming of the Lord in glory (1:16-21; 3:1-18)

IV. 1, 2 & 3 John

A. Author, Place of Origin and Date

Most commentators agree that John, the son of Zebedee, wrote the three epistles. Tradition has it that the apostle John (who was a Galilean) spent the last decades of his life in Ephesus and wrote the letters from there. They can be dated between 90 and 100 A.D.

The first epistle lacks the formal features of a letter - it has no personal greetings and does not indicate the name of the author or the recipient. It just starts with a personal testimony, much like the Gospel of John (1:1-4), and then directly addresses the content. The second and third letters do have initial greetings, and mention the recipients. Second John is directed to "the lady chosen by God and to her children" (1 John 1:1), and 3 John mentioned Gaius to whom John praises for his hospitality.

B. Purpose

John wrote these letters to warn the Christians to continue in the doctrine of Christ. The three Johannine letters were written to refute opposing arguments against the authority and teaching of the author that had arisen in the churches of Asia Minor. It was necessary to correct erroneous interpretations. The doctrine of the person of Jesus Christ was under threat. Several heretics denied the true incarnation of Christ (1 John 2:22; 4:1-3), and others denied the human nature of Jesus.

V. The Epistle of Jude

A. Author, Date and Recipients

Jude is mentioned among the brothers of Jesus (Mark 6:3; Luke 6:16). James, leader of the Jerusalem church during many years, is another brother (Acts 15:13; Galatians 2:9). However, the author does not claim to have apostolic authority

Despite his relationship with Jesus and with a leader in Jerusalem, he simply presents himself as "Jude, a servant of Jesus Christ and a brother of James" (v:1a). According to tradition, Jude died before 81 A.D.. Therefore, it's considered that he wrote his letter around 75 A.D..

Because of the scarcity of information and the brevity of the letter, it's impossible to know who the original recipients are.

B. Purpose

He writes to exhort Christians to contend earnestly for the faith because of the danger of false teachers, "I felt compelled to write and urge you to contend for the faith that was once for all entrusted to God's holy people. For certain individuals whose condemnation was written about long ago have secretly slipped in among you. They are ungodly people who pervert the grace of our God into a license for immorality and deny Jesus Christ our only sovereign and Lord" (vv. 3-4).

These letters teach us that in a rapidly changing society, the Christian faith should not renegotiate its purpose. A relevant church can confront the modern problems of society. This is achieved only by using the means of the grace of God, proclaiming the risen Christ through holy and committed lives.

Conclusion

The General epistles were inspired by God to teach with integrity the message of salvation in Jesus Christ. Although there are several authors, all have common themes - to remain in Jesus Christ, the author and finisher of our salvation, to obey the Word of God and to have the Bible as our foundation so as not to fall into false doctrines and false teachers.

Resources

Additional information

"The seven letters of James, 1 and 2 Peter, 1, 2, and 3 John, and Jude are often called the General Epistles because they seem to speak to the Christian church in general, rather than to individual churches. They are also united by their interest in practical matters such as organizational leadership, hard work, fairness, good relationships, and effective communication. The General Epistles reflect the essential challenge Christians faced in the Roman Empire—how to follow Jesus in a tough environment. Early Christians faced problems such as slavery, favoritism, and abuse by the rich and powerful. They dealt with harsh words and conflicts. They dealt with the real tensions between ambition and dependence on God, and the fear that doing things God's way would put them in conflict with those in authority. In general, they felt a sense of alienation living and working in a world that seemed incompatible with following Jesus." (https://www.theologyofwork.org/new-testament/general-epistles/)

Definition of Terms

Apostasy: "The word itself is from the Greek word "apostasia" and is very much like renouncing or disassociating oneself from a particular religion or certain religious beliefs. It's similar to a rejection of beliefs that were once held and accepting different beliefs and might even be a renunciation of the beliefs that were previously held. For example, if someone converts to another religion, they reject or turn away from their beliefs from something they once believed and turn to believing in another, much different religion, or it might be a falling away from anything to do with religion. Apostasy can also be considered abandonment or defiance of what was previously held to be true and practiced, and rebelling against those same beliefs and practices. Someone or some group who does this are considered an apostate" (http://www.patheos.com/blogs/christiancrier/2015/05/21/what-is-apostasy-a-biblical-definition-of-apostasy/)

"*Heresy* comes from a Greek word signifying (1) a choice, (2) the opinion chosen, and (3) the sect holding the opinion. In the Acts of the Apostles (5:17; 15:5; Isaiah 24:5 Isaiah 24:14; 26:5) it denotes a sect, without reference to its character. However, elsewhere in the New Testament it has a different meaning attached to it. Paul ranks "heresies" with crimes and seditions (Galatians 5:20). This word also denotes divisions or schisms in the church (1 Corinthians 11:19). In Titus 3:10, a "heretical person" is one who follows his own self-willed "questions," and who is to be avoided. Heresies thus came to signify self-chosen doctrines not emanating from God (2 Peter 2:1) (http://www.biblestudytools.com/dictionary/heresy/).

Septuagint: Translation of the Old Testament in Hebrew into Greek. The reading of the Septuagint presents the essential meaning of the original Hebrew, although the words are different.

Additional activity

Preparation before class:

Prepare some sheets with the initial information about the General Epistles (author, recipient, date and place of origin). Have several students read the assigned information and share it with the class in the order you indicate. If you have the chance, you can make sheets and add to the information.

Group activity

Take the names of the epistles and stick them on the board while you are talking about each of them; that will help the students remember the names of the books.

Divide the class into groups and assign each group one or two cards with the names of the epistles and have them try to extract as much data on that letter as they can (who wrote it, who, subject, etc.) in 3 minutes. The groups then share their findings with the rest of the class.

Revelation

Leonel de León (USA)

Memory Verse: "He who testifies to these things says, 'Yes, I am coming soon.' Amen. Come, Lord Jesus." Revelations 22:20.

Lesson Goal: That the students understand that the book of Revelation is a book that reveals fully who the Son of God is.

Introduction

You can start the lesson by reading Matthew 1:1, emphasizing that the revelation of Jesus Christ begins with his genealogy. Then jump to Revelation 1:1 and emphasize that in Revelation, his glory and the future of time is revealed.

I. The Last Book

The Revelation of John is the last book of the New Testament. Through it we see the culmination of everything we know, and the emergence of a new era. This book reveals everything that will happen. Although some may question it, God will fulfill everything he has said. Revelation is a book of signs and symbols and must be interpreted. It's interesting that both the beginning and the end of the book state that it was written by John (1:1 and 22:8).

Justin Martyr, Irenaeus, Clement, Origen and others (in the second and early third century) testified to the authorship of the apostle John for this book. John was on the island of Patmos; he writes about the vision he had "On the Lord's Day" when he was "in the Spirit" (1:10). There are two possible dates of writing; one in 65 A.D. during Nero's persecution of the Christians. And the other possible date is about 95 A.D., during Domitian's persecution.

John writes "To the seven churches in the province of Asia" (1:4). These churches are named in verse eleven. The purpose of Revelation was to comfort and motivate Christians who were experiencing persecution then, and those who would suffer afterwards. The writer through his message assures his readers of the ultimate triumph of Christ and his followers. He also warns the churches to review their doctrine and experiences and to remain faithful to the Lord.

There are three schools of interpretation for the book of Revelation, "The first, called preterist argues that Revelation refers to the period of the Roman Empire. The imperial persecution of Christians would be followed by the final collapse of imperial power. The second, known as historicism, sees the book as a prediction of a succession of significant events in the church age. The third, the concept futurist, argues that, from chapter four onwards, everything is yet to be fulfilled "(Beacon Bible Commentary, 1995 USA: CNP, p.481).

II. The Letters to the Churches Reveal the Lord of the Church

The first three chapters are dedicated to the description of the seven churches and contains seven specific messages. These messages were relevant for that time and remain relevant for us today. The author of the letters is the Lord. At the beginning, each is presented in a unique way (1:9-3:22).

1. Message to the church in Ephesus: Jesus Christ reveals his fidelity to the church, but has one thing against this congregation (v.4). This is a call to repentance and to leave behind a life of religious routine, and fall in love again with the Lord who saved them.

2. Message to the church in Smyrna: Jesus warns the church about their tribulation, and encourages them.

3. Message to the church in Pergamum: First tells them that he knows about their faithfulness, but warns them that some false doctrines are being taught and must be eradicated.

4. Message to the church in Thyatira: This church has many good things (3:19), but they need to continue sound doctrine.

5. Message to the church in Sardis: He emphasizes their hypocrisy and falsehood.

6. Message to the church in Philadelphia: He underscores the fidelity of this church and confirms that whoever keeps his word and doctrine faithfully, the Lord will also look after and keep well.

7. Message to the church in Laodicea: This is a warning against falsehood and unfruitful religion that has no foundation. It's a damning letter. They must repent

III. The Vision of the Throne Reveals the Glorious Lamb Sacrificed and Honored

Revelation 4:11 states, "You are worthy, our Lord and God, to receive glory and honor and power, for you created all things, and by your will they were created and have their being." Jesus Christ the Creator is the central message of this chapter. Every human being and every creature should pay and will render honor and glory to the Lamb. He deserves it because he gave his life and his body in sacrifice to redeem God's creation. These passages not only reveal what will be the glorious appearing of the Lamb on his throne, but represent what the Lord expects of us today as well.

In Revelation 5:1-14, we see Jesus Christ the redeemer. Observe the emphasis in verses 9, 10, 12 and 13. They reflect his dignity. He is worthy to open the forbidden book, and is worthy of all glory, wealth, power, etc. because he was slain. He was sacrificed to redeem people from every tongue, tribe, kingdom, people and nation.

IV. Jesus Christ is Judge and That Will Be Revealed in His Verdicts

The three symbols used to describe God's judgments are the sevens seals, seven trumpets and seven golden bowls.

A. The Seven Seals (6:1-8:5) Reveal:

1) The white horse which means peace, government and triumph; 2) the red horse, which is to be the opposite, it will take peace away, 3) a black horse, representing poverty and distress through scarcity; 4) a pale horse, representing illness, sickness and death; 5) the prayers and cries for justice of the saints; 6) natural disasters, destruction and judgment and; 7) the continuation of God's judgment. The announcement of the seven trumpets, each with its own meaning.

B. The Seven Trumpets (8:6-9:21, 11:15-19) Represent:

1) Judgment on a third of the vegetation is burned; 2) judgment on a third of the sea; 3) judgment on a third of the clean water, 4) a third of the lights in the universe will be darkened; 5) increased demonic activity; 6) a third of humanity dies and; 7) more trials, the seven golden bowls are announced.

C. The Seven Bowls (15:1-16:21) Represent:

1) Malignant sores; 2) the sea turned into blood; 3) Fresh water turns into blood; 4) men burned with fire; 5) the kingdom of the beast in darkness; 6) the invasion from the East and; 7) great destruction and earthquakes

V. Jesus Christ the Eternal King is Revealed in His Kingdom (19:1-20:15).

At this point in the class it would be good to sing a chorus, as a sign of our praise and worship of the Lord. Make special emphasis on the passage 19:1-5; He is worthy of all glory and honor. You can also take a small pause and ask your students to each silently raise a prayer of thanksgiving and praise to the Lord.

This is the climax of the book. Jesus is the conqueror; Satan will be destroyed. There will be a resurrection of the dead and those who haven't accepted the offer of salvation will be judged. It's time for the Lamb's wedding feast. John said: "Then I heard what sounded like a great multitude, like the roar of rushing waters and like loud peals of thunder, shouting: "Hallelujah! For our Lord God Almighty reigns. Let us rejoice and be glad and give him glory! For the wedding of the Lamb has come, and his bride has made herself ready..." (19:6-8).

VI. Jesus Christ is the Alpha and the Omega Revealed in Eternity (21:1-22:5).

In these last two chapters, the subject changes. We see the emergence of a new eternal order, the old one disappears forever. John saw "a new heaven and a new earth" (21:1).

Not everyone will get to heaven ... some will receive eternal punishment. None of those mentioned in verse 8 of chapter 21 will be in eternity with the Holy Lamb. But all those who have been faithful unto death, and have lived live according to the commands of the Lord, will be in the golden city forever. Nothing and no one will take away from them what the sacrificed Lamb has given them.

Conclusion

The book of Revelation unravels the story of God in Jesus Christ, what he wants from his church, and what will happen to the saints. The central message of Revelation is Jesus Christ, the Messiah who was slain but now is King of Kings and Lord of Lords, who will come back as judge to hold accountable the world and his church.

Resources

Additional Information

Revelation is one of the books of the Bible that is feared, ignored or simply avoided due to the complexity of its symbolism and its teachings. It's very easy to fall into moralism, or adapt each revelation to contemporary events, without taking into account its history and overall message throughout the Bible. We know of the curiosity that many people have about future events, but help your students see in this book the Christ who wants each of us to live holy lives in harmony with his body, the church, of which he is the head.

Definition of Terms

Alpha and Omega: A term that presents God as the cause and end of all things. It's derived from the first and last letters of the Greek alphabet. This expression emphasizes the divine action not only in the creation and consummation, but also in a continuous present (Revelation 1:8, Isaiah 44:6). In Revelation, this phrase applies not only to the Father (1:8), but also the Son (21:6, 22:13).

Revelation: Comes from the Greek (apokálypsi). It serves as the title of the last book of the New Testament.

Lamb of God: "The Christology of the Lamb of God rises to its zenith in the last canonical book, where "lamb" appears in the Greek text twenty-nine times. In the heavenly vision of chapter 4, the choir of twenty-four elders and four living creatures worship the "Lord God" who sits on the throne, for he is worthy (v.11) ... Through the ages, people like John had been expecting a militant, divine warrior "the Lion of the tribe of Judah" to appear in a magnificent display of power against evil. The triumph of God, however, came through his Son, a Son of David, who appeared like a Lamb. The Lamb, looking as if it had been slain stood in the center of the throne. He alone was worthy to open the scroll. When he took the scroll, the prayers of the saints were fulfilled and all heaven erupted in praise: "Worthy is the Lamb, who was slain, to receive power and wealth and wisdom and strength and honor and glory and praise!" Therefore, Jesus, the Lamb of God, is "Lord of lords and King of kings!" (Melvin H. Shoemaker, in Baker's Evangelical Dictionary of Biblical Theology - Lamb, Lamb of God).

Additional Activities

Before people come to class, hide under the chairs some biblical promises from Revelation written on bits of paper. When you finish the class, invite students to receive Christ, especially mentioning (Rev. 22:17). It doesn't matter if all are professing Christians, perhaps you may get a surprise. Then take time to pray for those who already know the Lord so that they might affirm their faith.

Tell them to look under their chairs and read what they find there. Tell them that the Lord reveals His promises, and that he himself is speaking. If you have time you can ask two or three people to share how they felt when they read their promise and knew it was the Lord through the revelation of His Word who had spoken with them. This can be very impressive when one emphasizes that Revelation is the revelation of God to his church.

Discovering the Message

Write the following phrase in a secret language on the board and ask your class to interpret it. Then apply this interpretation to the content of Revelation. Emphasize that the purpose of writing this book in forbidden language was to prevent enemies of the gospel from intercepting it and preventing it from coming to the churches.

The phrase is: fardfaoffaGodfaisfarevfaealfaedfatofathefadisfacipfalesfa ..."

Introductory Activity

To illustrate this lesson, you'll need the following objects or drawings: A temple, a decorated chair to seat a king, a hammer, a crown and a golden city with glowing light. Use all your creativity for each of these elements. Present these objects or pictures at each point of II to VI and ask your students what each of them could represent. Then you can tell them that Jesus Christ is revealed in five functions, according to the book of Revelation.

1. A temple representing the Church of the Lord (Jesus as the Lord of the church).
2. A chair that will represent the Lord's throne adorned for a king (Jesus as the Lamb immolated and glorified).
3. A wooden hammer, which represent a judge (Jesus as judge).
4. A crown that will represent his lordship, (Jesus revealed eternal king in his kingdom).
5. A city of gold with light shining represents eternity (Jesus the alpha and omega revealed in eternity).

The Book of Books

Lesson 13

Martha de Bradna (Guatemala)

Memory Verse: "All Scripture is God-breathed and is useful for teaching, rebuking, correcting and training in righteousness, so that the servant of God may be thoroughly equipped for every good work." 2 Timothy 3:16-17

Lesson Goal: That the students confirm their conviction that the Bible is the foundation of our Christian faith.

Introduction

The Bible is the inspired Word of God that reveals His will. It's the best book ever to have been written, the Book of books, and the book that has had more influence in the history of mankind. The Bible has been translated into more than a thousand languages. It's the book that all human beings ought to look to and search for because it reveals the plan of salvation for humanity. It's the book that guides us to our Redeemer and provides the doctrinal foundation of the Christian church.

I. The Unique Book

A. What is the Bible?

The Bible is the inspired Word of God. Its author is God Himself. We call the Bible 'holy' and 'inspired' because it was written by men consecrated to God and inspired by the Holy Spirit. The apostles Paul and Peter taught that the Bible "is inspired by God" (2 Timothy 3:16; 2 Peter 1:21) and was brought about by God's will, not by human will.

"The Christian faith comes from the Bible. It's the foundation of faith, salvation and sanctification. It's the guide for character and Christian behavior. 'Your word is a lamp for my feet, a light on my path' (Psalm 119:105) ... The Bible is a book that everyone should read, understand, obey and share with others (Bible Commentary Beacon, NPH, tr. from Spanish).

B. Purpose of the Bible

The purpose of the Bible is to reveal the will of God concerning our salvation and the way we should conduct ourselves daily. The Bible guides us to relate to God according to his will, that is, to live in obedience to God. God speaks to us through His Word. He allowed it to be written so that all people could share his Word, no matter the age or place where they live.

C. The Great Theme

The great theme of the Bible is God's redemptive plan for man, accomplished in the perfect sacrifice of Jesus Christ, and communicated by the work and the will of the Holy Spirit.

"The cross of redemption is situated in the heart of the Bible. The Old Testament and the four Gospels look towards this. All the rest of the New Testament, from the Gospels, look back at it as the supreme basis of faith and trust "(Exploring the Old Testament, NPH, p. 41, tr. from Spanish).

D. Division of the Bible

The Bible is divided into two parts:

1. The Old Testament (written before Christ) containing the old covenant of God with his people Israel.

2. The New Testament, whose content is the life of our Lord Jesus Christ, the origins of the early church, and the final victory of the kingdom of God over the forces of evil.

Since the late second century A.D., the terms 'Old Testament' and 'New Testament' were used to differentiate between the Hebrew and Christian Scriptures. A testament or covenant (gr. Diatheke), refers to an unalterable declaration of the will of God in relation to man. The final covenant between God and man is based on the blood of the great mediator, the lamb without spot or blemish, already provided before the foundation of the world (1 Peter 1:19-20) (Matthew Henry Commentary).

E. What are the Languages Used in the Bible?

The Old Testament was written in Hebrew almost entirely, although some parts in Aramaic. The entire New Testament was written in Greek, the common language spoken in the time of Jesus and his disciples

II. Panorama of the Old Testament

The books of the Bible began to be written between 1200 and 900 BC. At first they were written on separate rolls. The collection of manuscripts of the Pentateuch was found in 300 BC. Around the year 200 B.C. the second collection called "prophets" was formed and finally the "writings" appeared including the historical books, the poetic and the Minor Prophets. So the Hebrew division is: the Law, the Prophets and the Writings.

A. The Books of the Old Testament

According to the Christian division, the Old Testament contains 39 books, and is divided into five parts:

1. The Pentateuch contains the first five books of the Bible: Genesis, Exodus, Leviticus, Numbers and Deuteronomy.

2. Historical books (12 books) Joshua, Judges, Ruth, 1 and 2 Samuel, 1 and 2 Kings, 1 and 2 Chronicles, Ezra, Nehemiah and Esther.

3. Poetic Books (5 books) Job, Psalms, Proverbs, Ecclesiastes and Song of Solomon.

4. Major Prophets (5 books) Isaiah, Jeremiah, Lamentations, Ezekiel and Daniel.

5. Minor Prophets (12 books), Hosea, Joel, Amos, Obadiah, Jonah, Micah, Nahum, Habakkuk, Zephaniah, Haggai, Zechariah and Malachi.

B. Its Importance

1. The Old Testament is the basis of the New. The foundation on which rest both the teaching of our Lord, as well as the testimony of the apostles, is the recognition of God's revelation in the law, the prophets and the psalms. If we reject the Old Testament, we destroy the New ... In the pages of the New Testament, there are over 250 direct quotations from the Old Testament (Exploring the Old Testament, NPH tr. from Spanish). Jesus and the apostles used the Scriptures, the Old Testament.

2. The entire Old Testament points to God's redemptive plan for humanity.

III. Panorama of the New Testament

A. The Books of the New Testament

It contains 27 books and can be classified as follows:

1. Four Gospels: Matthew, Mark, Luke and John, which contain the life, ministry and ascension of Jesus Christ.

2. Acts of the Apostles is the first written history of the church, and also gives us the historical framework for the Pauline epistles.

3. The Epistles: There are 21 letters that are divided into two groups.

   a. Pauline Epistles: There are 13 letters that were written by the apostle Paul: Romans, 1 and 2 Corinthians, Galatians, Ephesians, Philippians, Colossians, 1 and 2 Thessalonians, 1 and 2 Timothy, Titus and Philemon.

   b. General Epistles: There are eight letters written by different authors. In this group are the books of Hebrews, James, 1 and 2 Peter, 1, 2 and 3 John and Jude.

4. Prophecy: The New Testament ends with a book of prophecy, directed towards the future, the book of Revelation.

Conclusion

The Bible contains everything God wanted to reveal of himself and his will to mankind. The Bible is his love letter revealing his Son Jesus Christ, who gave his life to save mankind. Christians must share the knowledge of the Word of God because "Consequently, faith comes from hearing the message, and the message is heard through the word about Christ" (Romans 10:17).

Resources

Additional Information

Definition of Terms

The Bible: The Bible is a collection of 66 books written by about 40 authors, in three different languages, on three different continents, over approximately 1600 years. The Bible claims to be inspired and inerrant. This means that the Bible claims to be from God and that it's without error in everything it addresses. The 66 books of the Bible are divided into two major sections, known as the Old and New Testament. The term "testament" in this case has the meaning of "covenant" or "agreement". Well into the Christian era, what we know as the Old Testament was known as "Scripture" or "The law and the prophets." From the moment that the books of our New Testament were all written and accepted into the canon, the title "Old Testament" was applied to the Hebrew Scriptures before Christ and the "New Testament" to the writings of the apostles and his companions (Exploring the Old Testament, NPH, tr. from Spanish).

The Unity of the Bible: "The study of the nature of the relationship of the sixty-six canonical books of the Bible. The unity of Scripture claims that the Bible presents a non-contradictory and consistent message concerning God and redemptive history. The fact of diversity is observed in comparing the individual authors' presentations of God and history" (Bakers evangelical Dictionary).

Biblical Aramaic: "The form of Aramaic that was the common language of Palestine in New Testament times. It was widespread throughout the Persian Empire from the 5th century and is found in the later books of the Old Testament (esp. Daniel 2:4–7:28)" (British Dictionary Definitions).

Additional Activity

Review

1. Encourage the students to memorize the books of the Bible. Ask them to name the list in class.

2. Write on separate cards the following topics: Pentateuch, historical books, poetry books, Major Prophets, Minor Prophets; Gospels and Acts, Pauline Epistles, universal Epistles and Prophecy. Have each person take a card and ask them to name from memory the books that correspond to each card.

What Do We Believe?

The Triune God
Jesus Christ
The Holy Spirit
The Bible and Sin
Atonement, Grace, and Repentance
Justification, Regeneration and Adoption
Entire Sanctification
The Church
Baptism and The Lord's Supper
Divine Healing
Second Coming of Christ
Resurrection, Judgement and Destiny
What Do We Believe?

The Triune God

Lesson 14

Eduardo Aparicio (USA)

Memory Verse: "Hear, O Israel: The Lord our God, the Lord is one." Deuteronomy 6:4

Lesson Goal: That the students will understand the biblical doctrine of the Trinity as a fundamental doctrine of the Christian faith.

Introduction

We recognize that the example we're going to suggest is a human, rational way to explain what the Bible teaches us in relation to the triune nature of God.

Write on the board the chemical formula for water, "H_2O". Ask, what are the three states in which water can be presented? The answer will be 'solid' when it's ice, or 'liquid' when it in the form of water, and 'gas' when heat is added and it evaporates. If we analyze separately each state in which we find the water, we'll always find the same H_2O formula.

This explains, though not exactly, what we mean when we say that God is one (like water) but manifested in three persons (as the three states of water: solid, liquid and gas).

Jehovah or Yahweh is the personal name of the God of Israel. It's a name that, in addition to identifying God as a person, also reveals his character. For Jews the name of Jehovah or Yahweh was so sacred that they dared not pronounce it, and instead they called him Adonai. For them, there was no other Lord Creator for all to listen to and obey in everything.

Every time the people of Israel gathered to worship, they repeated the Shema which reads as follows: "Hear, O Israel: The Lord our God, the Lord is one. Love the Lord your God with all your heart and with all your soul and with all your strength"(Deuteronomy 6:4-5). Take a moment to memorize the Shema.

I. God is a triune God

The biblical doctrine of the Trinity of God is the deepest doctrine of the Christian faith, the root of all the others, but it's also the most difficult to explain. Over the years, many have wanted to give a logical and rational expression of the Triune

God's existence, but their conclusions were not always the best.

We must understand that this doctrine is rooted in the Bible itself and in the spiritual experience of Christians. So basically it's a matter of faith. To this end, as believers we know we cannot speak of God without us having to refer to the doctrine of the Trinity.

In the Gospel of Mark 12:29-30, one of the religious leaders asked Jesus what is the first commandment of all? Jesus responded with the Shema. We can see that the Jewish confession of "one God" was transmitted to the Christian community through the synagogue and Christ's teachings.

From this confession, the first century church realized that Jehovah God is also manifested in three persons. And so, beginning with the Gospels, the sacred authors teach us through the Trinitarian formulas, that we have a God who manifests himself as Father, Son and Holy Spirit.

A. The Christian Church and the Doctrine of the Trinity

The New Testament writers understood that God is one, and at the same time three. This does not mean that there are three gods, but God is manifested as we said before, as Father, Son and Holy Spirit. We'll quote some examples:

1. The Great Commission (Matthew 28:19). Before returning to the Father, Jesus gave them the next task or ministry: "Therefore go and make disciples of all nations, baptizing them in the name of the Father and of the Son and of the Holy Spirit."

2. Paul's teachings. The same Trinitarian formula in Matthew appears in the letters of Paul: 1 Corinthians 12:3; 2 Corinthians 1:21-22; 2 Corinthians 13:14; 2 Thessalonians 2:13-17.

3. The apostle Peter refers to the trinity in I Peter 1:2.

B. The Christian Concept of the Trinity

It is true that the word 'Trinity' does not appear in the Bible, but throughout the New Testament we find the Trinitarian formula, and then later the concept of Trinity was given to explain God and the three forms in which he is manifested.

We believe in God the Father, God the Son, and God the Holy Spirit, who share one common nature or essence. We understand that God is triune, but at the same time is one in essence or nature. That means that although we speak of three people, we're not talking about three gods, but one.

II. The Attributes of God

A. God is Sovereign

When we express that God is sovereign, we're saying that He is not only the creator of all that exists, but the master of everything, and He has power over all things. Deuteronomy 10:14 says, "To the LORD your God belong the heavens, even the highest heavens, the earth and everything in it". The psalmist expresses in Psalm 24:1: "The earth is the Lord's, and everything in it, the world, and all who live in it." It's important that as children of God, we should understand that God owns everything that exists in the world. We must apply this truth in all areas of our life.

When we accept that God owns everything, every decision we make becomes a spiritual decision. When we cut down trees indiscriminately, when we pollute the environment, when we use disposables plastics bags (without thinking that nature will take hundreds of years to recycle them) and when we waste paper, we're hurting God's creation. In everything we do, we must recognize that our God is the owner of everything and that He has supreme and independent authority over all creation.

B. God is Holy

What does it mean that God is holy? It means that in Him there is no sin, no evil, and no deception. God is perfect and pure. Throughout the Bible we learn that God is holy. First we see that God states that He is holy: Leviticus 11:44, 19:2; 20:7; Hosea 11:9. Also, the holy prophets declared it: Isaiah 5:16; Jeremiah 50:29; 51:5. The spiritual forces also declared Him to be holy: Isaiah 6:1-3. In the New Testament, the apostle Peter declares that God is holy in I Peter 1:15; and the apostle John in I John 2:20.

C. God is Eternal and Omnipresent

All creation, including human beings, are limited in terms of space, origin, size and power. Therefore, we're finite. Eternal or infinite means that there will never be an end and that all is full of His presence. The Bible tells us that our God is an infinite God. This is one of the absolute attributes of God (Psalm 90:2; I Timothy 1:17). This attribute is closely related to eternity. We say that our God is eternal because He had no beginning nor will He have an end. So He is infinite and eternal.

In Genesis 1:1, Scripture declares that God created all things and that He existed from the beginning. The Bible does not explain the beginning of God because according to John 1:1, God's action is continuous without having a beginning or an end.

In Revelation 1:8, 11a; 21:4-6 and 22:13, God is represented as the Alpha and Omega. This not only express eternity, but complete infinity. God embraces all; there is no place or time where He started, or will there any place and a time where He will finish.

Here we can say that the fact that God is eternal and infinite and that He exists in all time and space. He is omnipresent. His presence fills everything; we cannot hide from Him (Psalm 139:7-12).

D. God is Omniscient

Omniscience is the perfect knowledge of God. He knows everything that should be known. God knows all about Himself and all that exists. Nothing escapes his knowledge. God knows all about us and our existence. His knowledge is perfect (I Samuel 16:7; I Chronicles 28:9; Job)

E. God is Omnipotent

By saying that God is omnipotent, we refer to His perfect power. God can do anything He wants (Psalm 115:3; Luke 1:37). The Bible presents God as "the Almighty." We see his power in creation (Jeremiah 32:17); in the miraculous works (Matthew 19:26) and in salvation (Romans 1:16; Ephesians 1:19-23).

Conclusion

The Bible clearly teaches that there is one God, manifested as Father, Son and Holy Spirit with the same attributes. The doctrine of the Trinity is fundamental in the Christian faith.

Resources

Additional Information

How can we care for God's creation? Between 500,000 million and a trillion plastic bags are used worldwide every year. Less than 1% of the bags are recycled. It's more expensive to recycle a plastic bag than to produce a new one. Processing and recycling a ton of plastic bags costs $4,000. The same goes for paper. To make new paper we damage trees, and the process of recycling is very expensive and unprofitable. But it's becoming an alternative (National Geographic News September 2, 2003).

Definition of Terms

Polytheism: Literally means "many gods". It's the belief in and worship of many gods. The neighboring countries of Israel were polytheists. The prophets, judges and priests of Israel spoke out for God, condemning polytheism.

Monotheism: Indicates the belief in one God. "Monotheism is distinguished from Polytheism, a belief in many gods and monolatry, the worship of a god without denying the existence of other gods. Among the world's religions Judaism, Christianity and Islam are monotheists "(Theological Dictionary Beacon, p.45, tr. from Spanish).

The Shema: Israel was the only monotheistic people living in the midst of polytheistic peoples. Faced with this influence, they testified that Yahweh was the only true God. The people recited the Shema constantly underscoring their belief that their Lord was the true and only God. The Shema says: "Hear, O Israel: The Lord our God, the Lord is one" (Deuteronomy 6:4). It's the affirmation of Judaism declaring faith in one God. Even today a Jew is required to recite the Shema in the morning and at night (Deuteronomy 6:7). It's the first sentence that is taught to a Jewish child, and should be the last words a Jew says before dying.

Triune: A term used to designate the divine Trinity: God is one in essence and three in person.

Sovereign: Someone who uses or has the supreme authority.

- Holy: Perfect and pure; separated from sin.
- Eternal: That which has no beginning or end, that which is perpetual.
- Omnipresent: to be always present in any place.
- Omniscient: to know everything.
- Omnipotent: to be all-powerful.

Additional Activity

Group Work

Before starting point II, ask the class to form into six groups. Have students look up the following passages and write what they say about God: Genesis 1:1; John 1:1; Revelation 1:8,11a; 21:4-6; 22:13.

Jesus Christ

Lesson 15

Eduardo Aparicio (USA)

Memory Verse: "We know also that the Son of God has come and has given us understanding, so that we may know him who is true. And we are in him who is true by being in his Son Jesus Christ. He is the true God and eternal life" 1 John 5:20.

Lesson Goal: That the students will understand that Jesus Christ is the Son of God, the second person of the Trinity, and that he actively participates in the redemptive work.

Introduction

How can we express what we believe about Jesus Christ in a single paragraph? Let's try. Allow a few minutes for the students to write their own statement of faith about Jesus Christ. It should be something like this: "Jesus Christ is the second person of the Trinity. He was incarnate by the Holy Spirit and born of the Virgin Mary. He is truly God and truly man. He died for our sins, rose again and ascended into heaven where he is interceding for us."

I. The Person of Jesus Christ

Who is Jesus Christ? He is God, the second person of the Trinity.

A. The Second Person of the Trinity

When asking people who Jesus is, the answers one might often get are as follows: "He is the Son of God," "the son of Mary", "God". And they are right, that is what the Bible teaches. In Matthew 3:17, God the Father says about Jesus: "… This is my Son, whom I love; with him I am well pleased." And in Luke 1:31, the angel announces to Mary that she will bear a son whose name will be Jesus.

The word "trinity" is not found in the Bible. It's just a term to explain the faith in God the Father, God the Son and God the Holy Spirit, and is a central doctrine of Christianity. In the early centuries, it was necessary to use that term to counter the false teachings concerning the person of Christ which began to appear in the Church of the first centuries. For example, the teaching of Arius of Alexandria around 325 A.D. said that Christ was created by God. There were also other sects and doctrines, like Gnosticism and Neoplatonism, which had similar positions to those of Arius.

Why do we say that Christ is the second person of the Trinity? Is there such a concept in the Bible? The Bible does not name Christ as "the second person of the Trinity". So, why do we say that Christ is the second person of the Trinity?

First, because every time the Bible mentions the triune nature of God, they do so in the following order: Father, Son and Holy Spirit (Matthew 28:19). Second, this Trinitarian confession is in various Christian faiths. For example, the "Apostles' Creed" which starts out: "I believe in God the Father Almighty and in Jesus Christ his only son …" For that reason we say that Christ is the second person of the Trinity.

B. He is One With the Father

All the time that Jesus was with the disciples, he told them that he knew the Father (John 1:18). However, we see that the last time he shared with his disciples, they were curious to know the Father and didn't understand what Jesus had taught them. So, despite Jesus' statement in John 14:7 which says: "If you really know me, you'll know my Father as well. From now on, you do know him and have seen him." Philip insists saying, "Lord, show us the Father and that will be enough for us" (verse 8). Jesus again emphasizes that He and the Father are one (verse 9). In Jesus' priestly prayer, there are several indications to this unity with the father (John 17:11, 21-23).

II. The Incarnation of God in Christ

Matthew 1:18-25, tells us the special

circumstances of the conception and birth of Jesus Christ, or what we call the "virgin birth". What is the message of this truth for us today?

A. Jesus was Conceived of the Holy Spirit (Matthew 1:18, 20). This passage corroborates the important teaching of the virgin birth of Jesus Christ. Why? For three main reasons: firstly, to free mankind from their sinful nature; he had to be free of that nature that all human beings are born with since Adam. Secondly: the birth of Jesus was the work of the Holy Spirit; it was a supernatural event, and Matthew wanted to emphasize that truth, (vv.18, 20). And thirdly: through his birth by a woman, Jesus was a human being, and being conceived of the Holy Spirit, he was born without sin. Thus Jesus Christ, the second person of the Trinity, was human and had the divine nature; as a man he was completely free from all sin.

B. He Was to be Called Jesus (Matthew 1:21, 25). In addition to highlighting the supernatural event of the birth of Jesus Christ, the angel who appeared to Joseph wanted him to understand that the child in Mary's womb would be our savior. This was why he was to be called "Jesus." "She will give birth to a son, and you are to give him the name Jesus, because he will save his people from their sins" (v.21).

On the other hand, Matthew tells us that the birth of Jesus is the fulfillment of the prophecy through Isaiah: "The virgin will conceive and give birth to a son, and they'll call him Emmanuel (which means "God with us") (Matthew 1:23; cf. Isaiah 7:14).

III. The Ministry of Jesus Christ

Why is it that today we don't need to offer animals as sacrifices to God? Animal sacrifices couldn't take away the sin of the people of Israel (Hebrews 10:4), let alone the consequences of sin (Romans 3:23; 6:23). It needed something radical to take away human sin. Therefore, God became incarnate in Christ to save us from sin once and for all (Romans 5:8; Hebrews 10:10, 12-14).

What sacrifices are pleasing to God? According to Romans 12:1-2: "Therefore, I urge you, brothers and sisters, in view of God's mercy, to offer your bodies as a living sacrifice, holy and pleasing to God—this is your true and proper worship. Don't conform to the pattern of this world, but be transformed by the renewing of your mind. Then you'll be able to test and approve what God's will is—his good, pleasing and perfect will ".

A. He Died for Our Sins

The death of Jesus Christ is the main theme in the New Testament. This is related to the general plan of God to save mankind from sin (John 10:14-15, Philippians 2:5-8). In his public ministry on at least three occasion, he clearly announced his death (Mark 8:31; 9:31 and 10:33-34). Jesus offered himself for us, to save us from sin, and this was done once and for all (Hebrews 9:24-28), not continually through the ministry of the high priest with the blood of animals (Leviticus 6:8-13).

B. He Rose Up From the Dead

If the death of Jesus had been the end, it really would have been a very sad story. The fact that Jesus died is an important part, because without the shedding of blood, there is no forgiveness of sins (Hebrews 9:22). But the resurrection is what completed the redemptive work of Christ in us, as the Apostle Paul wrote in 1 Corinthians 15:12-22. The resurrection of Christ opened the way for our resurrection.

C. He Intercedes for Us

After his resurrection, Jesus returned to heaven. "When he had led them out to the vicinity of Bethany, he lifted up his hands and blessed them. While he was blessing them, he left them and was taken up into heaven" (Luke 24:50-51).

Years later, the Apostle Paul in his letter to the Romans states: "Who then is the one who condemns? No one. Christ Jesus who died—more than that, who was raised to life—is at the right hand of God and is also interceding for us" (Romans 8:34). The apostle presents Christ as the one who intercedes for us. The writer of the letter to the Hebrews says: "Therefore he is able to save completely those who come to God through him, because he always lives to intercede for them" (Hebrews 7:25).

Finally, the apostle John introduced him as our lawyer saying: "My dear children, I write this to you so that you'll not sin. But if anybody does sin, we have an advocate with the Father—Jesus Christ, the Righteous One" (1 John 2:1). Jesus Christ is the mediator between God and humankind. He brings our case before God.

Conclusion

Jesus Christ is the second person of the Trinity; He was incarnate by the Holy Spirit and born of the Virgin Mary; He is truly God and truly human; He died for our sins, rose again and ascended into heaven and is there interceding for us.

Resources

Additional Information

The childhood of Jesus: The gospel accounts (Matthew, Mark, Luke, and John) tell us very little about the childhood of Jesus. We know only a handful of events: the family's escape to Egypt (Matthew 2:14) and return to Nazareth (Matthew 2:23; Luke 2:39); His increasing wisdom (Luke 2:40-52); and His visit to the Temple in Jerusalem at age 12, and obedience to His parents (Luke 2:41-51). It's possible that Joseph died early on, which would explain why Mark calls him the carpenter (Mark 6:3). He appears not to have done any miracles before the start of his public work.

Jesus Christ: This title speaks of his humanity and divinity. Jesus, his human name given to him by his parents as instructed by the angel, means "God is salvation," and the word Christ, or Messiah, means "the anointed one".

Definition of terms

Early Christian Gnosticism: "Gnostics believed that matter, whether it be the physical universe or the humanly body, is evil. It's obvious that there is a great tension between spirit and matter. This affects many of their beliefs and especially the way they perceived the world and God's interactions with it.... Gnostics considered themselves Christians and saw Jesus as a heavenly messenger. However, they rejected the idea of God becoming incarnate (God becoming a man), dying and rising bodily. These beliefs were considered unspiritual and against true wisdom because they entangled spirit with matter. Most Gnostics believe that whoever entered Jesus at his baptism left him before he died on the cross (http://www.theopedia.com/gnosticism).

Neoplatonism: This term refers to the revival of the teachings of Plato which began in the third century A.D. and ended in the sixth century. Neoplatonism influenced Christian theology especially Origen, Augustine and the work of Pseudo-Dionysius. (Theological Dictionary Beacon, USA: Nazarene Publishing House, p.463, tr. from Spanish).

Additional Activity

Copy the article of faith in the Manual of the Church of the Nazarene entitled "Jesus Christ" (see below) onto a card or make a copy for each of the students. When you start the lesson, ask them to read this statement and mark the main points. You can ask them to explain why they chose their main points.

Articles of Faith from the Manual

"We believe in Jesus Christ, the Second Person of the Triune Godhead; that He was eternally one with the Father; that He became incarnate by the Holy Spirit and was born of the Virgin Mary, so that two whole and perfect natures, that is to say the Godhead and manhood, are thus united in one Person very God and very man, the God-man. We believe that Jesus Christ died for our sins, and that He truly arose from the dead and took again His body, together with all things appertaining to the perfection of man's nature, wherewith He ascended into heaven and is there engaged in intercession for us" (Manual of the Church of the Nazarene, 2013-2017, pp. 28-29).

The Holy Spirit

Eduardo Aparicio (USA)

Lesson 16

Memory Verse: "But very truly I tell you, it is for your good that I am going away. Unless I go away, the Advocate will not come to you; but if I go, I will send him to you. When he comes, he will prove the world to be in the wrong about sin and righteousness and judgment." John 16:7-8

Lesson Goal: That the students will understand that the Holy Spirit is the third person of the Trinity and has an active ministry in the church.

Introduction

Make copies for students, or bring written on a large sheet of paper, the following statement about the article of faith on the Holy Spirit from the Manual of the Church of the Nazarene

"We believe in the Holy Spirit, the Third Person of the Triune Godhead, that He is ever present and efficiently active in and with the Church of Christ, convincing the world of sin, regenerating those who repent and believe, sanctifying believers, and guiding into all truth as it's in Jesus" (Manual 2013-2017, p. 29).

Ask the students to read it. When finished reading, question them: What are the main topics of this statement of faith concerning the Holy Spirit? Give them some time to respond.

I. The Holy Spirit, the Third Person of the Trinity

God is a being that transcends our intellectual capacity, even the most privileged. Teaching or doctrine of the Trinity is a biblical truth that is very difficult to understand through our natural abilities or human reasoning; we believe it through faith.

Not only do we have to believe by faith the doctrine of the Trinity, there are also other great biblical truths that go beyond our rational understanding, such as the doctrine of the creation. We don't understand, nor do the most famous scientists, how the world was created from nothing, but it was (Genesis 1:1). We accept it by faith. The same is the case of the virginal conception of Jesus Christ, which goes beyond our human comprehension (Matthew 1:20). We accept it by faith because it's in the Bible, which is the Word of God. In the same way, the doctrine of the Trinity cannot be understood rationally, but we accept it by faith.

The Bible shows us that the Holy Spirit is the third person of the Trinity in a number of passages in the following passages.

A. In the Great Commission: After Jesus was resurrected, he met with his disciples in Galilee and said, "All authority in heaven and on earth has been given to me. Therefore go and make disciples of all nations, baptizing them in the name of the Father and of the Son and of the Holy Spirit" (Matthew 28:18-19).

B. In Paul's Letters:

1. "Therefore I want you to know that no one who is speaking by the Spirit of God says, "Jesus be cursed," and no one can say, "Jesus is Lord," except by the Holy Spirit" (1 Corinthians 12:3).

2. "May the grace of the Lord Jesus Christ, and the love of God, and the fellowship of the Holy Spirit be with you all" (2 Corinthians 13:14).

3. There are other quotes from Paul that refer to the Holy Spirit as the third person of the Trinity: 2 Corinthians 1:21-23 and 2 Thessalonians 2:13.

C. In Peter's First Letter.

In his greetings to the church, Peter tells the believers in Christ: "who have been chosen according to the foreknowledge of God the Father, through the sanctifying work of the Spirit, to be obedient to Jesus Christ and sprinkled with his blood" (1 Peter 1:2).

The New Testament authors understood that just as God is manifested as the Father. He is also manifested through Jesus Christ, his Son bringing salvation, and through the Holy Spirit for sanctification.

II. The Holy Spirit Convinces the World About Sin

Jesus said referring to the Comforter: "When he comes, he will prove the world to be in the wrong about sin and righteousness and judgment" (John 16:8). Some people think that the ministry of the Holy Spirit is limited only to the sanctification of the believer. However and according to the Word of God, his ministry is broader. From the first verses we read about him in creation "Now the earth was formless and empty, darkness was over the surface of the deep, and the Spirit of God was hovering over the waters" (Genesis 1:2). The Holy Spirit is present even before a person hears the message of salvation or first reads the Bible, convincing them about their sinfulness (John 16:5-8).

To illustrate what we mean, we mention the report that a missionary gave about a visit to an Indian village. He projected slides of the crucifixion on a whitewashed wall. When he projected the image of Christ on the cross, one of the members of the village stood up and exclaimed, "Come down! I'm the one who should be there, not you".

We would not know of our need for a savior if someone had not convinced us of sin. Why did the projection of the image of someone who was crucified more than two thousand years ago in Palestine move the hearts of men and convict them of sin? It's simply the work of the Holy Spirit.

III. The Holy Spirit Sanctifies Believers

The Bible asks us to be sanctified completely, at any time and situation (1 Peter 1:15). Some would say, "wholly sanctified" (1 Thessalonians 5:23-24). This work of God in us is always in relation to the ministry of the Holy Spirit (Romans 15:16; 2 Thessalonians 2:13; 1 Peter 1:2). We obtain Sanctification as a work of grace because of the death of Christ and His work on the cross of Calvary.

How can we be sanctified or receive the fullness of the Holy Spirit in this life? First, we must receive Christ as our Lord and Savior (John 3:16). Then secondly, after accepting Christ as our Savior, we must dedicate our lives to Him (Romans 6:13, 19; 12:1-2). In third place, we must ask God for the Holy Spirit to come to us and to cleanse us and take control of our life (Luke 11:13). Just as we receive salvation by faith in Jesus Christ, so we receive by faith the fullness of the Holy Spirit in our lives. At this time the Holy Spirit sanctifies our lives and cleanses us from our sin nature (our predisposition to sin) so that we can live pure lives before God, who is holy.

IV. The Spirit Guides Us To All Truth

To guide us to all truth is one of the ministries of the Holy Spirit (John 16:13). And who is the truth? The Bible tells us that truth is Jesus Christ, the Son of God. That truth, which is Jesus Christ, cannot be discovered through theological, historical or anthropological research, but through the revelation of the Holy Spirit, who is God.

In the Bible, truth is not a philosophical or theological concept, but a person, and that person is the Son of God, Christ. In John 14:6, Jesus said: "I am the way and the truth and the life. No one comes to the Father except through me."

When a person is convinced of his sin, the next step to take is to go to the Lord, confess his/her sin, ask for forgiveness and receive Christ as Lord and Savior. That is also a work of the Holy Spirit, since He guides to the truth that is Jesus Christ.

Conclusion

We see in the Bible that the Holy Spirit has been present in creation (Genesis 1:2); in conception (Matthew 1:20) and baptism of Jesus (Matthew 3:16); He was manifested on the day of Pentecost when the disciples were baptized with the Holy Spirit (Acts 1:4-5). Since then, the Holy Spirit is in the church, which is the body of Jesus Christ, and in us, that "we are the temple of the Holy Spirit" (1 Corinthians 6:19-20).

Resources

Additional Information

Regarding the concept of "truth" we can see that from the biblical point of view, everything that has been revealed to us comes from God, because He has the whole truth. That truth:

- Is Jesus Christ, the Son of God, John 14:6.
- It shows the plans God has for us.
- It frees us (John 8:31-32).
- It's revealed by the Holy Spirit (John 16:13).

Regarding the concept of the Holy Spirit as "Comforter": In the memory verse (John 16:7-8), Jesus tells his disciples that it's necessary that he should return to his Father, otherwise the Comforter won't come; that referring to the Holy Spirit.

Anecdote

In one of his novels, William J. Locke describes a woman who had a large amount of money and had spent half her life visiting museums around the world. But she got tired and bored. In that situation, she met a Frenchman who had very few material possessions, but a great love for art. When the Frenchman accompanied the woman to a museum, she realized that by his side, everything seemed to make sense. That same day the woman told him: "I never knew how things were until you taught me how to look at them".

Application: We can know the Bible very well, but only when the Holy Spirit comes into our lives will he teach us to look at it and apply its teachings to our lives.

Holy Spirit:

"His personality is proved (1) from the fact that the attributes of personality, as intelligence and volition, are ascribed to him (John 14:17, John 14:26; 15:26; 1 Corinthians 2:10-11; 12:11). He reproves, helps, glorifies, intercedes (John 16:7-13; Romans 8:26). (2) He executes the offices peculiar only to a person. The very nature of these offices involves personal distinction (Luke 12:12; Acts 5:32; 15:28; 16:6; 28:25; 1 Corinthians 2:13; Hebrews 2:4; 3:7; 2 Pet 1:21). His divinity is established (1) from the fact that the names of God are ascribed to him (Exodus 17:7 ; Psalms 95:7 ; Compare Hebrews 3:7-11); and (2) that divine attributes are also ascribed to him, omnipresence (Psalms 139:7; Ephesians 2:17-18;

1 Corinthians 12:13); omniscience (1 Corinthians 2:10-11); omnipotence (Luke 1:35 ; Romans 8:11); eternity (Hebrews 9:4). (3) Creation is ascribed to him (Genesis 1:2; Job 26:13; Psalms 104:30), and the working of miracles (Matthew 12:28; 1 Corinthians 12:9-11). (4) Worship is required and ascribed to him (Isaiah 6:3; Acts 28:25; Romans 9:1; Revelation 1:4; Matthew 28:19).

The most common name is the third person of the Trinity; divine power created but not creator, transcendent man but able to dwell in the heart and the human spirit. It's not merely a benign influence, as fully engaged in life and authority of God, and through him, God is most frequently manifested in the cosmos and human experience. He is also known as the Spirit of God, Spirit of Christ, and Spirit of the Lord and the symbols of breath, wind, dove, fire and finger of God.

The Holy Spirit is manifested as a person has intellect (Isaiah 11:2; 1 Corinthians 2:10-11); emotions (Isaiah 63:10; Ephesians 4:30) and will (1 Corinthians 12:11).

Regarding the deity of the Holy Spirit and his equality with the Father and the Son. They affirm their titles: the Spirit of God (Genesis 1:2); Spirit of the Lord (Judges 3:10); Spirit of the Lord (Luke 4:18); Spirit of Christ (Romans 8:9). The baptismal formula relates directly to God the Father and Christ (Matthew 28:19). His attributes also claim their deity: He is eternal (Hebrews 9:14); holy (Romans 1:4); wise (Isaiah 11:2); omnipotent (Psalm 139:7-12) and omniscient (1 Corinthians 2:10-11) (Illustrated Bible Dictionary, USA: Revell, p.209).

Definition of Terms

Comforter: It comes from the Greek word parakletos meaning advocate or helper. In Christianity, the term 'comforter' most commonly refers to the Holy Spirit.

Truth: The Greek word alétheia does not refer merely to spoken truth; it means more truth of idea, reality, sincerity, truth in the moral sphere, divine truth revealed to man, straightforwardness (Strong's Concordance). According to the Bible, Christ is the supreme truth, and He will guide us into all truth.

The Bible and Sin

Eduardo Aparicio (USA)

Memory Verse: "All Scripture is God-breathed and is useful for teaching, rebuking, correcting and training in righteousness..." 2 Timothy 3:16.

Lesson Goal: That the students understand that the Bible is inspired by God for the purpose of showing the plan of salvation and thus free us from the sin that separates us from God.

Introduction

Of all existing books, none has had as much influence as the Word of God. Thousands of studies have been written about the Bible. Famous authors have taken themes of the Bible for their works, and poets and singers have been inspired by it. Since the advent of the printing press, the Bible has been translated into over two thousand languages.

Scripture reveals to us who God is. Also it shows us what human beings are like and the relationship between God and people. The Bible shows us God's faithfulness and the unfaithfulness of man (sin). It shows what went wrong but also points to the remedy.

I. The Bible

The Articles of Faith of the Church of the Nazarene states concerning the Bible: "We believe in the plenary inspiration of the Holy Scriptures, by which we understand the 66 books of the Old and New Testaments, given by divine inspiration, inerrantly revealing the will of God concerning us in all things necessary to our salvation, so that whatever is not contained therein is not to be enjoined as an article of faith" (Manual of the Church of the Nazarene 2013-2017, p.29).

We must emphasize three important points regarding the Bible:

A. The Bible is the Inspired Word of God

In 2 Peter 1:20-21, the apostle Peter clearly teaches that the Bible was not written because people wanted to write something. It's not a product of human initiative; if so, it would cease to be God's Word to become only the word of man. We believe in the plenary inspiration of the Bible. That is, we believe that the Bible is totally God's inspired Word.

The plenary inspiration of the Bible was not dictated to the biblical writers without their intervention. It was God who inspired the writers, who, from their full humanity and circumstances, reported the will of God. Therefore, the Bible is a book that does not hide human imperfections or show only stories of triumph and happy endings. Rather, it lets us see how, in everyday situations, God reveals his will to people.

B. The Bible Reveals God's Will

The Bible is the Word of God, inspired by the Holy Spirit, that reveals the will of God for our salvation and our daily lives. Luke 24:44-47 shows us that the purpose of Scripture is that we should get to know the gospel message of salvation. Although written by different people in different cultural contexts, its purpose is not to impose the customs of those cultures. All God wants through His Word is let us know the message He has for our salvation (2 Timothy 3:14-15).

The Bible shows us how we can have a right relationship with God. From the moment that we read and understand its message, God through the Holy Spirit opens our minds to see where we stand before Him. Thanks to the work of the Holy Spirit, we repent and confess our sins and He helps us to live each day in holiness (1 Thessalonians 4:3; Hebrews 12:14).

C. The Bible Shows Us How to Live Victoriously

In the church we must teach only what the Bible says. The same Holy Scriptures warn us of this in Deuteronomy 4:2 and Revelation 22:18-19. All we need to live in victory are in the 66 books that make up the Bible. In them there are valuable principles that help us to live in obedience to God. The value of these principles is that they are always for our good. They are impartial and applicable to any time and situation.

II. Sin

The Article of Faith of the Church of the Nazarene with respect to sin says: "We believe that sin came into the world through the disobedience of our first parents, and death by sin. We believe that sin is of two kinds: original sin or depravity, and actual or personal sin" (p. 29).

A. The Concept of Sin

The scriptural basis to say how sin entered the world is found in Genesis 3. This chapter shows us that by the disobedience of the first man and first woman, Adam and Eve, they were expelled from the presence of God.

How did that happen? God told Adam and Eve they could eat the fruit of the trees of Eden except the fruit of that tree in the middle of the garden, and if they did they would die (Genesis 3:2-3). However, Satan, snakelike, said, "You won't certainly die…For God knows that when you eat from it your eyes will be opened, and you'll be like God, knowing good and evil" (Genesis 3:4-5).

What did they do?

1. They believed the serpent (Satan) more than God.

2. They disobeyed God's command and ate the fruit.

This passage teaches us that sin is to obey Satan and disobey God. Romans 6:23 says, "For the wages of sin is death…" Sin is living far from God in disobedience to His commandments. Jesus said in John 8:34 "… everyone who sins is a slave to sin."

James 4:17 goes further when he says: "If anyone, then, knows the good they ought to do and doesn't do it, it's sin for them." This passage teaches us that if we know something pleases God and we don't do it (disobey), we also commit sin. In one sense, this is a way to see sin from another point of view. We often think passively that if we don't commit sin, it's enough. Yet the Bible teaches us that faith in Jesus Christ is a call to action for good. In that sense, sin is much more than doing evil. As the Apostle James says, knowing what is right and not doing is also sin.

B. Original Sin

Theology professors define original sin as the first transgression of mankind to the will of God, and that first transgression was committed by Adam and Eve. Since then, the desire has always been present in mankind to go against God and disobey him. According to the Beacon Theological Dictionary, "…original sin is generally defined as the universal and hereditary sinfulness of man since the fall of Adam" (p. 504).

In Genesis 1 and 2, we see that we were created to have fellowship with God. That is what differentiates us from the other species that God created (Genesis 1:26-28). But human beings, in their quest to be like God (Genesis 3:5,) fell into disobedience which resulted in separation from God (Genesis 3:8-24).

This sin was passed from generation to generation. For that reason, King David stated that sin was something which is transmitted (Psalm 51:5). Psalm 58:3 says: "Even from birth the wicked go astray; from the womb they are wayward, spreading lies."

Many years later, Jesus said that moral problems of man are the result of what is inside us (Matthew 15:18-19). Paul also makes a contrast between Adam and Christ in Romans 5:12-21, explaining that as by one man (Adam) all inherited sin, by one man (Jesus Christ) all can be set free from sin.

C. Personal Sin

Sin, which entered through Adam and Eve, opened the doors to let into human nature disobedience and rebellion against God, which leads to spiritual death. But it depends on us if we continue to follow the example of Adam and Eve, or follow the example of Christ who by his obedience to God the Father makes it possible for us to have eternal life. Then, if after knowing Christ we follow the example of Adam and Eve, we're rebelling against God. Knowingly we're rejecting His will and the love He has for us.

The apostle Paul, in his letter to the Romans, clearly explains this problem. The Good News Translation says: "God's anger is revealed from heaven against all the sin and evil of the people whose evil ways prevent the truth from being known. God punishes them, because what can be known about God is plain to them, for God himself made it plain. Ever since God created the world, his invisible qualities, both his eternal power and his divine nature, have been clearly seen; they are perceived in the things that God has made. So those people have no excuse at all! They know God, but they don't give him the honor that belongs to him, nor do they thank him. Instead, their thoughts have become complete nonsense, and their empty minds are filled with darkness"(Romans 1:18-21). Personal sin is when we act knowing that we're disobeying God.

Conclusion

The Bible is inspired by God and reveals His plans for our lives. The Bible shows us sin and its consequences as well as Jesus Christ, our savior, who frees us from sin.

Resources

Additional Information

"How did the Bible come to us? In the days of Christ, they had in the literature of the Jewish nation a group of writings, called "The Scriptures" (now the Old Testament) which people commonly recognized as coming from God. They called this literature the Word of God. Jesus himself recognized this to be so. It was read and taught regularly in the synagogues.

Christian churches, from the beginning, accepted these Jewish scriptures as the Word of God, and in their assemblies they gave them the same place as had prevailed in the synagogue. As the writings of the apostles appeared, they were added to those Hebrew Scriptures, and they had equally sacred veneration. Within the New Testament itself, there are indications that while the apostles were still alive, and under their supervision, collections of their writings appeared in the churches, which were placed with the Old Testament as inspired Word of God.

Paul claimed to have God's inspiration in his teachings (1 Corinthians 2:7 to 13.14:37; 1 Thessalonians 2:13); also John in Revelation (Revelation 1:2). Paul wanted his epistles to be read in the churches (Colossians 4:16; 1 Thessalonians 5:27; 2 Thessalonians 2:15).

Peter wrote "I will make every effort to see that after my departure you'll always be able to remember these things" (2 Peter 1:15). Paul quoted verses from Luke and Matthew as scripture (1 Timothy 5:18 cf. Matthew 10:10 and Luke 10:7) which suggests that these gospels might have been circulating when Paul wrote 1 Timothy. Peter includes Paul's epistles with the other Scriptures (2 Peter 3:15-16). (Henry H. Halley's Bible Handbook, USA. Editorial Moody, p. 652, tr. from Spanish).

Definition of Terms

Inspiration establishes that the Bible is a divine product. In other words, Scripture is divinely inspired in that God actively worked through the process and had his hand in the outcome of what Scripture would say. Inspired Scripture is simply written revelation. "Scripture is not only man's word but also, and equally God's word, spoken through man's lips or written with man's pen" (J.I. Packer, The Origin of the Bible, p. 31).

Additional Activities

Questionnaire for group work.

You can use this exercise before starting the development of section II.

Divide the class into groups of three. Then get each group to read James 4:17; Romans 1:18-20, 23, and 25 and answer the following questions:

1. What is sin?

2. What does Paul regard as personal sin?

3. What are the consequences of personal sin?

Application: Give three practical examples of how these teachings apply to your personal life (family, work, etc.)?

Group work:

Plan: to discover the need of guidance

Materials: A roadmap and two dark scarves.

Time: Five minutes

Choose two people in the class to leave the classroom. The two people involved are blindfolded. The aim of the activity is that both people have to go in and sit down in a place previously designated for them. One of them will be told that he is on his own. He can ask the class questions. The other person will have been given a sheet with exact directions to the place. The people in the class can only help the person without the map. It's desirable to come to an agreement that some people will act indifferently, others will give them wrong information, while others only say 'yes' or 'no' and give very little help. No one can stand up to help. Some obstacles can be placed in the space of the classroom to make it more fun.

Application: Discuss with the class the value of the Bible for us. Have the people involved tell their experiences. What is the value of having an exact map to help us to reach the destination?

Atonement, Grace and Repentance

Lesson 18

Eduardo Aparicio (USA)

Memory Verse: "But God demonstrates his own love for us in this: While we were still sinners, Christ died for us." Romans 5:8

Lesson Goal: That students will understand how atonement, prevenient grace and repentance are applied in their lives.

Introduction

The Bible contains great truths that are the fundamentals of the Christian faith. In relation to three of them, the Bible says:

1. The Doctrine of Atonement tells us that Christ died for our sins (Romans 5:8). Had it not been for the death of the son of God, right now we would not have salvation.

2. Prevenient grace is God's mercy acting even before we understand what Christ did on the cross for us (Ephesians 2:4-9). It's God's initiative for our salvation; we need to take care of our salvation because we may lose (consciously reject) it.

3. Repentance is recognizing that we have sinned against God, turning to Him and living according to His will (Romans 10:9).

So let's get ready to understand, through this lesson, more about the love and plan of salvation that God has for us.

I. Christ Died for Our Sins (Doctrine of Atonement)

The Articles of Faith of the Church of the Nazarene on Atonement states: "We believe that Jesus Christ, by His sufferings, by the shedding of His own blood, and by His death on the Cross, made a full atonement for all human sin, and that this Atonement is the only ground of salvation, and that it's sufficient for every individual of Adam's race. The Atonement is graciously efficacious for the salvation of those incapable of moral responsibility and for the children in innocence but is efficacious for the salvation of those who reach the age of responsibility only when they repent and believe" (Manual, 2013-2017, p. 28). This statement is in harmony with the teachings of the Bible.

A. The Condition of Man in Relation to God

Human beings, after the disobedience of Adam and Eve, lost their relationship with God. Sin blocked this relationship. From that moment we were left outside the presence of God as Paul says in Romans 3:23. Psalm 14:3 teaches us that men and women have turned away from God, denying His existence: "All have turned away, all have become corrupt; there is no one who does good, not even one. They are corrupt, their deeds are vile". When men and women close their eyes to the evidence that God exists, and live in a disobedient manner, they are rejecting their Creator.

B. Christ Died for Our Sins

Despite the situation in which men and women find themselves, and their indifference to God, He decided to send his only Son to die for our sins. In other words, God Himself came to restore our relationship with Him. He came to tear down the separation that existed between mankind and their Creator. He atoned for our sins by shedding his blood on the cross of Calvary. This was done once and for all as the author of Hebrews says: "And by that will, we have been made holy through the sacrifice of the body of Jesus Christ once for all" (Hebrews 10:10). This allowed us to have eternal life and communion with God.

Why did Christ die for us? Romans 5:8 says, " But God demonstrates his own love for us in this: While we were still sinners, Christ died for us." If we have salvation, it's not by our initiative or good works, but because God loves us. John in his gospel communicates this truth when he says: "For God so loved the world that he gave his one and only Son, that whoever believes in him shall not perish but have eternal life" (John 3:16).

60

In addition to salvation, God demonstrates His own love toward us by giving us abundant life here (John 10:10) and eternal life after death (John 3:16).

II. Our Salvation Was God's Idea (The Doctrine of Prevenient Grace)

A. Saved by Grace

But could men and women attain salvation on their own merits? NO. Why not? The reasons are as follows:

- *Human beings are slaves of sin.*

Sin controls people's lives, enslaving them and turning them away from God. Being enslaved to sin prevents them from doing what is good; their lives lean continually towards evil (Matthew 12:34-35; John 8:34).

- *Apart from Christ we can do nothing.*

While we're slaves to sin, it's impossible to have a relationship or fellowship with God. In John 15:5, Jesus Himself tells us that "apart from me you can do nothing".

- *God loved us first.*

God knew that although He gave us the freedom to make our own decisions, we would never have been able to return to God by our own means. This is where we understand the doctrine of "Prevenient Grace"; that is, God took the initiative to free us from the bondage of sin and to come to Christ (John 6:44; 1 John 4:19).

B. We Can Reject This Gift

The grace of God is seeking us out before we're saved. God's grace is what saves us and forgives our sins. God's grace sanctifies us. God's grace will allow us to enter his presence if we remain faithful.

As we're saved by choice, we can also reject salvation (known as free will). We won't lose out if we watch and care for this gift of God (John 15:1-7). We need to remain faithful to the will of God if we don't want to reject this gift of God (1 Corinthians 9:27; 10:12; Hebrews 2:1-3; 10:26-29).

III. Our Return To God (The Doctrine Of Repentance)

A. What does repentance mean?

On many occasions, we can confuse repentance with at least two states. While these may be contained in repentance, they are not to be confused with it. Repentance is not simply feeling very remorseful for committing an action; neither is it feeling shame after being discovered in a fault. Repentance means being aware of one's personal guilt and making a voluntary decision to separate oneself from consenting to sin, and allowing God to help one to change. Repentance means a change of direction. I went north, now I'm going south. It's to have a 180 degree turnabout in our lives. It's to stop doing what was wrong, which offended God, and resolutely do what is right and pleases Him, doing his will.

B. God Calls Us To Repent

When Israel turned away from God, the prophet Jeremiah called the people to return to God. The prophet required them to recognize their wickedness and turn to God (Jeremiah 3:12-14). Repentance is the first step to getting closer to God and restoring a relationship with Him. In his first sermon, Peter spoke about it. When people asked him what they must do to be saved, Peter replied that the first priority was to repent (Acts 2:37-38).

Conclusion

Kenneth Grider says: "God does not wait for us halfway along the road, but goes all the way to where we are, and starts creating in us the first desires to be saved" (Theological Dictionary Beacon, USA: Nazarene Publishing House, p. 316, tr. from Spanish). The Bible teaches that God's grace makes us see that the sacrifice of Christ happened in our place in order that we can turn to God, and through His sacrifice we're freed from sin and have salvation through genuine repentance.

Resources

Additional information

Articles of Faith of
the Church of the Nazarene
(Manual 2013-2017)

- **Article VI - Atonement**
  (see # 1 at the beginning of this lesson)

- **Article VII - Prevenient Grace:**

"We believe that the human race's creation in Godlikeness included ability to choose between right and wrong, and that thus human beings were made morally responsible; that through the fall of Adam they became depraved so that they cannot now turn and prepare themselves by their own natural strength and works to faith and calling upon God. But we also believe that the grace of God through Jesus Christ is freely bestowed upon all people, enabling all who will to turn from sin to righteousness, believe on Jesus Christ for pardon and cleansing from sin, and follow good works pleasing and acceptable in His sight. We believe that all persons, though in the possession of the experience of regeneration and entire sanctification, may fall from grace and apostatize and, unless they repent of their sins, be hopelessly and eternally lost" (p. 31).

- **Article VII Repentance**

"We believe that repentance, which is a sincere and thorough change of the mind in regard to sin, involving a sense of personal guilt and a voluntary turning away from sin, is demanded of all who have by act or purpose become sinners against God. The Spirit of God gives to all who will repent the gracious help of penitence of heart and hope of mercy, that they may believe unto pardon and spiritual life" (p. 31).

Definitions

Atonement: It means reconciliation. In the Old Testament, it was associated with sacrificial offerings to remove the effects of sin, and in the New Testament the word refers specifically to the reconciliation between God and humanity effected by the death, burial, and resurrection of Christ.

Grace: "Grace may be defined as the unmerited or undeserving favor of God to those who are under condemnation" (Paul Enns. Moody Handbook of Theology, p. 196)

Prevenient grace refers to the grace of God in a person's life that precedes conversion (or salvation).

Activity

Use at the beginning of the class

Read the following story:

"When Mr. Hannes Zimmerman visited an evangelical church in Frankfurt, Germany, everything was new to him. He continued to attend for a month, spending every Sunday at the church. One morning, Hannes told the pastor: 'I come each Sunday because I need more time to understand what they teach here'.

One Sunday morning the Holy Spirit broke down Mr. Zimmerman's heart. When the pastor invited people to go to the altar and receive Christ as Lord and Savior, Mr. Zimmerman stood up, but it was not to the altar that he went, but rather he walked slowly toward the wall where there was a cross. He stayed for a good time in front of the cross. He moved his mouth but no one could hear what he said. The pastor came to pray with him, and Mr. Zimmerman said, "Thank you, please I just need to be here a little longer. There are many things I have to fix."

The Holy Spirit spoke to Mr. Zimmerman, leading him to the cross. In that church and in front of the cross, the physical representation of Christ's death, Mr. Zimmerman found forgiveness of his sins and came to be at one with God."

Let the students think about the story for a few moments then ask them: What other ways or means does the Holy Spirit use to help us to recognize what God has done for us? Write down the answers on the board.

Justification, Regeneration and Adoption

Lesson 19

Eduardo Aparicio (USA)

Memory Verse: "Therefore, since we have been justified through faith, we have peace with God through our Lord Jesus Christ ..." Romans 5:1.

Lesson Goal: That the students understand that justification, regeneration, and adoption are simultaneous in those who seek God through the work of Jesus Christ.

Introduction

Justification is for all those who want to live according to the will of God; the same is true with regeneration and adoption. Before studying these three states of grace, we must remember the following:

1. We receive these blessings as a gift from God because He first loved us (1 John 4:19). They come from divine initiative or what we called in the previous lesson "prevenient grace".

2. We receive them if we respond positively to the divine call through Christ and repent of our sins.

3. Justification and regeneration don't come in chronological order, but are simultaneous blessings that bring us into a right relationship with God.

Let us study each of these three states of grace.

I. It's God Who Justifies Us

A young man told me: "Pastor, I need your help. I'm in trouble and I must go next week to the judge. Please, I would like you to accompany me." That day at the appointed time, we were facing the judge. The charge against the young man was serious; He had broken two traffic laws: not stopping at the red light, and not obeying the police officer who had told him to stop.

After hearing the allegations, the judge asked the young man if he was guilty, and he acknowledged his guilt. But that's not all over, the judge told the young man to pay the fine that the law indicated. He had to do 20 hours of community work and study the traffic laws of the city. The young man accepted the judge's ruling and was cited to be presented in court again after four weeks. When the judge saw that the young man had carried out all the court orders he said: "Since you have complied with excellence the orders of the court, I declare you today to be without guilt." He was free and made sure that he didn't break the traffic rules of his city again.

"We believe that justification is the gracious and judicial act of God by which He grants full pardon of all guilt and complete release from the penalty of sins committed, and acceptance as righteous, to all who believe on Jesus Christ and receive Him as Lord and Savior" (Manual of the Church of the Nazarene 2013-2017, p. 32).

A. What Is Justification?

Justification is the judicial act of God that gives the sinner complete forgiveness of all guilt. Romans 5:1 tells us that God justifies us by faith. He makes us righteous, no matter what we have done. When we come to the Lord and repent, we're guiltless. This can be achieved thanks to the sacrifice Jesus made on the cross of Calvary. Justification gives us peace with God.

B. Why Do We Need To Be Justified?

In Isaiah 59:2, the prophet speaks of the sin which had separated the people of Israel from God. "But your iniquities have separated you from your God; your sins have hidden his face from you, so that he won't hear."

Centuries later the apostle John said, "Whoever believes in the Son has eternal life, but whoever rejects the Son won't see life, for God's wrath remains on them" (John 3:36). Paul wrote to the church in Rome that "the wages of sin is death" (Romans 6:23a). The only result that sin brings with it is death. We all deserve death because we're guilty. We need to be justified by God for salvation and eternal life. We need God to absolve us and make us free from guilt (Romans 3:23-26).

C. How Do We Obtain Justification?

Justification is based on the work of Christ. All the credit goes to God, so we say it's by grace. It's a gift of God for everyone. We get it only by faith in the Son of God (Ephesians 2:8-9).

II. It Is God Who Regenerates

"We believe that regeneration, or the new birth, is that gracious work of God whereby the moral nature of the repentant believer is spiritually quickened and given a distinctively spiritual life, capable of faith, love, and obedience" (Manual of the Church of the Nazarene 2013-2017, p. 32).

Regeneration occurs when a person repents and confesses his sins before God through Christ. That is when we pass from spiritual death to spiritual life.

A. Regeneration Is To Be Born Again

When Jesus was talking to Nicodemus, he said, "... no one can see the kingdom of God unless they are born again" (John 3:3). Jesus spoke of the new birth as a necessary requirement to belong to the kingdom of God. This new birth indicates that the change must be radical. Before knowing Christ, men and women are dead in sin, but then through the work of the Holy Spirit, they can be born anew and live (John 5:24; Ephesians 2:1; Colossians 2:13).

What do the following passages tell us about this? Because of our sin (lies, slander, theft, fraud, adultery, deception, etc.), we cannot come to God on our own. Paul in his letter to Titus explains: "He saved us, not because of righteous things we had done, but because of his mercy. He saved us through the washing of rebirth and renewal by the Holy Spirit (3:5).

Ephesians 2:1-9 tells us that salvation and regeneration are divine works that we don't deserve, and that we receive by grace. I Peter 1:23 states that we have been "born again, not of perishable seed, but of imperishable, through the living and enduring word of God."

B. Regeneration Also Implies Transformation

The prophet Ezekiel makes this clear. To put it into our own words, God will take our hard and stubborn will and change it for a heart willing to obey his will (11:19-20). This great work of transformation is made possible by Christ through the Holy Spirit that makes us "new creatures" (2 Corinthians 5:17).

III. It Is God Who Adopts Us

"We believe that adoption is that gracious act of God by which the justified and regenerated believer is constituted a child of God" (Manual, p. 32).

What is adoption? From the biblical point of view, adoption is when God receives those who were not his children as his own sons and daughters (Romans 8:14-15; Galatians 4:6-7).

A. Adoption Is A Work Of God

Again we must return to the doctrine of "prevenient grace". Adoption is God's initiative. The moment we accept Christ as our Lord and Savior, by His grace we're part of his family, the church. We have not done anything to earn it, nor deserve it, it's just through the love and mercy of God the Father, "He predestined us for adoption to sonship through Jesus Christ, in accordance with his pleasure and will" (Ephesians 1:5).

Through this work of God, we're heirs with Christ, of all the treasures, resources and privileges of the kingdom of God, Paul says: "Now if we're children, then we're heirs—heirs of God and co-heirs with Christ, if indeed we share in his sufferings in order that we may also share in his glory" (Romans 8:17).

B. How Do We Know That We're Children Of God?

It is a work God does in us. The apostle Paul says that the Spirit of God bears witness with our spirit that we're children of God (Romans 8:14-16). If we're willing to live according to the demands of the gospel, we'll inherit an eternity with Jesus Christ.

Conclusion

Ask the students what they think should be the conclusion of this lesson. Let them express it in their own words. This will help you determine how much they learned from the lesson.

"Thank God for His love, for His forgiveness of our sins, and for new spiritual life and for making us his children."

Resources

Additional Information

With regard to adoption, according to the commentary by William Barclay, the apostle Paul used here the figure of Roman adoption. "The adoption ceremony, according to Roman law, took place in the presence of seven witnesses. Now suppose that the adoptive father died. In that event, should any dispute arise regarding the rights of the adopted child, one or more of the seven original witnesses would come forward and swear that the adoption was genuine and true. Thus they guaranteed the rights of the adopted person to receive his inheritance. "According to the teachings of Paul, the Holy Spirit itself is the witness of our "adoption into the family of God" (William Barclay, Commentary on the New Testament, Romans, Vol. 8, p. 121, tr. from Spanish).

Definition of Terms

Justification: A sovereign act of God's grace, declaring a person to be just or righteous. It's a legal term signifying acquittal.

Regeneration: The English word "regeneration" is the translation of palingenesia, from palin (again) and genesis (birth). It simply means a new birth, a new beginning, a new order. The person leaves the dominion of sin to the domain of the Spirit, and initiates growth and spiritual progress whose goal is perfection, becoming like Christ.

Adoption: act of leaving one's natural family and entering into the privileges and responsibilities of another family.

Additional Activity

Questionnaire for group work

The final paragraph of the Article of Faith of the Church of the Nazarene in relation to biblical teaching on justification, regeneration and adoption says as follows:

"We believe that justification, regeneration, and adoption are simultaneous in the experience of seekers after God and are obtained upon the condition of faith, preceded by repentance; and that to this work and state of grace the Holy Spirit bears witness" (p. 32).

Ask your students to analyze this statement and answer the following questions:

1. Who are justified, regenerated and adopted?

[Only those who seek God wholeheartedly will be justified, regenerated and adopted through faith in Christ].

2. How do we get these blessings of God?

[Through repentance of sins and faith in Jesus Christ.]

3. Who is the one who bears witness to this work of grace in us?

[The Holy Spirit of God, which confirms this grace.]

Entire Sanctification

Eduardo Aparicio (USA)

Memory Verse: " May God himself, the God of peace,(AL) sanctify you through and through. May your whole spirit, soul(AM) and body be kept blameless(AN) at the coming of our Lord Jesus Christ." I Thessalonians 5:23

Lesson Goal: That the students understand that the will of God is our sanctification, made by faith in Jesus Christ through baptism with the Holy Spirit.

Introduction

The Article of Faith of the Church of the Nazarene in relation to the doctrine of Entire Sanctification reads as follows:

"We believe that entire sanctification is that act of God, subsequent to regeneration, by which believers are made free from original sin, or depravity, and brought into a state of entire devotement to God, and the holy obedience of love made perfect.

It is wrought by the baptism or infilling of the Holy Spirit, and comprehends in one experience the cleansing of the heart from sin and the abiding, indwelling presence of the Holy Spirit, empowering the believer for life and service.

Entire sanctification is provided by the blood of Jesus, is wrought instantaneously by grace through faith, preceded by entire consecration; and to this work and state of grace the Holy Spirit bears witness.

This experience is also known by various terms representing its different phases, such as "Christian perfection," "perfect love," "heart purity," "the baptism with or infilling of the Holy

Spirit," "the fullness of the blessing," and "Christian holiness" (2013-2017, pp. 32-33).

In the first part of the Article of faith, we see three important truths regarding the doctrine of entire sanctification:

1. It's an act or work of God.
2. It's subsequent to regeneration; that is, that sanctification comes after we're regenerated by God.
3. The sanctification is wrought by the baptism with the Holy Spirit.

Before continuing with the study of sanctification, and to better understand this issue, we need to understand the scope of the work of Christ on the cross of Calvary.

I. The Scope of the Work of Christ on the Cross

When we talk about the work of Christ on the cross of Calvary, we immediately think of the forgiveness of our sins and the salvation He brought us. Christ died for our salvation, but he also died for our sanctification and glorification. Let us briefly look at what the Bible teaches us about this.

A. Salvation

Ask your students to read Acts 4:12 and 16:31, and get them briefly to explain what these verses teach. The central truth is that we can only be saved through Christ.

B. Regeneration

From the moment that God, through His Son Jesus Christ, forgave us our sins and declared us righteous, we're regenerated; that is to say:

1. Spiritually, we're born again (John 3:3).
2. We pass from death to life (John 5:24).
3. We're new creatures (2 Corinthians 5:17).

Regeneration is brought about through Jesus Christ

C. Sanctification

Christ died for our sanctification. In I Thessalonians 4:7, the apostle tells us: "For God didn't call us to be impure, but to live a holy life." God has not called us to live in the uncleanliness of sin, but to a life of holiness. All this thanks to the work of Christ on the cross of Calvary.

D. Glorification

If we confess that Christ is our Lord and Savior, we testify that we have passed from death to life and live in holiness, we shall see God "face to face".

In Romans 8:16-17:29-30 Paul says that when Christ comes, or if the Lord leads us first to be with Him, we'll stand before Him with glorified bodies seeing him "face to face".

II. Sanctification Is A Divine Work

As we said earlier, after our regeneration or spiritual rebirth, we need to walk every day in the Spirit; that is, we must let the Holy Spirit have control of our lives. That is sanctification.

A. It's The Will Of God

Paul tells us that like salvation and regeneration, sanctification is the work of God and that is what He wants for us. In 1 Thessalonians 4:3 and 5:23-24, the apostle tells us that God's will is that we live in holiness, away from sin, and that God sanctifies us completely: spirit, soul and body. Paul ends by declaring that God is faithful, He calls us to be sanctified and will do it in us.

B. We Obtain Sanctification Through Baptism With The Holy Spirit

Salvation is what Christ does for us and sanctification what Christ does in us. Only then can we live free from the contamination of sin. And that is possible only through the baptism of the Holy Spirit. The apostle Paul tells us in Ephesians 3:14-16 that we must be strengthened by his Spirit, and in Ephesians 5:18 that we should seek to be filled with Him.

In Luke 11:13, Jesus said that if we want to receive the Spirit, all we have to do is ask: " If you then, though you are evil, know how to give good gifts to your children, how much more will your Father in heaven give the Holy Spirit to those who ask him!"

In this work of grace, we're wholly sanctified by the baptism with the Holy Spirit. John the Baptist said to the people: "I baptize you with water for repentance. But after me comes one who is more powerful than I, whose sandals I am not worthy to carry. He will baptize you with the Holy Spirit and fire" (Matthew 3:11). This is possible if we ask God for faith. The Lord will cleanse us from all impurity of sin through the constant presence of the Holy Spirit in our lives.

How do we know that we're fully sanctified? Acts 1:8 says that we'll receive power and will be witnesses, and 2 Corinthians 7:1 says that we'll live in fear (authority) of God, perfecting holiness.

C. Names Used To Refer To Entire Sanctification

There are other terms to explain the work of grace of Christ in entire sanctification; for example: "Christian perfection," "perfect love," "purity of heart", "baptism with the Holy Spirit," "Fullness of the blessing" and "Christian holiness."

III. Growth in Grace

The article of faith of the Church of the Nazarene on this issue continues:

"We believe that there is a marked distinction between a pure heart and a mature character. The former is obtained in an instant, the result of entire sanctification; the latter is the result of growth in grace.

We believe that the grace of entire sanctification includes the divine impulse to grow in grace as a Christlike disciple. However, this impulse must be consciously nurtured, and careful attention given to the requisites and processes of spiritual development and improvement in Christlikeness of character and personality. Without such purposeful endeavor, one's witness may be impaired and the grace itself frustrated and ultimately lost" (Manual, 2013-2017, p.33).

Entire Sanctification is a work which occurs when we ask in faith. Then, we must continue to grow in the grace that is given to us in Christ until achieving "... the whole measure of the fullness of Christ..." Ephesians 4:13.

Growth will help us to be mature in the faith and not be carried away by any current of thought. In addition we'll walk in truth and grow in love. "Then we'll no longer be infants, tossed back and forth by the waves, and blown here and there by every wind of teaching and by the cunning and craftiness of people in their deceitful scheming. Instead, speaking the truth in love, we'll grow to become in every respect the mature body of him who is the head, that is, Christ" (Ephesians 4:14-15).

Conclusion

Baptism with the Holy Spirit is the blessed experience of entire sanctification. Thanks to the Holy Spirit, we can live in complete consecration and holiness before God and our neighbor. If you already have this experience, thank God. If you don't have it and want it, ask in faith and tell your leader or pastor to guide you and pray with you.

Additional information

Biblical references to other names for Entire Sanctification, (Manual 2013-2017, pp.33-34).

- "Christian perfection," "perfect love": Deuteronomy 30:6; Matthew 5:43-48; 22:37-40; Romans 12:9-21; 13:8-10; 1 Corinthians 13; Philippians 3:10-15; Hebrews 6:1; 1 John 4:17-18

- "Heart purity": Matthew 5:8; Acts 15:8-9; 1 Peter 1:22; 1 John 3:3

- "Baptism of the Holy Spirit": Jeremiah 31:31-34; Ezekiel 36:25-27; Malachi 3:2-3; Matthew 3:11-12; Luke 3:16-17; Acts 1:5; 2:1-4; 15:8-9

- "Fullness of the blessing": Romans 15:29

- "Christian holiness": Matthew 5:1-7:29; John 15:1-11; Romans 12:1-15:3; 2 Corinthians 7:1; Ephesians 4:17-5:20; Philippians 1:9-11; 3:12-15; Colossians 2:20-3:17; 1 Thessalonians 3:13; 4:7-8; 5:23; 2 Timothy 2:19-22; Hebrews 10:19-25; 12:14; 13:20-21; 1 Peter 1:15-16; 2 Peter 1:1-11; 3:18; Jude 20-21)

Core Values of the Church of the Nazarene

"We Are a Holiness People. God, who is holy, calls us to a life of holiness. We believe that the Holy Spirit seeks to do in us a second work of grace, called by various terms including "entire sanctification" and "baptism of the Holy Spirit"- cleansing us from all sin, renewing us in the image of God, empowering us to love God with our whole heart, soul, mind, and strength, and our neighbors as ourselves, and producing in us the character of Christ. Holiness in the life of believers is most clearly understood as Christlikeness"

(http://nazarene.org/ministries/administration/visitorcenter/values/holiness/display.html).

Definition of terms

Sanctification, or in its verbal form, sanctify, literally means "to set apart" for special use or purpose, that is, to make holy or sacred. Therefore, sanctification refers to the state or process of being set apart, i.e. made holy

Additional Activity

Find the key phrase

Before starting the lesson, ask students to read the following scriptures, and in their own words say briefly what the message is that God wants to give us today. Philippians 1:6; 1 Thessalonians 4:3, 5:23.

What are the key concepts or phrases found in the passages read?

[The Lord will perfect the work He began in us. God's will is our sanctification. It's God that sanctifies us completely].

The Church

Eduardo Aparicio (USA)

Memory Verse: "...let us consider how we may spur one another on toward love and good deeds,..." Hebrews 10:24.

Lesson Goal: That the students understand that the church is the community that confesses Jesus Christ as their Lord and Savior, and its mission is to continue the message of salvation in Jesus Christ.

Introduction

Vern and Luz Tamayo helped found the church in Taytay near Manila, Philippines. That ministry grew rapidly, and even though on a tragic day criminals killed Vern, the church continued its mission. The Sunday after his death, fifty people completed five weeks of discipleship and were welcomed as members of the church. That same Sunday, the church of Taytay surrounded Luz and her three children to show them their love and support; they also asked Luz to be their pastor. Today that church has 2,423 active members and is serving God and the community in various ministries.

I. The Church Is Made Up Of A People Who Confess Jesus Christ As Lord

In New Testament times, during the Roman Empire, Caesar was the lord of the world, and those who didn't recognize and proclaim his lordship were punished or sentenced to death. What did the Christians do? Once they had accepted Christ as Lord, they became part of the new people of God and became partakers of the new covenant. Therefore, they had to be obedient and serve Jesus Christ as their Lord (1 Peter 2:9-10).

The early Christians didn't fear the persecutions. Although they understood the danger they were in, they chose to recognize and confess Christ as Lord (Romans 10:8-9 and Philippians 2:11). They made that confession because their lives belonged completely to God and He was watching over them. Today where we live, are we confessing with conviction that Jesus Christ is Lord of our lives? Are our lives different from others because we live according to the that which God asks of us?

The story of God and his people is marked by different covenants. He made a covenant with Adam, Noah and Abraham; also with his people on Mount Sinai. A covenant is an agreement between God and us through which we can obtain salvation (Jeremiah 31:33). These covenants are initiated by God, and we can become part of it by our own choice. In the New Testament, we find the specifications of this new covenant that provides our justification through faith in Christ Jesus. The old covenant didn't allow us to enter the presence of God, but the new covenant does, through the blood the Son of God shed for us (Hebrews 10:19-23).

In Christ God has made a new covenant with His people, the church. What is this new covenant? This new covenant has been made through Jesus Christ's death on the cross. Being part of this new agreement brings benefits and obligations to fulfill.

II. The Church Expresses Its Life In The Unity And Fellowship Of The Spirit

It is important to understand that as Christians we're not isolated beings. God saved us, not to live apart from the world and from other Christians; On the contrary, he called us to live in community. We asked to be part of his church (Hebrews 10:24-25).

A. In Worship And Through The Preaching Of The Word

At this time, when many say they preach the Word, we must be careful and remain steadfast to the true Word of God: Examining the Word, not accepting everything that we're told (Acts 17:11), encouraging one another with the Word of God, and giving and receiving teaching (1 Thessalonians 2:3-6; 1 Timothy 4:13).

B. In Observance Of The Sacraments

Jesus knew what we're like and how fragile is our thinking. In the Old Testament, God again and again asked parents to remind their children of the wonders that He had done. However, with the passing of generations, the people forgot. So to help us remember, he gave us the Sacrament of the Holy Communion. Jesus wanted to celebrate this last Passover with his disciples to remember the departure from slavery for Egypt, symbolizing the departure of sin that they soon would experience. Jesus wants his disciples to remember the forgiveness of sins every time we share the Lord's Supper (Luke 22:14 -18, 20).

C. The Church Is Called To Minister In His Name

This is not just philanthropy, or help for help's sake, but rather service in the name of Jesus (Colossians 3:17). All our daily work must extol the name of our God. We should serve as representatives of Christ on earth.

D. The Church Must Live In Obedience To Christ And Mutual Accountability

Obedience to Christ is obeying the Word of God. This must be accomplished faithfully following Christ's example when he lived in this world (John 15:10; Philippians 2:8).

III. The Church Continues the Redemptive Work of Christ in the Power of the Holy Spirit

Christ's death was not the end of the redemptive work of Christ, but the beginning. From then on we should accept this work and share it with the rest of humanity.

A. Through Holy Living

Holiness basically means set apart; in other words, the Christian is part of God's people. Separate from the world (John 17:15-16); keeping clear of anything that displeases God and at the same time living a life of good influence in the world (Matthew 5:14-16). The Holy Christian is devoted to obey God in everything and at all times (1 Peter 1:14-15).

B. Through Evangelism

Unlike the situation of the church in the first century, we must recognize that in many of our countries, nothing prevents us from saying that Christ is Lord and Savior of our lives; however, very few dare to do so. Why?

1. Perhaps for fear of being criticized.

2. Because if we confess that He is Lord, we're recognizing that we have to obey him fully and are not willing to do so.

What does Mark 16:15 say on the same subject? Here there is a clear mandate: Jesus said

to them, "Go into all the world and preach the gospel to all creation." As members of a church, we have the responsibility to carry out the task of evangelization of humanity, starting with the person closest to us and continuing to the ends of the earth (Acts 1:8).

C. Through Discipleship

The meaning of the word "disciple" in Greek is "pupil" or "student". A disciple is a student or apprentice studying under the guidance of a teacher. This term was extended to all followers of Christ. From the word disciple comes the concept of discipleship, which implies the formation of the disciple.

In the ministry of Jesus, 'discipleship' was a key word. This is because Jesus took three years making disciples. From the time that Jesus called the twelve, he didn't depart from them until the day he began his suffering and crucifixion. Day and night he was with them, and never missed an opportunity to teach them.

In Matthew 16:24, he says that we're his disciples and we must take up our cross and follow him. The cross means what it meant for Christ: obedience, humiliation and salvation; and we must take that cross and make disciples as Christ did (Matthew 28:16-20).

D. Through Our Testimony

Every privilege brings responsibility. The privilege of Christians is to be the people of God. We have a responsibility to testify that He is our Lord and Savior (Mark 13:9; John 15:27; Acts 4:33).

E. Through Service

Service is the work we do for another person. As a church we must work carrying out God's orders. God asks us as a church to serve each other, no matter what it involves, without counting the cost and always serving with joy and as if we were doing it for the Lord (Colossians 3:23). As our Lord's representatives, the service of the church must go beyond the walls of the temple, serving others in their needs, following our Lord's example (Luke 4:18-19). The church must serve the Lord at all times, even in difficult circumstances (Acts 20:19). Service is a hallmark of the Lord's Church (John 12:26).

Conclusion

We are part of a large church, and we must live each day as people worthy of representing it. Being part of God's people gives us privileges and responsibilities that we must fulfill with the help of the Holy Spirit.

Resources

Additional Information

Characteristics of the church

    A. Unity (Ephesians 4:1-6).

    B. Holiness (Ephesians 4:17; 5:25-27).

    C. Authority (Acts 2:14).

    D. Faith (Acts 2:44; 5:14).

    E. Fellowship (Romans 12:5).

Definition of terms

Biblical Definition Of The Church

The word *"church"* in the Bible comes from the Greek word ecclesia, which means "a called out company or assembly." Wherever it's used in the Bible, it refers to people. It can be a mob (Acts 19:30-41), the children of Israel (Acts 7:38), and the body of Christ (Ephesians 1:22; Ephesians 5:25, 32).

We see the word church used three different ways: First, as the body of Christ, the church is often defined as a local assembly or group of believers (1 Corinthians 1:2; 2 Corinthians 1:1; Galatians 1:1-2). Second, it's defined as the body of individual living believers (1 Corinthians 15:9; Galatians 1:13). Finally, it's defined as the universal group of all people who have trusted Christ through the ages (Matthew 16:18; Ephesians 5:23-27) (Dr. Michael Williams, http://www.patheos.com/).

A *sacrament* is a religious ceremony or act of the Christian Church that is regarded as an outward and visible sign of inward and spiritual divine grace.

Philanthropy is the desire to promote the welfare of others, expressed especially by the generous donation of money to good causes.

Additional Activity

Prepare three or four copies, depending on the number of groups or students, of the Articles of Faith "XI. The Church" from the Manual of the Church of the Nazarene. Ask students to divide into groups and to carry out the following tasks:

- Read the Article of Faith on the church.

- Look for three separate themes in this declaration.

- Briefly express its relevance today.

Article:

"We believe in the Church, the community that confesses Jesus Christ as Lord, the covenant people of God made new in Christ, the Body of Christ called together by the Holy Spirit through the Word.

God calls the Church to express its life in the unity and fellowship of the Spirit; in worship through the preaching of the Word, observance of the sacraments, and ministry in His name; by obedience to Christ, holy living, and mutual accountability.

The mission of the Church in the world is to share in the redemptive and reconciling ministry of Christ in the power of the Spirit. The Church fulfills its mission by making disciples through evangelism, education, showing compassion, working for justice, and bearing witness to the kingdom of God.

The Church is a historical reality that organizes itself in culturally conditioned forms, exists both as local congregations and as a universal body, and also sets apart persons called of God for specific ministries. God calls the Church to live under His rule in anticipation of the consummation at the coming of our Lord Jesus Christ" (2013-2017, p. 34).

[Theme & Message for Today (answers to point 3)]

When reading the statement of the church we must understand that the church is the community:

Theme 1: A community that confesses that Jesus Christ is Lord.

    Message for Today: We must live according to the ordinances of Christ at all times and everywhere.

Theme 2: In which we express our lives in the unity and fellowship of the Spirit.

    Message for Today: In walking together helping each other and in group worship (singing, prayer, etc.)

Theme 3: Where the church continues the redemptive work of Christ through the Holy Spirit.

    Message for Today: We need to live holy lives, serving, evangelizing and discipling.

Baptism and The Lord's Supper

Eduardo Aparicio (USA)

Lesson
22

Memory Verse: "And he took bread, gave thanks and broke it, and gave it to them, saying, "This is my body given for you; do this in remembrance of me." Luke 22:19

Lesson Goal: That the students understand that baptism and the Lord's Supper are means of grace that we observe in obedience to Christ.

Introduction

The church has two sacraments: baptism and the Lord's Supper. What is a sacrament? It's something common that takes on a special meaning for us. It's something visible and external which, when we participate in it, reminds us of a spiritual and inner truth. There is nothing mysterious about it.

I. Baptism

We don't know what the origin of baptism is. Some believe it's a continuation of the ancient washings described in the book of Leviticus (13:6; 14:8-9; 16:24). On the other hand the Jews baptized proselytes, or Gentiles who converted to Judaism. That was before Christ began his ministry.

"We believe that Christian baptism, commanded by our Lord, is a sacrament signifying acceptance of the benefits of the atonement of Jesus Christ, to be administered to believers and declarative of their faith in Jesus Christ as their Savior, and full purpose of obedience in holiness and righteousness.

Baptism is a symbol of the new covenant, so young children may be baptized, upon request of parents or guardians who shall give assurance for them of necessary Christian training.

Baptism may be administered by sprinkling, pouring, or immersion, according to the choice of the applicant" (Manual of the Church of the Nazarene, 2013-2017, pp.34-35).

Baptism in the New Testament is the entrance into the community of the New Covenant, the new family of Christian faith. John the Baptist was the one who called the Jews to baptism (Matthew 3:1-6). It was John himself who baptized Jesus (Matthew 3:13-17). Jesus was later led by the Spirit into the wilderness (Matthew 4:1-11) and began his messianic ministry that culminated in the cross.

A. Baptism in Early Christianity

In Acts 8:26-29, we read the story of Philip and the Ethiopian eunuch. The fact that the eunuch was baptized after receiving Christ means that baptism gives public witness of faith and salvation in Jesus Christ.

Baptism is a command of Jesus. With power and authority he said: "Therefore go and make disciples of all nations, baptizing them in the name of the Father and of the Son and of the Holy Spirit…" (Matthew 28:19).

No doubt Peter remembered the words of Jesus Christ and repeated them to the crowd that was listening to his message: "Repent and be baptized, every one of you, in the name of Jesus Christ…" (Acts 2:38). Therefore, to participate in baptism we need to believe in Jesus Christ as Lord, repent and confess our sins, and be forgiven by God.

B. The Meaning of Baptism for Christians in Apostolic Times

In Israel, water was always a symbol of purification. Christ marks a new beginning in the lives of those who have been baptized. The new Christian leaves that life without God to begin life with God through Christ. It's evident that the early church practiced baptism as a sacrament of initiation into the Christian family. Lots of passages give evidence of this: Acts 2:41; 8:12-13.16; 9:18; 16:15.33; 19:5. At different times, people of different classes and in various ways were baptized in response to Jesus' commanded (Matthew 28:18-20).

On the other hand, baptism symbolized the true union with Christ; when we're immersed in the baptismal waters, we die (symbolically) to our former life, like Christ, rising to a new life (Romans 6:3-4; Colossians 2:12). If you want to, you can share your experience of your baptism as well as ask one or two of the class to share their memories and experiences too.

II. The Lord's Supper

"We believe that the Memorial and Communion Supper instituted by our Lord and Savior Jesus Christ is essentially a New Testament sacrament, declarative of His sacrificial death, through the merits of which believers have life and salvation and promise of all spiritual blessings in Christ. It's distinctively for those who are prepared for reverent appreciation of its significance, and by it they show forth the Lord's death till He come again. It being the Communion feast, only those who have faith in Christ and love for the saints should be called to participate therein" (Manual, p. 35)

The Lord's Supper as a spiritual feast is where we have communion with Christ, commemorates the sacrifice he made for us on the cross of Calvary, and reminds us of the glory to come.

"The Lord's Supper is a meeting place between the visible church and the church triumphant. These two dimensions of the Lord's Supper make it a real celebration. Looking back we focus so passionately in the redemptive work of Christ we experience again his saving grace in our lives. Looking forward we have a glimpse of the perfect and eternal life that awaits us when we die. The sharing of Communion together takes on meaning from what has been and what will be! (Steve Harper, 1999, The life of devotion in the Wesleyan tradition, p. 83, tr. from Spanish).

A. A Spiritual Feast of Communion With Christ

In 1 Corinthians 10:16-17, the apostle speaks of "communion" with Christ. That word means "to have something in common", and often means "sharing what one has." Professor Adam Clarke explains: "Those who partake of this Supper are partakers of the body and blood of Jesus Christ, that way we have fellowship with Him ... All who gather to participate and celebrate the Lord's Supper testify with him that they are Christians and have communion with Christ" (Adam Clarke,

Commentary on the Holy Bible, Volume III, pp. 407-408, tr. from Spanish).

In 1 Corinthians 10:18-22, Paul contrasts between communion with the pagan idols and Christian communion with Christ. In this, the apostle teaches that we cannot share the things of God with the things of the devil. If we practice sin, we should not partake of the Lord's Table without repenting and forsaking sin.

B. A Spiritual Commemoration Feast

In 1 Corinthians 11:23-26, Paul tells us that the Lord's Supper is a remembrance of what Christ did for us. The apostle says:

1. It is a teaching that has been received directly from the Lord. From the point of view of the apostle, the Lord's Supper replaced the Jewish feast of Passover.

2. Through the sacrament we remember with gratitude what Christ did for us, for the forgiveness of our sins, and to give us eternal life.

3. It's a feast where he is remembered and celebrated, and where we look forward to the return or second coming of our Lord Jesus Christ.

Each time we partake of the sacrament, we make public our faith; we reaffirm the forgiving grace of God in our life, and give evidence of our hope in the glorious return of Jesus Christ for his church.

Conclusion

The sacrament of baptism is a command of Jesus Christ to give public testimony of forgiveness of our sins and symbolically to die to the old life and be born to new life with Christ as our Lord and Savior.

The Lord's Supper is a spiritual feast of communion with Christ and the church. We remember the Lord's death for the forgiveness of our sins and remind ourselves of his second coming for His church.

Resources

Additional information

1. Baptism

Baptism of John the Baptist: "In Matthew 3:11, John the Baptist mentions the purpose of his baptisms: "I baptize you with water for repentance." Paul affirms this in Acts 19:4: "John's baptism was a baptism of repentance. He told the people to believe in the one coming after him, that is, in Jesus." John's baptism had to do with repentance—it was a symbolic representation of changing one's mind and going a new direction.

"Confessing their sins, they were baptized by him in the Jordan River" (Matthew 3:6). Being baptized by John demonstrated recognition of one's sin, a desire for spiritual cleansing, and a commitment to follow God's law in anticipation of the Messiah's arrival" (http://www.gotquestions.org/baptism-of-John.html).

Christian Baptism: It's an act of obedience symbolizing the believer's faith in a crucified, buried, and risen Savior, the believer's death to sin, the burial of the old life, and the resurrection to walk in newness of life in Christ Jesus. It's a testimony to the believer's faith in the final resurrection of the dead. Baptism is the one sacrament that all Christian denominations share in common.

In the Catholic Church, infants are baptized to welcome them into the Catholic faith and to free them from the original sin they were born with.

The mode of baptism: "There are three modes (or methods) of water baptism used in Christian churches today: immersion (in which the person is completely submerged), affusion (that is, pouring), and aspersion (sprinkling). Evangelical Christians are divided on the question of which mode or modes are proper forms of baptism. Some Christians (typically those who believe that only believers should be baptized), think that immersion is the only valid mode, while other Christians (usually those who recognize the validity of infant baptism) consider all three modes to be acceptable" (http://www.equip.org/article/the-mode-of-baptism/).

The Nazarene Church sees beyond the mode to the significance and accepts all three modes as possible ways of being baptized (see article above).

2. The Lord's supper

Catholic position: Transubstantiation is the process by which the bread and wine of the Eucharist is transformed into the Body and Blood of Jesus Christ. Catholics believe that through transubstantiation, the risen Jesus becomes truly present in the Eucharist.

John Wesley: Lord's supper as a means of Grace

Wesley believed and Christian tradition teaches that the Lord's Supper is the paramount means of grace. The sharing of bread and wine that represent the body and blood of our Savior conveys forgiveness of sins, reconciliation, and healing that is tangible and real. Wesley puts it this way:

"The grace of God given herein confirms to us the pardon of our sins by enabling us to leave them. As our bodies are strengthened by bread and wine, so are our souls by these tokens of the body and blood of Christ. This is the food of our souls: this gives strength to perform our duty, and leads us on to perfection. If therefore we have any regard for the plain command of Christ, if we desire the pardon of our sins, if we wish for strength to believe, to love and obey God, then we should neglect no opportunity of receiving the Lord's Supper" (Sermon 101: The Duty of Constant Communion).

Definition of Terms

Affusion is a method of baptism where water is poured on the head of the person being baptized. The word "affusion" comes from the Latin affusio, meaning "to pour on".

Sprinkling or aspersion is the act of sprinkling with water. Aspersion is a method used in baptism as an alternative to immersion or affusion.

Immersion baptism is a method of baptism that is distinguished from baptism by affusion (pouring) and by aspersion (sprinkling). The person is totally submerged in the water.

Additional Activity

Dramatization and Questions

At the beginning of the class, ask two students to read the story of Philip and the Ethiopian in Acts 8:26-29. It can be read in a dramatic way with one student reading the part of Philip and another one the part of the Ethiopian.

Then ask them the following questions:

- Who are the main characters?
  [Philip and an Ethiopian]
- What was Ethiopian doing?
  [He was sitting in his chariot reading the prophet Isaiah, v.28].
- What was Philip's question?
  [Do you understand what you read?" v.30]
- According to Acts 8:35, what did Philip do next?
  [Then Philip opened his mouth, and began to explain this Scripture and told him about Jesus].
- After receiving Christ, what did the eunuch ask Philip?
  [What prevents me from being baptized? v.36]
- What was Philip's response?
  [When he saw the eunuch's determination to be baptized, he asked him if he believed wholeheartedly in Jesus Christ. The eunuch's response was: "I believe that Jesus Christ is the Son of God" (v.37). Based on that confession, Philip baptized the eunuch.]
- Was the eunuch baptized before or after receiving Christ as his Lord and Savior?
  [After receiving Christ; this means that baptism is not for the remission of sins, but for public witness of faith and salvation in Christ.]

Recommendation

After teaching point II of the lesson, it's appropriate to motivate those who have not yet been baptized to think about what prevents them from doing so, and to make a decision. It can also be of help and blessing if your class, in consultation with the pastor, is able to share with the church lessons learned about the Lord's Supper with the congregation.

Divine Healing

Eduardo Aparicio (USA)

Memory Verse: "But he was pierced for our transgressions, he was crushed for our iniquities; the punishment that brought us peace was on him, and by his wounds we are healed" Isaiah 53:5.

Lesson Goal: That students understand the place of the miracles of healing in the ministry of Jesus Christ and the ministry that the church has today for the sick.

Introduction

If you have a testimony of healing, share it with the class. If not, announce the subject and allow someone to testify about how God has worked healing in their lives. Or if there is someone in your congregation who has a testimony of healing, invite them to come and share it briefly.

I. What the Word of God Teaches Us

The teaching of the Word of God on the issue of healing is abundant. Both the Old and New Testaments have stories of divine healing. For reasons of space, it's not possible to study all of them, but we do believe in healing and its importance today.

A. Jesus Christ and the Healing Ministry

In relation to Jesus Christ and the ministry of healing, Luke 4:18-21 reads: "The Spirit of the Lord is on me, because he has anointed me to proclaim good news to the poor. He has sent me to proclaim freedom for the prisoners and recovery of sight for the blind, to set the oppressed free, to proclaim the year of the Lord's favor." That is, the healing that God wants for his people is not only physical, "sight to the blind," but also the emotional and spiritual freeing of people who are oppressed. In many cases, Jesus healed and at the same time forgave the sins of the person. Matthew 9:27 tells us that Jesus first forgave the sins of the paralytic, and then healed him. However, this does not mean that the disease is the result of sin.

In Luke 4:18-21, Jesus makes two statements:

1. "The Spirit of the Lord is on me..." (v.18); this means that the power and authority of God was on him for the ministry entrusted to him.

As we read in Luke 4:18-19, Christ was anointed for five reasons:

- To proclaim good news to the poor.
- To proclaim freedom for the prisoners.
- Recovery of sight for the blind
- To set the oppressed free
- To proclaim the year of the Lord's favor

2. In verse 21, Jesus continues: ""Today this scripture is fulfilled in your hearing."

The miracles of healing during the ministry of Jesus Christ were a confirmation of his divinity and the promise that God gave through Isaiah, saying, "The Spirit of the Sovereign Lord is on me, because the Lord has anointed me to proclaim good news to the poor. He has sent me to bind up the brokenhearted, to proclaim freedom for the captives and release from darkness for the prisoners, to proclaim the year of the Lord's favor and the day of vengeance of our God, to comfort all who mourn" (Isaiah 61:1-2).

The "year of the Lord's favor" announced by Isaiah was fulfilled in Jesus Christ, who announced freedom and healing. Matthew also referred to the prophecy of Isaiah 53:4 in Matthew 8:17 when he said: "This was to fulfill what was spoken through the prophet Isaiah: 'He took up our infirmities and bore our diseases.' "

B. The Sick

The healing ministry of the church should be fulfilled through us. The ministry of the twelve should also be our ministry.

1. The mission of the twelve. The twelve disciples simply continued the ministry that Jesus Christ had left them. Their responsibility was to preach the message of the kingdom of God, but also to address the physical and emotional needs of people.

Luke tells us: "When Jesus had called the Twelve together, he gave them power and authority to drive out all demons and to cure diseases, and he sent them out to proclaim the kingdom of God and to heal the sick." (Luke 9:1-2).

2. The mission of the church today. In many biblical passages, we can discover a common denominator: the ministry of healing, salvation and restoration is possible through the power and authority of God. That power and authority comes only with the anointing of the Holy Spirit.

Remember that on the cross, Jesus Christ took on himself the sin of all mankind. This was a unique and sufficient sacrifice. "He was pierced for our transgressions, he was crushed for our iniquities; the punishment that brought us peace was on him, and by his wounds we're healed" (Isaiah 53:5). The idea is that by his wounds, there is healing for us. The sufferings of the Servant are not only vicarious, but redemptive and healing.

But we must also remember that illness and pain will only be completely eradicated when the kingdom of God comes fully. So, while this promise is being fulfilled, we must pray for the sick and ask Jesus for healing for them.

II. Healing In Daily Life

Through the ministry of Jesus and his disciples, the Bible teaches that Christians should pray for healing. At the same time, we recognize that God gives human beings the ability to study, investigate and discover cures for many diseases. So, we understand that God also uses other means to heal people, which we should not stop using.

A. Christians Should Pray For Healing

God's Word says: "Is anyone among you sick? Let them call the elders of the church to pray over them and anoint them with oil in the name of the Lord" (James 5:14). The following Article of Faith affirms this: "We believe in the Bible doctrine of divine healing and urge our people [to seek] to offer the prayer of faith for the healing of the sick. We also believe God heals through the means of medical science" (Manual of the Church of the Nazarene 2013-2017 p. 35).

With this statement, we're saying that we need to pray for each other for healing. We believe God as our creator can restore us physically, emotionally and spiritually.

B. Christians Must Recognize That God Has Other Means Of Healing

In John 9:6-7 we read how Christ restored sight to a blind man: "…He spat on the ground, made some mud with the saliva, and put it on the man's eyes. 'Go,' he told him, 'wash in the Pool of Siloam' (this word means 'Sent'). So the man went and washed, and came home seeing."

This story leads us to ask two questions:

1. Why didn't Jesus just speak to the blind to regain his sight, even though his word would have been enough?

2. Why did Jesus Christ make mud with his saliva, anoint his eyes and then ordered him to go to the pond to wash to restore the man's sight? The answer is because Jesus Christ, the Son of God, is sovereign. He promised to heal us, and for that he will use whatever means necessary for our restoration.

Jesus repeatedly performed miracles only by a word, but he also used his hands placed on the sick or he used mud as in the previous case. John 4:46-53 says that Jesus healed the son of a noble without even being near him. At other times, as in Matthew 9:29; Mark 10:52 and Luke 17:19, he asked people to use their faith.

We on our part must be obedient, pray for the sick and ask for their healing in the name of Christ, and seek the means available, letting God do his work by His perfect and pleasing will.

Conclusion

Healing is a work of God in us. We must pray for the sick, believing that God can work a miracle. But we must also go to doctors, understanding that God also works through them.

Resources

Additional Information

In 1936, Dr. Orpha Speicher went to India as a missionary. Two years earlier, a church had donated land that had an abandoned in Washim, India, to be used for a four-classroom school. Dr. Speicher saw the ground and had the vision to remodel the school to build a hospital. That vision became a reality and the hospital opened its services to the community in 1938. Dr. Speicher then had only the support of a single nurse; but, as the hospital earned the people's trust, she saw the need to build a nursing school and expand the hospital.

The project took 15 years. Dr. Speicher was not there, but left in her place missionary Jean Darling, and in 1946, she founded the first school for nurses. Today, the University for training nurses and Reynolds Hospital is managed by Christians in India as a powerful witness of God's love and healing to thousands of people.

Definition of Terms

Healing is the process of making or becoming sound or healthy again.

Divine Healing is when someone is healed, restored to health, by miraculous divine intervention.

Supplementary Activity

Read the following Article of Faith on healing and help your students discover the two basic teachings.

"We believe in the Bible doctrine of divine healing and urge our people [to seek] to offer the prayer of faith for the healing of the sick. We also believe God heals through the means of medical science."

(2 Kings 5:1-19; Psalm 103:1-5; Matthew 4:23-24; 9:18-35; John 4:46-54; Acts 5:12-16; 9:32-42; 14:8-15; 1 Corinthians 12:4-11; 2 Corinthians 12:7-10; James 5:13-16)

1. It teaches that Christians should pray for healing.

2. It teaches that God also has other means of healing.

The Second Coming of Christ

Lesson 24

Eduardo Aparicio (USA)

> **Memory Verse:** "You also must be ready, because the Son of Man will come at an hour when you do not expect him" Luke 12:40
>
> **Lesson Goal:** That students affirm the biblical promise of the second coming of Christ and what the responsibilities of his people (the church) are when the time comes.

Introduction

The Article of Faith on the Second Coming states: "We believe that the Lord Jesus Christ will come again; that we who are alive at His coming shall not precede them that are asleep in Christ Jesus; but that, if we're abiding in Him, we shall be caught up with the risen saints to meet the Lord in the air, so that we shall ever be with the Lord" (Manual of the Church of the Nazarene 2013-2017, pp. 35-36).

Let us look at two great truths found at the beginning and end of this Article of Faith:

1. The declaration of faith begins with the following statement: "We believe that the Lord Jesus Christ will come again." On what is this belief based? It's the teaching of the Bible, and we have no doubt that this promise will be fulfilled. Bible promises have been fulfilled and will be fulfilled to the letter (Matthew 24:35; John 14:3; 2 Peter 3:10; Revelation 1:7).

2. The declaration ends with the following statement: "we shall be caught up with the risen saints to meet the Lord in the air, so that we shall ever be with the Lord."

I. The Second Coming Of Christ

For those who are not Christians and intentionally deny God, the second coming of Christ will be to eternal death; but for us who we have accepted Christ as our Lord and Savior and live according to the will of God, the second coming of Christ is eternal life. In Luke 21:28, the evangelist warns us to be alert to the signs that take place before the second coming.

A. The Signs Of His Coming

After Christ announced the destruction of the Temple in Jerusalem (Luke 21:1-4), the disciples asked him this question: "when will these things happen? And what will be the sign that they are about to take place?" (v. 7). The Jews were always waiting for signs of major events that would occur, so it was not surprising that they raise this question. We Christians also want to know the signs that will announce the coming of Jesus Christ. The good news is that the Word of God has the answer to our questions.

In Luke 21:25-28, we see that Jesus said that the events before his second coming will include:

1. "There will be signs in the sun, moon and stars" (v.2 5). What are the signs? The answer is Matthew 24:29, "The sun will be darkened, and the moon won't give its light; the stars will fall from the sky, and the heavenly bodies will be shaken."

2. "People will faint from terror, apprehensive of what is coming on the world, for the heavenly bodies will be shaken (Luke 21:26). For those who don't recognize Christ as Lord and Savior, it will be a day of terror.

B. God Will Fulfill His Promise

Jesus Christ told his disciples that He would come, and that they had no reason to doubt; for that reason he told them the parable of the fig tree (Luke 21:29-36).

1. Among the Jews, the fig tree always had been used to represent Israel. Luke adds, "and all the trees" (v. 29), indicating that the message is not only for Israel but also for all nations.

2. We'll have to be alert (v.31); we're preparing to enter God's presence.

II. How Can We Be Prepared For The Second Coming Of The Lord?

A. We Need to Live Holy Lives

Peter in his second letter explains the promise of the second coming of Christ. In 2 Peter 3:10-14 we read:

1. "Since everything will be destroyed in this way, what kind of people ought you to be? You ought to live holy and godly lives as you look forward to the day of God and speed its coming. That day will bring about the destruction of the heavens by fire, and the elements will melt in the heat. But in keeping with his promise, we're looking forward to a new heaven and a new earth, where righteousness dwells (11-14).

2. We expect a new heaven and the new earth where there will be righteousness: "But in keeping with his promise, we're looking forward to a new heaven and a new earth, where righteousness dwells" (v. 13). As we await this new order we need to live justly.

3. Peter concludes: "So then, dear friends, since you are looking forward to this, make every effort to be found spotless, blameless and at peace with him"(v. 14)

So as we await the second coming of Jesus Christ, we must live in holiness, in justice and in peace.

In Titus 2:11-14, Paul warns Christians: "For the grace of God has appeared that offers salvation to all people. It teaches us to say 'No' to ungodliness and worldly passions, and to live self-controlled, upright and godly lives in this present age, while we wait for the blessed hope—the appearing of the glory of our great God and Savior, Jesus Christ, who gave himself for us to redeem us from all wickedness and to purify for himself a people that are his very own, eager to do what is good." The apostle warns us that the Lord not only died to save us but also for us to be a holy people, dedicated to do good, live in justice, and piety and self-control while waiting for his second coming.

B. We Must Be Vigilant in Prayer

When will be the exact day of the coming of Christ? Only God knows. According to Mark 13:32, "But about that day or hour no one knows, not even the angels in heaven, nor the Son, but only the Father."

So how should we expect the return of Christ? Mark 13:33-35 warns us to be vigilant, waiting expectantly and praying before the coming of Christ: "Be on guard! Be alert! You don't know when that time will come. It's like a man going away: He leaves his house and puts his servants in charge, each with their assigned task, and tells the one at the door to keep watch. Therefore, keep watch because you don't know when the owner of the house will come back— whether in the evening, or at midnight, or when the rooster crows, or at dawn."

III. How Will The Lord Come Back?

In 1 Thessalonians 4:13-18, the apostle Paul gives us a preview of this fact so important for followers of Christ.

According to the commentator Adam Clarke: "It is assumed that the apostle had come to know that the Thessalonians mourned for their dead, as did the pagans who had no hope in the resurrection of the body and were confused as to the doctrine of Resurrection". Verse 13 says: " Brothers and sisters, we don't want you to be uninformed about those who sleep in death, so that you don't grieve like the rest of mankind, who have no hope." We understand that if Christ was resurrected, we have the promise that we too will be raised up.

The Lord will return, but won't come like the first time as a lamb, but with all power, as the king of kings: "For the Lord himself will come down from heaven, with a loud command, with the voice of the archangel and with the trumpet call of God, and the dead in Christ will rise first" (v. 16).

Those who know Christ, on that day we'll become the reality that we have waited for for so long. Jesus said: "When these things begin to take place, stand up and lift up your heads, because your redemption is drawing near" (Luke 21:28).

Conclusion

Christ will come a second time. We don't know the day or the hour when this will happen, therefore we must live each day as if it were the last and be prepared to receive the Son of God when He returns for us.

Resources

Additional Information

The Second Coming of Christ to the earth will be as literal as his coming in the flesh to work out our redemption, through the sacrifice of his own life for us (John 14:3; Acts 1:11).

"Our Lord Jesus Christ presents the purpose of his coming in two familiar parables of the ten virgins and the talents. The important truth emphasized in these two parables is that of the coming of a trial in which the righteous will be rewarded and the wicked punished (Matthew 25:31-34)" (Introduction to Christian Theology, Wiley, Culbertson, USA:1976, p. 463, tr. from Spanish).

Definition of Terms

The Second Coming: A term used to refer to the glorious manifestation of Jesus Christ, when he returns at the end of this epoch to start the last acts of redemption and judgment. The term 'Second Coming' does not appear in the Bible, but is implied in such passages as Hebrews 9:28 ("...he will appear a second time"). The second coming of Jesus Christ has had a permanent value for Christianity, and through the centuries has been a source of inspiration and confidence. It exhorts us to purity, faithfulness, holiness, supervision and responsibility (Illustrated Bible Dictionary, tr. From Spanish).

The return of Christ in glory is the *Parousia:* The Greek word *Parousía* derives from *parōn,* "be present, arrive to enter into a situation." Properly, it means coming, especially the arrival of the owner who alone can deal with a situation. Parousía is a technical term, with reference to the visit of a king or some other official, 'a royal visit' in the NT, specifically of the Advent or Parousia of Christ" (Strong's Concordance).

The 'rapture': Some evangelical Christians believe in a sort of secret rapture where the Christian believers will be taken out of the world, while the world passes a period of tribulation. This is a position of those that have a pre-millenialist interpretation of the last things. As is clear in the Article of Faith, the Church of the Nazarene takes no position on either the millennium or the rapture in dispensationalist or pre-millennial terms. It does not define the nature of the Second Coming, only that it will occur using the biblical metaphors from 1 Thessalonians.

Additional Activity

If you would like to, use this activity before explaining or teaching point II of the lesson. Give this example and leave a few minutes to think about the answer.

Suppose you live in another city or country, and for almost ten years you have not seen your parents. One morning you receive the great news that they'll be coming to visit you. At last, after many years you'll see your loved ones. The visit is announced for next month, but they didn't say exactly when; despite that, you are very happy because you'll see your parents. While awaiting the arrival of this great family event, what do you need to do? How will you prepare? Allow your students to express four or five ideas.

Resurrection, Judgment, and Destiny

Lesson 25

Eduardo Aparicio (USA)

Memory Verse: "And if Christ has not been raised, our preaching is useless and so is your faith." 1 Corinthians 15:14.

Lesson Goal: That students understand biblically what we believe about the resurrection of the dead, the judgment of God and eternal destiny.

Introduction

When someone mentions the word "judgment", we usually pay attention to what they are saying. This is a word that we would like to overlook because of its own connotations. We must recognize that the subject of judgement, along with the doctrines of resurrection and eternal destiny, affirm the plan of salvation for humanity. So, let's look briefly at each of these issues starting with the doctrine of resurrection.

I. The Resurrection of the Dead

The Article of Faith of the Church of the Nazarene on the doctrine of the resurrection states: " We believe in the resurrection of the dead, that the bodies both of the just and of the unjust shall be raised to life and united with their spirits—"they that have done good, unto the resurrection of life; and they that have done evil, unto the resurrection of damnation" (Manual of the Church of the Nazarene 2013-2017 p.36).

"St. Paul puts the second coming in close relationship with the resurrection by the resurrection of the righteous dead something that immediately precedes the rapture of the living saints (1 Thessalonians 4:14-17). The resurrection immediate effect following the second coming of Christ is truly distinctive and elemental ... The term Resurrection means the return to life again, that is, the raising up of what had been in the grave. It also means a restoration to life of that which had previously died. As the soul does not die with the body, it cannot be subject to the resurrection. So it's the body of man that revives" (Wiley and Culbertson, Introduction to Christian Theology, USA:1976 pp.463, 474, tr. from Spanish).

A. Resurrection in the Old Testament

A rabbi's viewpoint "There are only two biblical references to the resurrection of the dead, in passages generally held by biblical scholars to be of late date, so that it has been conjectured that the doctrine owes something to Persian influence. The first is: "But your dead will live, Lord; their bodies will rise—let those who dwell in the dust wake up and shout for joy—your dew is like the dew of the morning" (Isaiah 26:19); and the second: "Multitudes who sleep in the dust of the earth will awake: some to everlasting life, others to shame and everlasting contempt" (Daniel 12:2)" (Rabbi Louis Jacobs, The Jewish Religion: A Companion).

B. Concept of Resurrection in the Christian Era

The assurance of resurrection is based on the resurrection of Christ. The apostle Paul in 1 Corinthians 15:20-23 tells us that as Christ was raised, so we too will rise. As through the sin of Adam we all become sinners and die; but through the death of Christ, all those who repent and do his will can be saved and rise again to be in eternity with Him (2 Corinthians 4:14; Romans 8:11).

The disciples saw the resurrected Jesus, and the church taught the resurrection as the foundation of salvation (Acts 2:32; 3:15; 4:10-12; 26:23; Colossians 1:18). Christ's resurrection means that death was defeated. That's why Paul said, "And if Christ has not been raised, our preaching is useless and so is your faith" (1 Corinthians 15:14).

We believe in the resurrection because Christ was raised from the dead, "...the first fruits of those who have fallen asleep..." (1 Corinthians 15:20).

II. Divine Judgment

"We believe in future judgment in which every person shall appear before God to be judged according to his or her deeds in this life" (Manual of the Church of the Nazarene 2013-2017, p. 36).

George was a young man who had been imprisoned. While in prison, he made an obscene tattoo on his arm. He argued that he could do what he liked and didn't care whether it was good or bad. One day, Jorge was released from prison and accepted Christ as his Savior. Wearing the tattoo on his arm embarrassed him and for that reason he always wore long sleeves. He tried to remove the tattoo but could not. Eventually he pondered and said: "God forgave my sins, he justified me but there are consequences of my past decisions that I cannot erase."

Before God, we're all important; therefore, everything we do and decide matters to our Creator. All our actions and decisions have consequences that affect us and affect those around us. So, the Bible says we'll be judged. And maybe, like Jorge, there are things in our lives that we cannot erase and we have to live with them, but if we repent, God forgives and they'll not affect the decision of God at the final judgment.

A. The Meaning of the Day of Judgment

When we talk about judgment, it does not mean God will rejoice when he must judge those who disobeyed him. The story of Matthew 23:37 shows us just the opposite. There will be judgment, and God will judge with justice. When that day comes, it will be a day of sadness for all those who rejected him. Some argue that if God is love, He won't really judge anyone. Yes, God is indeed love (1 John 4:8), but He is also just and He will keep His Word. That is why he won't fail to punish those who didn't want to obey him, and reward those who obeyed (Romans 2:5-11).

B. We'll All Stand Trial Before God

The Bible says that God will judge everyone, both Christians and unbelievers. He will judge everyone according to what they have done (Matthew 7:21-23; 25:21, 23; 2 Corinthians 5:10; Hebrews 9:27; Revelation 20:11-13).

III. The Gift Of Eternal Life

"We believe that glorious and everlasting life is assured to all who savingly believe in, and obediently follow, Jesus Christ our Lord; and that the finally impenitent shall suffer eternally in hell" (Manual of the Church of the Nazarene 2013-2017, p. 36).

A. God Offers Us Eternal Life

The Bible tells us a lot about the quality of life that Jesus Christ brought here on earth as well as in eternity. The characteristics of life that Christ offers us are as follows:

1. Eternal life: "For God so loved the world that he gave his one and only Son, that whoever believes in him shall not perish but have eternal life" (John 3:16).

2. Life in his presence: "After this I looked, and there before me was a great multitude that no one could count, from every nation, tribe, people and language, standing before the throne and before the Lamb. They were wearing white robes and were holding palm branches in their hands... Therefore, they are before the throne of God and serve him day and night in his temple; and he who sits on the throne will shelter them with his presence" (Revelation 7:9, 15).

3. Abundant Life: Jesus said, "... I have come that they may have life, and have it to the full" (John 10:10).

B. The Eternal Destiny: Heaven And Hell

In the Bible, the word "heaven" is used in three different senses:

1. Genesis 1:7 to 8.20; Psalm 19:1; Matthew 34:30 speak of heaven as the atmosphere around us, the sky.

2. Genesis 1:14; 15:5; Joshua 10:13 refers to heaven as unlimited space where the sun and the stars are.

3. 2 Corinthians 5:1-2; Hebrews 10:34 refer to heaven as the place where the saints go after this present life.

Heaven, the eternal home of God, is unchangeable and unshakable (Hebrews 12:28). It's where God is said to be and Christ is exalted. God's children shall dwell there for eternity (2 Corinthians 5:1), with an incorruptible body (1 Corinthians 15:42). We cannot describe or imagine what heaven will be like. Its measurements will have no limits, and there is no time in eternity.

Hell is eternal punishment. The Jews didn't accept the idea that life had a purpose. They believed that the dead continued to exist in a world of shadows and silence. The punishment of hell is separation from God. Those who don't accept the salvation that Jesus Christ offers are rejecting Him and God; therefore their end will be far from His presence (Matthew 7:23; 25:41, 46; 2 Thessalonians 1:6-9; Revelation 20:15).

Conclusion

Finally, you can ask the students to think about these questions and then leave a few minutes in prayer for students to reflect on the following questions: Have you thought about your eternity today? If you die today, where would you go? What are you doing today to enjoy an eternity with God? Invite everyone to pray for a few moments as they think about these things.

Resources

Additional Information

A new heaven and a new earth: "This phrase is used several times in the Bible to describe the ultimate destiny of the redeemed. The popular Christian idea of the ultimate salvation is that the Christian will die and go to heaven. Redemption includes the redemption of the body in the resurrection, and also includes the redemption of the earth (Romans 8:21). In creation, the earth was made to be the place where man dwelt, and ultimately, the earth will be redeemed and transformed to be the dwelling place of the saints after the resurrection" (Theological Dictionary Beacon, USA:1995 NPH p.127, tr. from Spanish).

Definition of Terms

Judgment: "Generally when the Bible speaks of judgment, it's assumed that the judge is God. God's judgment is, of course, infallible. He judges the world in two dimensions, historically and eschatologically ... Most of the biblical teaching about the Day of Judgement, however, refers to the future, that is the eschatological dimension. The author of the book of Hebrews states: "Just as people are destined to die once, and after that to face judgment" (9:27). The final judgment is the Great White Throne (Revelation 20:11) when all those whose names are not written in the book of life will be cast into the lake of fire (Revelation 20:15). The judgment establishes the terrible and eternal difference between heaven and hell. Those who will spend eternity in hell will be condemned by their own sin (Romans 6:23; Revelation 20:12). Those who go to heaven don't go for their own good works (Ephesians 2:8, 9), but for their faith in Christ, which is the basis of salvation and the heart of the gospel (Romans 3:21-24; 1 Corinthians 15:3; 1 John 1:7)" (Illustrated Bible Dictionary, pp.358,359, tr. from Spanish).

Supplementary Activity

Questions for Group Work

Before starting the lesson, divide the class into three or four groups. Make sure that each group has a secretary to take note of the replies of the group to the following questions. Assign each group a question and biblical texts.

Question 1: What will happen to those who die before the Second Coming of Christ? John 5:25-29; 11:21-27; 1 Corinthians 15:12-58; 1 Thessalonians 4:13-18; Revelation 20:11-13 (answer: they'll be raised from the dead).

Question 2: Who will God the Father choose to be the judge? John 5:22-23, 26-27; 2 Timothy 4:1 (answer: Jesus Christ).

Question 3: Who will be judged? Matthew 25:31- 32; 2 Corinthians 5:10. (answer: all nations).

Question 4: What is the final destination as a result of the trial? Matthew 25:46; Romans 2:5-11; Revelation 20:15 (answer: those who have done well to the resurrection of life, and those who have done evil go to hell for ever).

When the class gets together again, encourage each group to read the question and briefly explain what their answer is based on the assigned Bible passages. If you prefer, you can ask the groups to give their answers as an introduction to each point of the lesson.

What Do We believe?

Martha de Bradna (Guatemala)

Introduction

We often call the teaching of the Word of God 'doctrine.' God's teaching is manifested in statutes and decrees (Deuteronomy 4:1), words (Deuteronomy 4:10) and in His expressed will, contained mainly in the Law (Exodus 20:1-17). "Teaching" has the purpose of leading us to the more intimate experience with the divine will, because doctrine affects both the intellect and the human will.

In Matthew 7:28-29, we're told that the people were astonished at the doctrine of Jesus Christ. The apostles continued the teachings of Jesus, and the early church persevered in the doctrine of the apostles (Acts 2:42; Romans 6:17). Paul, in his epistles, continually exhorted the leaders to be firm and teach good and sound doctrine, which would result in godliness (1 Timothy 4:6-7, 13, 6:3-5; 2 Timothy 4:1-5; Titus 2:1, 8). The apostle John warns of the importance of doctrine (1 John 1:9-11).

It is important to study the Articles of Faith of our church (the doctrinal body), which have been based on the Word of God, to remain steadfast in sound doctrine, and to be sanctified in the Word of God (John 17:17, 19).

I. The Trinity and Its Attributes

A. God is a Triune God

The Trinity expresses the truth that God is one in essence, manifested in three persons. The word "trinity" is not found in the Bible. It is a term used to explain the faith in God the Father, God the Son and God the Holy Spirit, who share one common nature or essence. God is triune, but at the same time is one in essence or nature. That means that although we speak of three persons, we're talking about one God who manifests himself as Father, Son and Holy Spirit (Matthew 3:13-17, 28:19; 2 Corinthians 1:21-22, 13:14; 1 Peter 1:2; 1 John 5:7).

1. The Father is the first Person of the Trinity. God revealed himself as the Father of Israel, so Israel turns to God as her father (Isaiah 64:8). In the New Testament, we speak of God as "Father of our Lord Jesus Christ" (Romans 15:6). Through Jesus Christ, believers can address God as "Our Father".

2. Jesus Christ is the second person of the Trinity; He is eternally one with the Father. He was incarnate by the Holy Spirit and born of the Virgin Mary. Jesus Christ is true God and true man; He is our Savior and He died for our sins, rose again and ascended into heaven and is there interceding for us (Matthew 1:18-25, Romans 5:8; Philippians 2:5-8; Hebrews 10:10, 12-14; 1 Corinthians 15:12-22; Hebrews 7:25).

3. The Holy Spirit is the third person of the Trinity. He dwells in believers and sanctifies, convinces us of sin and leads us into all truth (1 Corinthians 6:19; Romans 15:16; John 16:5-8, 13).

B. God's Attributes

Through Scripture we learn that God is unique, good, great, mighty, merciful, faithful, just, creator and sustainer, worthy of all praise, honor and glory. The following are some of His attributes:

1. God is sovereign: He possesses and exercises supreme authority (Deuteronomy 10:14; Psalm 24:1, 103:19.)

2. God is holy: In Him there is no sin, no evil or deceit. God is perfect and pure. (Leviticus 11:44, 19:2, 20:7; Hosea 11:9; Isaiah 5:16; Jeremiah 50:29, 51:5; Isaiah 6:1-3; 1 Peter 1:15; 1 John 2:20.)

3. God is eternal and omnipresent: Our God had no beginning, nor will never end. (Psalm 90:2; I Timothy 1:17). Because He is in all time and space, He is Omnipresent (Psalm 139:7-12).

4. God is omniscient: God knows everything about himself, about us and all that exists. Nothing escapes his knowledge (I Samuel 16:7; I Chronicles 28:9; Job 37:16,42:2; Psalm 139:1-4).

5. God is almighty: His power is perfect, He can do everything He wants to (Psalm 115:3; Jeremiah 32:17; Luke 1:37; Romans 1:16; Ephesians 1:19-23).

II. The Scope of the Redemptive Work of Jesus Christ

The Bible is God's Word, inspired by the Holy Spirit; it reveals the will of God for our salvation and our daily life, and guides us to have a right relationship with God. The Bible reveals who God is; also who we humans are and the relationship that exist between us and God. The Bible shows us God's faithfulness and the unfaithfulness of men and women, in other words our sinfulness.

What is sin? It's an act of disobedience to God, motivated by our desire to establish our own rules and become master of our own destiny. The most distinctive feature of sin is rebellion against God (Psalm 51:4).

The Genesis 3 shows us the main characteristics of sin and its consequences. At the same time, it establishes God's faithfulness to His purpose of having fellowship with men and women, manifesting the beginning of His redemptive work. The first word of hope appears in Genesis 3:15 where God promises a Savior who will annul the consequences of sin.

The apostle Paul expresses in Romans 6:23: "For the wages of sin is death, but the gift of God is eternal life in Christ Jesus our Lord." In Romans 5:12-21, he makes a contrast between Adam and Christ. Paul explains that as a result of the sin of disobedience of the one man (Adam), death came, we all inherit sinfulness, we should be judged and condemned; but in contrast, through the perfect obedience of another man (Jesus Christ) we're free from sin, we're justified and receive eternal life. Jesus Christ conquered death and sin; so if we repent, we'll have forgiveness of our sins and eternal life.

Prevenient grace is God's mercy acting even before we understand what Christ did on the cross for us. It's the initiative of God for our salvation, and we need to take care of it because it's possible to reject it. Ephesians 2:8-9 says, "For it's by grace you have been saved, through faith—and this is not from yourselves, it's the gift of God— not by works, so that no one can boast." Repentance is recognizing that we have sinned against God, returning to Him and walking according to his will.

When Jesus Christ died on the cross of Calvary, he paid the full price for our salvation. We need to thank God for the divine miracle of spiritual freedom from the guilt of sin and death, and the possibility of enjoying an eternal life of renewed communion with God. Among the scope of the death of Jesus on the cross, are the following:

A. Atonement

Through the sacrifice of Christ on the cross, by the shedding of his blood, God takes away our sin (Hebrews 9:26; I John 1:7).

B. Justification

We are declared righteous before God, blameless before his throne, and this gives us peace with God (Romans 5:1).

C. Regeneration

Regeneration is the process of moving from spiritual death to spiritual life. This new birth indicates that the change must be radical (John 3:3, 5:24). This also implies transformation (2 Corinthians 5:17).

D. Adoption

It is the gracious act of God by which the justified and regenerated believers are constituted as sons and daughters of God, becoming part of His family, the church (Romans 8:16).

E. Sanctification

To be sanctified is to live consecrated to God, turning away from sin. God's will is that His people be holy (Hebrews 10:10; 2 Peter 1:15-16).

F. Healing

Through the sacrifice of Jesus Christ on the cross, God gives us physical, emotional and spiritual healing (Luke 4:18-21). Isaiah 53:4-5 says, "Surely he took up our pain and bore our suffering ... and by his wounds we're healed." In James 5:14-16 we're encouraged to ask God for the healing of the sick.

III. The Church and the Sacraments

A. The Church

The church is made up of the people who confess Jesus Christ as their Lord and Savior; the people of the new covenant; the body of Christ

(Ephesians 1:22-23) called together by the Holy Spirit. God calls the Church to express its life in the unity and fellowship of the Holy Spirit; in worship, through the preaching of the Word, observance of the sacraments, ministry in His name; and, by obedience to Christ and mutual accountability.

The mission of the church in the world is to continue the redemptive work of Christ in the power of the Spirit through holy living, evangelism, discipleship, our witness and service.

B. The Sacraments: Baptism and the Lord's Supper

1. Baptism

Jesus commanded us to be baptized (Matthew 28:19) and to give public witness to our faith and salvation in Him. In order to participate in baptism, it's necessary to believe in Jesus Christ as Lord and Savior, repent and confess one's sins, and be forgiven by God. The early church practiced baptism as a sacrament of initiation into Christianity (Acts 2:3,41; 8:12 to 13.16; 9:18; 16:15,33; 19:5; 1 Corinthians 1:14-17). When the believer is immersed in the water, it symbolizes his/her identification with Christ's death and resurrection (Romans 6:3-4; Colossians 2:12).

2. The Lord's supper

It's a spiritual feast of communion with Christ and a commemoration of the sacrifice he made for us on the cross. Jesus instituted the sacrament, teaching us as we take part to remember Him with gratitude for the work of redemption carried out on our behalf (Luke 22:19-20; 1 Corinthians 11:23-26). Each time we partake of this sacrament, we make public our faith and the hope in the return of Jesus Christ.

IV. Future Events

A. The Second Coming of Jesus Christ

This is the glorious return of Christ to earth in the end times for the last acts of redemption and judgment. In his first coming, he came as Savior, but he will return as a judge. No one knows the day or the hour when he will return.

"We believe that the Lord Jesus Christ will come again; that we who are alive at His coming shall not precede them that are asleep in Christ Jesus; but that, if we're abiding in Him, we shall be caught up with the risen saints to meet the Lord in the air, so that we shall ever be with the Lord" (Manual of the Church of the Nazarene 2013-2017, p. 35-36).

How should we live in expectation of the Second Coming of Christ? Living in holiness, justice and peace (1 Peter 3:10-14); vigilant and constant in prayer (Mark 13:32-37).

B. Resurrection

"We believe in the resurrection of the dead, that the bodies both of the just and of the unjust shall be raised to life and united with their spirits—"they that have done good, unto the resurrection of life; and they that have done evil, unto the resurrection of damnation" (Manual, 2013-2017, p. 36)

We believe in the resurrection because Christ rose again (1 Corinthians 15:20). The assurance of resurrection is based on Christ's resurrection (Romans 8:11; 1 Corinthians 15:20-23; 2 Corinthians 4:14). Christ's resurrection overcame death. Paul teaches that after the second coming of Jesus Christ, the dead in Christ shall rise and then the living saints will be caught up to heaven (1 Thessalonians 4:14-17).

C. The Divine Judgment and Eternal Destiny

1. Divine Judgement

"We believe in future judgment in which every person shall appear before God to be judged according to his or her deeds in this life" (Manual, p.36).

On the Day of Judgment, God will judge with justice, punishing those who didn't obey him and rewarding those who obey (Romans 2:5-11). That day God will judge everyone, Christians and unbelievers (Matthew 25:31-32; 2 Corinthians 5:10), based on what they have done (Matthew 7:21-23; 25:21, 23; Hebrews 9:27; Revelation 20:11-13).

2. Eternal Destiny

"We believe that glorious and everlasting life is assured to all who savingly believe in, and obediently follow, Jesus Christ our Lord; and that the finally impenitent shall suffer eternally in hell" (Manual, p. 36).

There are only two places of eternal destiny: heaven and hell. Heaven is the eternal abode of God, and His children shall dwell there for eternity (2 Corinthians 5:1), with an incorruptible body (1 Corinthians 15:42).

Hell is eternal punishment that implies eternal separation from God. Hell will be for whoever didn't accept Christ's salvation, rejecting him; therefore, they will be permanently removed from God's presence (Matthew 7:23; 25:41, 46; 2 Thessalonians 1:6-9; Revelation 20:15).

Stewards
of Our Bodies

Third Quarter

Your Body-The Temple Of The Holy Spirit

Eating For God's Glory

HIV And Aids: A Major Challenge

Eating Disorders: More Than Just Food

Stressed Out!

Smoking And Health

Could Drugs Come Into Our Homes?

Are You Worried? Tomorrow Will Be Another Day!

Slaves Of Alcoholic Drinks?

Let's Talk About It!

Is Euthanasia Good Or Bad?

Stewards Of Our Bodies

Taking Care Of Our Bodies (Review)

Lesson 27

Your Body - The Temple of the Holy Spirit

Ernesto Bathermy (Dominican Republic)

Memory Verse: "Do you not know that your bodies are temples of the Holy Spirit, who is in you, whom you have received from God? You are not your own; ..." 1 Corinthians 6:19.

Lesson Goal: To help the students to understand that they should take care of their body because it's the temple of the Holy Spirit.

Introduction

Ask the students to give their opinion on whether the body is good or bad. If they say that the body is good, ask them why they think so, and if they respond that the body is bad, ask them why they think that?

Some Greeks held the Platonic concept that the body is a shell that oppresses the soul of mankind. They believed that the soul was good, while the body was evil. According to the Plato, the body was a prison that held the soul, and therefore should be released from the body. But the biblical view is that our bodies are good, because God created them.

Ask them to read the passage from 1 Corinthians 6:12-20 to gain a better understanding of the passage. If some of the class has other versions, get them to share what their version says.

I. The Principles of Christian Freedom (v.12)

"I have the right to do anything," (v.12a). All things are allowed, I have the right and freedom to do whatever I want. In other words, I have no prohibitions; it's legitimate to do whatever I want to. However, the verse continues "but not everything is beneficial" or helpful. Not everything brings blessing. Christian freedom must include the principle of appropriate behavior.

The second principle that should govern our actions is self-control. The apostle Paul says, "I have the right to do anything—but I won't be mastered by anything" (v.12b). To allow ourselves to be dominated by "freedom" is slavery disguised as freedom. There is no greater slavery than to be a slave to freedom, and no greater freedom than to be free from the bondage of "freedom".

So, there are two principles that govern Christian freedom and that must be present in every act of our lives: appropriate behavior and self-control.

II. Our Bodies Belong to the Lord (vv.13-18)

Ask the students to read 1 Corinthians 6:13-18 and 1 Thessalonians 5:23 and give their opinion regarding the importance of what the Bible says about our bodies. Then write on a blackboard or a large sheet of paper the characteristics that describe the importance of the physical body.

In verse 13, Paul is emphatic in stating that "the body is for the Lord." The Corinthians had what appears to be a common saying to try to justify immorality:

"Food for the stomach and the stomach for food..." (v.13a). Paul answered them, saying that, "the body, however, is not meant for sexual immorality but for the Lord and the Lord for the body" (v.13b). He was reminding the Corinthians that their body is holy and therefore needs to be cared for. Like the Corinthians, believers today must remember that our body belongs to the Lord.

In 1 Corinthians 6:14, the apostle says: "By his power God raised the Lord from the dead, and he will raise us also." Here it's clear that the apostle is referring to the resurrection of our body. Ask the students to read Philippians 3:21 and share what it says about the resurrected body. After hearing the views, explain that our resurrected body will be transformed to be like the body of Christ. We'll have bodies which are incorruptible, glorious, strong and spiritual.

In 1 Corinthians 6:15-18, Paul urges the believers to "Flee from sexual immorality". In verses 15-18, the apostle presents three reasons why we should do this:

1. Because we're members of Christ. Paul says: "Do you not know that your bodies are members of Christ himself? Shall I then take the members of Christ and unite them with a prostitute? Never!" (v.15).

2. Verse 16 says: "Do you not know that he who unites himself with a prostitute is one with her in body? For it's said, "The two will become one flesh." Have students read Genesis 2:24; Matthew 19:5 and Ephesians 5:31.

3. Verse 18 states: "All other sins a person commits are outside the body, but whoever sins sexually, sins against their own body." Ask one of the students to read Romans 6:12-13. What does this text say about how we should use our bodies?

III. We're Stewards of our Bodies (I Corinthians 19-20)

Ask the students to define the concept of stewardship. In a simple way, a steward is a person who manages the assets of someone else. In other words, a steward is an administrator who is in charge of property belonging to another person, and that at some point, the owner will ask an account from his steward. In I Corinthians 6:19, Paul presents three arguments why we should look after our bodies:

1. Because our body is the temple of the Holy Spirit (v.19). A temple is a building set apart for the service to divinity, a sacred place. There were many temples in Corinth, but the temple that Paul has in mind here is the temple that the Jews had built to worship the God of Israel. For this reason, the temple is considered holy. In the same way, our body is the temple of the Holy Spirit and should not be used in ways that dishonors God (v.16).

2. In the same way that the Jews said that God dwelt in his temple, the apostle Paul says that the Holy Spirit dwells in Christians, which is why Christians should take care of their bodies from contamination. The Bible states clearly that the Holy Spirit dwells in believers (John 14:17 and 2 Timothy 1:14).

3. Verse 20 states: "You are not your own; you were bought at a price. Therefore, honor God with your bodies." Because our body does not belong to us, we're stewards. Romans 14:8 says: "If we live, we live for the Lord; and if we die, we die for the Lord. So, whether we live or die, we belong to the Lord."

Paul concludes by saying: "Therefore honor God with your bodies" (I Corinthians 6:20). Glorifying God with our bodies goes beyond avoiding sex before marriage or adultery. It involves the way we use our bodies and the way we care for them.

Ask the students to reflect and say how they can use their body for the glory of God. Write the answers on the board.

Conclusion

Ask the class what practical lessons they learned for their daily lives? Let each person share their opinions. Then, make a recap of the lesson making it clear that:

1. In Christ we have freedom based on two fundamental principles: Appropriate behavior and self-control.

2. Our body is the Lord's.

3. We're stewards of our bodies.

Resources

Additional Information

"Christian stewardship is ... everything we think, say and do after we say "I believe." Christian Stewardship is how we invest God's 'stuff' for God's mission in God's world...

We are called as individuals and as congregations and communities into God's mission. We participate by giving the gifts that God has entrusted to us. These gifts are everything that we have: our time, our talents and skills, and our treasure or physical resources. Christian stewardship includes all aspects of our lives. It's about our personal, work, and family life. It's about the good management of donations, including those made to our church. It's about our congregational and denominational life, which flows from our individual and collective desire to be part of God's mission for the world" (http://www.stewardshiptoolkit.ca/what-is-stewardship)

"I am accountable to God for the way I control my body under His authority. Paul said he didn't "set aside the grace of God"— make it ineffective (Galatians 2:21). The grace of God is absolute and limitless, and the work of salvation through Jesus is complete and finished forever. I am not being saved— I am saved. Salvation is as eternal as God's throne, but I must put to work or use what God has placed within me. To "work out [my] own salvation" (Philippians 2:12) means that I am responsible for using what He has given me. It also means that I must exhibit in my own body the life of the Lord Jesus, not mysteriously or secretly, but openly and boldly. "I discipline my body and bring it into subjection . . ." (1 Corinthians 9:27). Every Christian can have his body under absolute control for God. God has given us the responsibility to rule over all "the temple of the Holy Spirit," including our thoughts and desires (1 Corinthians 6:19). We're responsible for these, and we must never give way to improper ones. But most of us are much more severe in our judgment of others than we are in judging ourselves. We make excuses for things in ourselves, while we condemn things in the lives of others simply because we're not naturally inclined to do them. Paul said, "I beseech you... that you present your bodies a living sacrifice..." (Romans 12:1). What I must decide is whether or not I will agree with my Lord and Master that my body will indeed be His temple. Once I agree, all the rules, regulations, and requirements of the law concerning the body are summed up for me in this revealed truth-my body is "the temple of the Holy Spirit" (Oswald Chambers, My Utmost for His Highest).

Definition of Terms

Sexual immorality (porneias) is a term used to describe any form of illicit sexual behavior (John 8:41; Acts 15:20, 29; 21:25; 1 Cor. 5:1; 6:13, 18; 2 Cor. 12:21; Gal. 5:19; Eph. 5:3; Col. 3:5; Rev. 2:21; 9:21). Any sexual activity that deviates from the monogamous relationship between a husband and a wife is immoral by God's standard. The Lord does bless the sexual relationship in matrimony: "Marriage is to be held in honor among all, and the marriage bed is to be undefiled" (Heb. 13:4a). But He is not pleased with sexual activity of any kind other than that, "for fornicators and adulterers God will judge" (Heb. 13:4b; cf. Rom. 1:24–32; 2:2).

Additional Activity

Activity: Temple of the Holy Spirit today

Materials: One or two sheets of paper or cardboard, markers and tape.

Objective: To understand, in practical terms, what it means to be a temple of the Holy Spirit today.

Time: No more than 10 minutes.

Development: Draw on the board or paper previously prepared a silhouette of the human body. It would be best if you can make it the actual size. Then ask the class 'what does it mean for you today to be a temple of the Holy Spirit?' Get them to write a word or two and stick these words inside the human body silhouette. If the outline is drawn on the blackboard, you can write the answers there. Then discuss the answers.

Variation: Divide the class into two groups. Give each group a sheet of paper or card and ask them to draw a silhouette of the human body. Ask one group to write down inside the outline everything implied in being a temple of the Holy Spirit today. Ask the other group to write down, inside as well as outside the shape, internal and external factors which currently affect people as temples of the Holy Spirit be. Then put the silhouettes up in the front of the classroom and discuss the answers.

Lesson 28

Eating for God's Glory

María Elena Ureña (Costa Rica)

> **Memory Verse:** "So whether you eat or drink or whatever you do, do it all for the glory of God." 1 Corinthians 10:31
>
> **Lesson Goal:** That the students become aware that good nutrition is part of our responsibility as Christians.

Introduction

Ask students:

1. Why don't Christians use drugs?

2. Why do we consider that smoking cigarettes or drinking alcohol is not appropriate behavior for a child of God? Allow for a little discussion.

Read the passage of 1 Corinthians 10:31 in as many versions of the Bible as possible.

It seems that we should not need to question such mundane things like eating and drinking. Paul tells us that when we eat and drink, we need to do it for the glory of God. However, if you think about it, most of the time we don't think about this. In fact, we often eat or drink too much, or conversely we choose to eat less than what we need.

Increased advertising and availability allows us to have at our disposal a lot of fast "Junk Foods" which require little or no preparation, and may well produce several negative consequences for our health.

I. How do We Nourish Ourselves?

Ask a student to read aloud the first chapter of Daniel. Then ask students why it was that Daniel insisted on not eating the food offered to him.

Daniel's example invites us to try to eat healthy foods that don't contaminate us. It's now known that high intake of foods high in fat, sugar and salt leads us to develop serious health problems.

Ask your class to mention some of these problems and their consequences.

Among the main problems which may be mentioned are:

1. Hypertension or high blood pressure.

2. Elevated levels of cholesterol and triglycerides in the blood.

3. Diabetes Mellitus (elevations of blood sugar).

If these health problems are not treated, they may become serious; they can trigger other major diseases such as heart problems and strokes. It's very important to note that just being overweight or obese usually leads to one or more of the aforementioned problems.

There are different types of cancer that are also being associated with a poor diet, both from excesses and deficiencies, the latter especially when vitamins and minerals are concerned.

We know that large food consumption damages our body, but what will happen if we do the opposite? What will happen if we eat less than we need?

Another nutritional problem afflicting our populations in these times is due to an excessive concentration of how we look. Many of our teenagers and young people, and even some of our children, are falling into the clutches of Eating Disorders. Ask the students if they know what Eating Disorders are. If you know someone in the class or in the church who works in healthcare, you can ask them to come to the class to give a short explanation on the subject.

The main Eating Disorders are associated with body image distortions that make people think they are fat when in fact they are extremely thin. Among these problems we find:

1. Bulimia. Here they eat huge meals and then find a way to get rid of what they have

eaten. They may force themselves to vomit, use laxatives or diuretics (medications that increase the amount of urine), or have a period of exaggerated physical exercise (in time and intensity).

2. Anorexia Nervosa. This is an eating disorder where the body image is so distorted that people severely limit the amount of food they eat. This limitation leads them to consume less than a quarter of what their body needs; they see themselves as obese. This way of eating results in severe malnutrition.

II. A Good Nourishing Diet

God definitely knows what we need, so since creation he has given us all the types of food that we need to consume. A healthy adult should have food three to five times every day. The latter is recommended: three bigger meals, breakfast, lunch and dinner and two snacks between meals, which preferably should be fruit.

We must also include vegetables at lunch and dinner; and animal products such as meat, cheese, or eggs once a day. We should also consume at least one glass of milk (250 ml) per day. The consumption of fatty or fried foods as well as sweet foods or packaged products must be reduced as much as possible or removed from our diet.

Paul writes in 1 Corinthians 6:19, 20: "Do you not know that your bodies are temples of the Holy Spirit, who is in you, whom you have received from God? You are not your own; you were bought at a price. Therefore, honor God with your bodies".

Six tips for healthy eating:

1. Eat at regular intervals (Ecclesiastes 3:1).

2. Eat to live and don't live to eat (Proverbs 23:1-2).

3. Keep your bodies clean (2 Corinthians 7:1).

4. Practice self-control, not eating too much, and sharing with others (Philippians 4:5; 2 Timothy 1:7).

5. Avoid eating fat (Leviticus 3:17; 1 Corinthians 6:12).

6. Give glory to God when eating, drinking and in everything you do (1 Corinthians 10:31).

III. We're Free to Eat Well

Read aloud James 4:17. It is very likely that we know if we're not eating well, eating too much, have a high consumption of "junk food", omit meal times, don't get enough exercise, or don't eat enough. The reality is that we always find excuses for not doing what we know we ought to do, often putting it off till "next week". However, James tells us that if we know that something is good and we don't do it, it's sin. Ask your class what are they doing with their diet? Give them a few seconds to think about it.

Have a student read aloud 1 Corinthians 3:16 and another read 1 Corinthians 6:19-20. When we asked Christians why they don't use drugs or alcohol, usually they answer something like this: "We don't do these things because they damage the body, because our body has been lent to us from God who made us, and we don't want to contaminate it with harmful substances". Paul reminds us that there is more to it than this. Our body is the temple of the Holy Spirit. Therefore, we must beware of anything that might contaminate or harm us in any way.

On the other hand, Christ called us to freedom. At this time, one can see how many people are losing their freedom even in this mundane case of eating. Either because they are obsessed with having a "perfect" body, which according to them inhibits them from eating freely; or else they have lost their freedom by being tied in mind and body to food, living to eat rather than eating to live.

We need to ask God to help us find the balance between what we eat and what our body needs. We need to become aware we're responsible for how we feed our body. Like Daniel, we must act sensibly and wisely taking care of our body even in extreme situations.

Conclusion

We cannot escape from the fact that we're responsible for our bodies. Again and again, God's Word confronts us with this truth. Nourishing our body is an important factor not only from the point of view of nutrition but because we must to everything to give glory to God.

Resources

Additional Information

Hectic lives. It's important to know that hectically rushing around each day directly affects our eating habits. Scientific studies show that many families no longer share meal times together. These studies also reveal that having at least one meal time together each day protects children and young people from risky situations such as sex at an early age, drug use and development of eating disorders.

Obesity is increasing at an alarming rate throughout the world. Today it's estimated that there are more than 300 million obese people world-wide. Obesity is defined as a condition of excess body fat, and is associated with a large number of debilitating and life-threatening disorders. Obesity is a serious medical condition which needs urgent attention throughout the world. The growing prevalence of obesity among children is also a major concern.

Junk Food is food that has low nutritional value, typically produced in the form of packaged snacks needing little or no preparation. Junk or Fast Food is high in calories, but low in nutrients. Filling your diet with junk food causes an array of problems in your body. Junk food is often high in sugar, fat and calories, while providing very few nutrients (healthyeating.sfgate.com).

Definition of terms

High blood pressure, or hypertension, rarely has noticeable symptoms. But if untreated, it increases the risk of serious problems such as heart attacks and strokes.

High cholesterol or hypercholesterolemia: Everyone should have a certain amount of cholesterol and triglycerides in the blood, but when normal levels are increased, this may cause hardening of the arteries, which lose their natural elasticity and become rigid, increasing the problems of blood circulation and increased odds of having a stroke or a heart attack. Abnormal levels of cholesterol are treated with a low-fat diet, exercise, and medications.

Diabetes Mellitus refers to a group of diseases that affect how your body uses blood sugar (glucose). Glucose is vital to your health because it's an important source of energy for the cells that make up your muscles and tissues. It's also your brain's main source of fuel.

Additional Activity

When you get to point II, you can divide the class into three groups and assign each group two of the tips for good nutrition. Have them search the scriptures for each of the tips and discuss in each group how in a practical way they can follow that good biblical advice offered. Tell them they have three minutes to do so.

Ask them to reach a short conclusion and then share it with the whole class. Take a minute to sum up what has been shared.

HIV and AIDS: A Major Challenge

Lesson 29

René Rivas Fernández (Guatemala)

> **Memory Verse:** "Religion that God our Father accepts as pure and faultless is this: to look after orphans and widows in their distress and to keep oneself from being polluted by the world" James 1:27.
>
> **Lesson Goal:** That the students understand that AIDS is a preventable disease, that for those infected with HIV there is hope in Christ, and that we must offer compassionate care through action.

Introduction

AIDS has been considered as the pandemic of the century, and although much has been written, there are still many stigmas about the disease. Together with your students, make a list of the myths and realities of AIDS.

Myth 1: There are enough resources to fight AIDS.

Fact: When working in an area as big as this, funds are not sufficient to meet the challenge. It's extremely expensive, no fund is sufficient because it involves extreme expense.

Myth 2: AIDS only affects drug users, homosexuals and sex workers.

Fact: Anyone can be infected by HIV/AIDS.

Myth 3: AIDS can be spread through kissing.

Fact: The contagion is only by contact with blood and through sex.

Ask the class if anyone knows or has met a person who is suffering from AIDS or has died from the disease.

Start the class by sharing the statistics of the disease in your country or region; you can get the information through the offices of Public Health or on the Internet.

I. What is HIV/AIDS?

The AIDS Virus that produced a hitherto unknown and apparently mortal disease was first identified in 1981. Treatment is now available in the form of Antiretroviral Therapy, but this tends to be expensive. In 2015, an estimated 100,000 new HIV infections and 50,000 AIDS-related deaths were reported in Latin America and the Caribbean. Initially this disease was associated only with sex and drug use, but now is a global epidemic that, if proper precautions are not taken, can affect anyone regardless of age, sex, religion, and educational economic level.

HIV (Human Immunodeficiency Virus) is the microbe that causes the AIDS. The acronym AIDS stands for Acquired Immune Deficiency Syndrome, a disease that causes a decrease in the defenses of the human body so that it cannot defend against opportunistic infections.

The virus can be transmitted by contact with body fluids such as blood, semen, vaginal secretions and breast milk. For that reason, sexual relations are still the most common cause of infection. It may also be spread through blood transfusions contaminated with HIV, but increasingly this is not so common due to the controls carried out by blood banks. A mother can transmit the virus to her child during pregnancy by the placenta and during lactation. Another way of transmission is the use of contaminated needles and sharp piercing instruments used on the skin that have not been properly sterilized. Hence the high rate of the disease in drug addicts.

Although the AIDS virus is contagious, it's not transmitted by mosquito bites, sharing food or eating utensils, through kissing, or by a casual contact with an infected person (touching or hugging).

II. Manifestations and Preventive Measures

After being infected with HIV, a person may experience symptoms similar to those of a cold or flu one or two months after being infected. After that, the person may not know he/she is

94

a carrier of the virus and may very well not feel other symptoms for a long time. But during that time, the infected person can transmit the virus to others.

In the initial stage of AIDS, signs begin to appear, such as weight loss, diarrhea and chronic cough for more than a month, lesions on the lips and skin, swollen glands, fever and night sweats, among others.

In the final stage, the person living with AIDS may suffer many symptoms such as extreme fatigue, painful rashes and mental disorders. They can also develop infections such as pneumonia and severe pulmonary tuberculosis, as well as some cancers such as "Kaposi sarcoma" manifested by the appearance of dark brown or reddish blue spots on the skin. Usually the person dies due to infections caused through having low body defenses.

At the moment, there is no vaccine or cure for HIV/AIDS. However, there are treatments that can slow down the replication of the virus and mitigate the damage caused. In any case, the treatment provides a better quality of life for patients. In marriage, fidelity to one's partner is not just obedience to God's commands, but guarantees personal safety against AIDS.

Currently, most laboratories use methods to detect HIV in the blood used for transfusions. Needles or sharps instruments previously used by infected persons, should be adequately disinfected. We know that 10% to 20% of breast-fed infants from an infected mother can be infected with the virus. Today with careful use of Antiretroviral Therapy during pregnancy and afterwards, this situation can be reduced. Another solution is to give the children powdered milk with a special formula for babies.

III. A Solemn Warning

The biblical concept of marriage is the unity between a man and a woman. This union is used by Paul as an illustration of the relationship of unity between Christ and the church. Humans were created with two different sorts of anatomies, each with distinct and defined organs for the purposes of procreation. Therefore, the marital relationship between two people of the same sex is inconceivable in thought and much less in practice. Paul presents a list of sins that apparently were temptations to the Corinthians as they are for many today. The Apostle mentions fornicators, adulterers, male prostitutes and sodomites (I

Corinthians 6:9; cf. Leviticus 20:13). We humans cannot allow our sexuality to become an idol that separates us from the true God. Paul states that such persons won't inherit the kingdom of God (I Corinthians 6:10).

AIDS has been linked to sexual disorders, and it has spread both among gay communities as well as through extra marital relationships. "The wages of sin is death," as we read in Romans 6:23a. However, those who are dominated by this kind of sin can change and become new creatures (2 Corinthians 5:17). Paul says referring to people who had practiced a series of sins: "But you were washed, you were sanctified, you were justified in the name of the Lord Jesus Christ and by the Spirit of our God" (I Corinthians 6:11).

IV. The Challenge for the Church

The question of AIDS can be approached with a judgmental and moralistic attitude, but as Christians we must base our response on the solid values of love and compassion. Some systematically associate HIV/AIDS with consequences of sin. To say that AIDS is a divine punishment is wrong, because God does not distinguish between sins of sex, sins of mind or sins of selfishness. One sin is no more serious than other sins, God condemns sin.

If AIDS was God's punishment to humanity for sin, nobody would still be alive; Paul says "for all have sinned and fall short of the glory of God" (Romans 3:23). There are many people who have been infected with HIV accidentally. Do these victims deserve divine punishment? Also 80% of women suffering from AIDS are victims of their husbands who have been infected after having extramarital affairs. So who would God punish? Would it be a sick prostitute, the unfaithful and irresponsible husband or the innocent wife?

God's Word teaches us that God's love for every human being is immense. It was his love for every individual, including those who are HIV-positive, which led him to sacrifice his own son on our behalf. AIDS patients need a lot of love, mercy and hope that only the church can give. Sometimes as Christians we're so concerned about the "salvation of souls" that we neglect the immediate needs of individuals (physical, material and relational). This contradicts the example Jesus gave us. According to James, pure and undefiled religion is demonstrated in practice by helping the needy (1:27).

Conclusion

The Lord calls us to preach to everyone, and that includes HIV-positive people. How can we do this? There are hospitals with many infected people just waiting to die and go to eternal damnation. What is holding us back from going and sharing with them the message of salvation? Let us be an active part of the church sharing the message of hope with those who have none.

Resources

Additional Information

In the General Assembly of the Church of the Nazarene International in 2001, an appendix was approved and added to the Manual of the Church of the Nazarene with the following statement about HIV-AIDS:

"Since 1981, our world has been confronted with a most devastating disease known as HIV/AIDS. In view of the deep need of HIV/AIDS sufferers, Christian compassion motivates us to become accurately informed about HIV/AIDS. Christ would have us to find a way to communicate His love and concern for these sufferers in any and every country of the world" (903.17, 2013-2017).

Some global information about AIDS. "In 2015, 36.7 million people were living with HIV; 2.1 million people were newly infected with HIV; 150,000 were under the age of 15; Every day about 5,753 people contract HIV—about 240 every hour; 1.1 million people died from AIDS-related illnesses; since the beginning of the pandemic, 78 million people have contracted HIV and 35 million have died of AIDS-related causes. As of December 2015, 17 million people living with HIV (46% of the total) had access to antiretroviral therapy." (http://www.amfar.org/worldwide-aids-stats/).

Definition of Terms

A *pandemic* is the spread of an infectious disease over a large area geographically, often worldwide. For a disease to be considered pandemic, it must have a high degree of infectiousness, some level of mortality and spread easily from one geographical area to another. This is the case of HIV/AIDS.

HIV-positive: Being HIV-positive means that the person has developed antibodies to the virus because they have been in contact with it, but probably have not yet developed the disease. This is determined by laboratory tests, and HIV-negative test result does not mean precisely that the infection is not present, because antibodies can develop in three to six months after exposure.

Additional Activity (5 minutes)

Activity: broken down telephone line

Objective: to see how information can be distorted by the interpretation that each gives.

Development: Place all the class in a circle. Whisper clearly in someone's ear the following phrase making sure that the rest cannot hear. "John's father went to the doctor with his mother and the doctor told him that her Pap is normal but that in six months she should return for a control test". That person must whisper what he/she has heard of the phrase as clearly as possible the next person on the left, and so on until the circle has been completed. The last person will then say out loud what he/she has heard. The teacher will then share what she said to the first person. The two sentences will very likely be very different.

Application: When information is passed between several people, facts become confused. It's important to have correct information, especially when it comes to protecting the health and life, as in the case of AIDS prevention

Practical Exercise

1. Find out if there are services for people with HIV/AIDS in the community and contact them to learn more about the disease.

2. Offer to babysit of patients with HIV/AIDS when they have appointments at the hospital.

3. As a group of Sunday school, schedule a visit to a hospital for patients with HIV/AIDS and bring gifts to the sick, and especially to share with them the love of Christ.

4. Organize a day in the church where as a Sunday School class you can share information on AIDS and pray for the salvation of these people.

Eating Disorders: More Than Just Food

Marcela Aguirre (Argentina)

> **Memory Verse:** "The Lord does not look at the things people look at. People look at the outward appearance, but the Lord looks at the heart." I Samuel 16:7b.
>
> **Lesson Goal:** To inform the students about anorexia and bulimia, understand the biblical view, and help people with behavior disorders related to food.

Introduction

Start by sharing this old story: "Narcissus was the son of a river and a nymph. And apparently, he was a very handsome boy. Narcissus grew and soon was a handsome young man. He rejected the proffered love and affection, and remained insensitive to others. He was only aware of himself. So the years went by until one hot day, after a hunt, this young man stopped at a fountain to cool down. As he bent to drink, Narcissus saw his reflection in the water and fell in love with his own image in the water. Narcissus stood there, indifferent to everything. Absorbed in his own contemplation, he let himself be consumed by hunger and loneliness and faded away and died." That is why the term 'narcissism' is used to define someone who lives thinking only of themselves and what they look like.

How did Narcissus relate to others? What was he waiting for? What made him only think about his reflection in the water? This legend shows the vanity of those who constantly admire themselves.

I. Too Thin or Too Fat - Does It Matter?

'Image' is a buzzword. Society in general is concerned about how we all look. People value this. Covers of magazines and television commercials all push us to stay young, to look good. Some people make superhuman efforts to achieve this image. Thousands of girls struggle for personal satisfaction, and believe that they'll it when they look like the models they see in the media.

The Internet has countless number of pages advertising special diets and drugs to slim, aimed especially at girls who want to change their image. Thus, they become slaves of the weighing scales, chasing stereotypes, and are in danger of falling into one of the two the most common types of eating disorders: anorexia and bulimia. In both cases, the person has a distorted image of her own body, and lives obsessed with food and fear of being fat.

Anorexia and bulimia tend to affect women more often than men. They usually occur in young women who have a low self-esteem, feel threatened by the changes that come with growth, depend on the opinion of others, or live in dysfunctional homes.

Social pressure is very strong today. Thin is considered to be beautiful and fashionable. It's easy to see how this social pressure leads some young women to excessive dieting, and eventually developing anorexia. The media continually presents us with miraculous diets and exercise plans that they say will give us the ideal figure.

Other factors that might lead young women to seek to be thin have to do with having a family with excessive preoccupation with the figure, or who are critical or make jokes about physical appearance.

If not controlled, anorexia may cause heart, liver or kidney problems. It can lower blood pressure, pulse and breathing rates. Also, the lack of energy leads to feeling dizzy and having a short attention span. It also causes anemia (lack of red blood cells), hair loss, brittle nails, and in extreme cases, severe malnutrition that may lead to death.

On the other hand, bulimia causes constant stomach pain. As a result of vomiting, teeth deteriorate as the gastric acid decays the dentine on the teeth. Salivary glands can swell because of continuous vomiting. People who have bulimia stop having menstruation cycles. A decrease in potassium may lead to the onset of heart problems, causing death. People with eating disorders become less sociable, meeting less with friends or family.

In assessing the value of our life, we must keep in mind what Genesis 1:31 says, "God saw all that he had made, and it was very good. And there was evening, and there was morning—the sixth day." This chapter also tells us that He created the plants, seeds, fruits and animals for food (Genesis 1:29-30). We ought to enjoy food and eat well without overdoing it, maintaining our weight according to the recommendation of the specialists and not by what fashion dictates.

II. How Can We Help?

What can we do for a person suffering from any of these diseases?

1. The first step is to help the person recognize that they have a problem. It's difficult to help a person who doesn't admit that they have a problem. God cannot heal diseases that we don't acknowledge (James 5:14-15).

2. These people need to have medical and therapeutic help because their lives could be in danger. The longer there's a delay in diagnosis, the longer it takes to heal.

3. The family needs understanding and assurance. We must provide support and guidance (James 5:16; Hebrews 13:16).

4. Rather than concentrate on how other people see us, it's more important to understand that God sees and accepts us (1 Samuel 16:7, Ecclesiastes 12:13).

5. We all need to recognize that while the body is important and is a beautiful creation of God (Genesis 1:26-27), what is really essential is invisible to the eyes (2 Corinthians 4:16-18).

6. We need to accompany these young people throughout the recovery process, showing love and confidence that they'll get better (Galatians 6:2).

III. How Does God Look At All Of This?

Ecclesiastes argues that time passes and everything continues, but that we're only here for a short time. The point the writer is saying is that "All our achievements disappear someday." If we don't understand this truth clearly, we can become proud or frustrated and depressed. The word 'vanity' in Hebrew means "all that is empty and fleeting." It's also defined as "the relative unimportance of life apart from God." The Message translates Ecclesiastes 1:4 in the following way: "One generation goes its way, the next one arrives, but nothing changes— it's business as usual for old planet earth". In Ecclesiastes 1:1-11, the preacher makes it clear that everything is fleeting and meaningless. Whatever we do, the world will keep on going. So, should we be worrying unnecessarily about how to invest our time or money? We shouldn't put so much attention on transient things, but rather put our eyes on eternal God. Searching for God provides full satisfaction.

God sees as vanity these evils that afflict modern society, placing too much of our attention on cares which are fleeting.

Let's reflect briefly on two biblical stories about David (1 Samuel 16:11-13; 17:14-18) and the prodigal son in Luke 15:11-32. Divide the class into two groups and give them a few minutes to answer these questions:

What did these two young men do when they were young? [Answer: David looked after sheep as a shepherd. The prodigal son spent his time in temporary pleasures and delights].

What was their place in the family? [Answer: David was the youngest and had the "unimportant job" as a shepherd. The prodigal son was spoiled, occupying his time amusing himself.]

What did each of them have? [Answer: David had a few sheep to look after. The prodigal son received an inheritance].

What did they become in the end? [Answer: David became a great ruler of a nation. The prodigal son was left with nothing and his status was less than a servant].

Listen to the answers from the groups to each of the questions.

The pursuit of vain things almost ended up destroying the life of the prodigal son. David, however, dealt with the value of the inner life, cultivating values that led him to be a great king later on.

When Samuel was to choose the future king, he was about to make the mistake of evaluating on appearance. God reminded him that this is not important (1 Samuel 16:7).

Many harm their health and spend hours a day in vain things. What really has value is to cultivate the inner being. Proverbs 4:23 says: "Above all else, guard your heart, for everything you do flows from it".

The prodigal son, when he was in a really bad way, recognized his problem and understood that his only way out was to return to the Father. Only God can liberate a person from that frustration and emptiness that generates vanity, and He can give them the abundant life that Jesus brings (John 10:10).

As Christians, we must look after our lives, keeping ourselves free of this world's vain things (Ephesians 4:17; Acts 14:15).

Conclusion

We shouldn't let vanity distance us from our salvation in God, and we need to help those who are trapped by it.

Resources

Additional Information

Would you like to see if your weight is healthy? Go to this internet page and work out your Body Mass Index. You could help your students to work out theirs.

(http://www.nhlbi.nih.gov/health/educational/lose_wt/BMI/bmicalc.htm)

Definition of Terms

Anorexia nervosa: a serious disorder in eating behavior primarily of young women in their teens and early twenties that is characterized especially by a pathological fear of weight gain, leading to faulty eating patterns, malnutrition, and usually excessive weight loss

Bulimia nervosa is a serious, potentially life-threatening eating disorder characterized by a cycle of binging and compensatory behaviors, such as self-induced vomiting, designed to undo or compensate for the effects of binge eating.

Case Studies:

Anorexia nervosa - Katie's story see http://www.nhs.uk/Conditions/Anorexia-nervosa/Pages/Realstorypg.aspx

Bulimia nervosa – for Shaye's story see http://www.your-bulimia-recovery.com/bulimia-case-study.html

Additional Activities

1. Before starting the lesson, you could ask each student the following questions:
    a. How do you think other people see you?
    b. How do you see yourself?
    c. How would you like others to see you?

Then comment on the answers as you start the lesson.

2. Drama

Before Point 1, you can use this little skit.

Daughter: Look what I bought, Mum (new jeans with a new blouse).

Mother: Don't you think those jeans are a bit low on the hips? And the blouse barely covers your navel. It's a bit revealing isn't it.

Daughter: Mum, how can you be so old fashioned! This is what everyone is wearing!

3. Debate

Before developing Point 3, you can read these questions and start a brief discussion.

What are the values for society today?

What is vanity?

What is image?

What is a good or bad image?

Stressed Out!

Lesson 31

Ana Paxtor de Yuman (Guatemala)

Memory Verse: "Cast all your anxiety on him because he cares for you." I Peter 5:7

Lesson Goal: That the students might recognize the symptoms of stress and how to handle it properly with God's help.

Introduction

Ask the students: Why do we get worked up and worry about things? Write on the board what the students suggest. Then proceed to the next point.

I. What Is Stress and What Causes It?

Stress is a growing problem in our society. We can define it as a state of mental or emotional strain or tension resulting from adverse or very demanding circumstances. One of the symptoms of stress is physical or psychological fatigue. Alternative names for stress are tension, apprehension or feeling nervous.

Stress is the body's response to external conditions (work, accidents, studying), and internal ones (fears, bad memories and traumas) that disturb a person's equilibrium. This may occur in spite of age, race or status in society.

On the positive side, stress is a way that the body becomes active in order to successfully accomplish things. Stress is part of our life; in fact, a little stress is good. Most humans, when they begin activities like sports, music, dance, work, or study, don't feel able to do well. This situation creates some degree of tension or stress that drives a person to strive and perform the task better. So, you cannot completely renounce stress.

Any emotional response, situation or thought (whether positive or negative) that makes a person feel frustrated, angry or anxious can cause stress.

II. General Symptoms Of Stress

There are different types of stressful events. Some are considered greater than others.

a. The major ones could be: wars, loss of a loved one, change in economic situation,

different types of violence, kidnapping, etc.

b. The minor ones could be: work related issues, health, accident, marriage, birth of a child, graduation, etc.

In any case, we must understand that situations that cause stress in one person won't necessarily do so in another person. The body's response to these situations can be disease, which will be different in each person according to family medical history or vulnerability to certain diseases. This response also depends on their mental state, in other words, whether a person is tough, somewhat anxious, depressed, etc. will influence how they perceive a particular event.

It's important to learn to recognize the symptoms of stress. Stress can affect how one feels, thinks, behaves and how the body works. The first signs that can be seen include tension in the shoulders and neck. There are other physical symptoms such as muscle tension, cold and clammy hands, nail biting, headaches, decreased energy, sexual impotence, etc. In other people, there may be symptoms such as psychological anxiety, nervousness, poor concentration and memory, changes in sleep patterns, decreased appetite, irritable mood, drug use, or alcohol abuse.

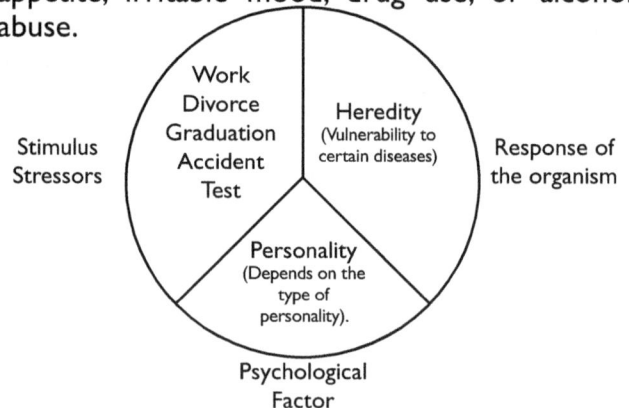

Stimulus Stressors — Work, Divorce, Graduation, Accident, Test — Heredity (Vulnerability to certain diseases) — Response of the organism — Personality (Depends on the type of personality). — Psychological Factor

Stress causes a surge of hormones to be released to help deal with pressures or threats – the so-called "fight or flight" response. Once the pressure or threat has passed, the stress hormone levels will usually return to normal. However, if someone is constantly under stress, these hormones will continue to be present, leading to the symptoms of stress.

Stress can bring some consequences. Stress acts in the body, triggering a large number of diseases and disorders at different levels, such as: high blood pressure, heart disease or heart palpitations, asthma, rapid development of infectious diseases, hypothyroidism, hyperthyroidism, peptic ulcer, constipation, excessive sweating, dermatitis, tics, tremors, impotence, etc.

III. What Does The Bible Say To Us Today?

What should we do about this problem that day by day is becoming more common? The most effective way to deal with stress is to find out and address the cause. The first step is to make an inventory of experiences and thoughts that may be making us "stressed out". We could ask: What situation makes us worry most? Is there something that is always on our mind? Is there anything in particular that is causing us grief?

Remember that Jesus said, "So don't worry, saying, 'What shall we eat?' or 'What shall we drink?' or 'What shall we wear?' For the pagans run after all these things, and your heavenly Father knows that you need them" (Matthew 6:31-32). We should be wary of the things that torment us! It's good to take time to write things down and analyze them, as this will help us see things more clearly and from the right perspective.

It's also good to find a trusted person (friend, relative, neighbor, counselor, pastor, or a psychologist) who will listen, because many times simply talking to a loved one or someone we trust helps decrease stress.

Proverbs 1:5 tells us: "Let the wise listen and add to their learning, and let the discerning get guidance." Good advice can help in some situations, only we have to be careful who we ask. "Listen to my instruction and be wise; don't disregard it" (Proverbs 8:33).

As Christians, we must give prayer the first place. Before, during and after seeking help, advice or anything else, we should pray to God and ask him to guide us to know what we must do (Luke 11:9-10).

The apostle Paul encouraged the Philippian church in Philippians 4:6-7, "Do not be anxious about anything, but in every situation, by prayer and petition, with thanksgiving, present your requests to God. And the peace of God, which transcends all understanding, will guard your hearts and your minds in Christ Jesus."

Finally, the Psalmist reminds us that the Christian life doesn't deliver us from problems or stressful situations. "The righteous person may have many troubles, but the Lord delivers him from them all" (Psalm 34:19). Jesus takes up this concept with his followers and tells them: "I have told you these things, so that in me you may have peace. In this world, you'll have trouble. But take heart! I have overcome the world" (John 16:33).

Conclusion

Ask the class what they have learned about stress? Finish, making it clear that while stress will always be present in our lives in one way or another, with the help of God we can learn how to handle it properly.

Resources

Additional Information

Stress Related Facts And Statistics

"The Stress in America survey results show that adults continue to report high levels of stress and many report that their stress has increased over the past year...Stress is a top health concern for U.S. teens between 9th and 12th grade, psychologists say that if they don't learn healthy ways to manage that stress now, it could have serious long-term health implications...80% of workers feel stress on the job and nearly half say they need help in learning how to manage stress. And 42% say their co-workers need such help – American Psychological Association.

Stress levels in the workplace are rising with 6 in 10 workers in major global economies experiencing increased workplace stress. With China (86%) having the highest rise in workplace stress – The Regus Group

An estimated 442,000 individuals in Britain, who worked in 2007/08 believed that they were experiencing work-related stress at a level that was making them ill – Labour Force Survey.

Depression is among the leading causes of disability worldwide... Fewer than 25% of those with depression world-wide have access to effective treatments – World Health Organization" (http://www.gostress.com/stress-facts/)

Definition of Terms

Stress hormones:

Cortisol is produced by the adrenal glands.

Adrenaline, commonly known as the fight or flight hormone, is produced by the adrenal glands after receiving a message from the brain that a stressful situation has presented itself.

Norepinephrine is a hormone similar to adrenaline, released from the adrenal glands and also from the brain,

The "fight or flight response" is our body's primitive, automatic, inborn response that prepares the body to "fight" or "flee" from perceived attack, harm or threat to our survival.

Additional Activities

1. Practical Exercise

To start point 2, encourage the class to have a brief relaxation exercise.

Ask students to work in pairs; ladies with ladies, men with men unless you have married couples. In turn, each one will give a shoulder massage to the other one.

Application: This is a practical way of relaxation and that can be carried out very easily in our daily lives.

2. Daily Map

You can ask your students to make a accounting of their day, from getting up until they go to bed. They should write all activities that they generally do (Examples: work, study, kitchen, cleaning, travel, shopping, etc.).

Application: This will make them aware of how busy they are and maybe will help them see which things cause stress and what they can do to reduce it.

3. Dynamic: "Simon Says"

Objective: To assess the importance of physical exercise to manage stress.

Time: Five minutes.

Development: Name a person (which could be yourself) to direct the activity. This person is Simon. With authority Simon will ask the people to stand up and make certain movements such as:

  a. Open your mouth and move it from side to side.
  b. Move your head from side to side.
  c. Walk in place.
  d. Put your hands in the air.

And so on.

Note: If you hear some joints cracking that may be because the muscles are very tight.

Application: Talk about how they felt doing the exercises.

Lesson 32 — Smoking and Health

Erika Rios Hasenauer (USA)

> **Memory Verse:** "If anyone destroys God's temple, God will destroy that person; for God's temple is sacred, and you together are that temple." I Corinthians 3:17
>
> **Lesson Goal:** To show that through scientific and biblical evidence, smoking affects our body, not only physically, but mentally and spiritually as well.

Introduction

Take the time to read I Corinthians 3:17; 10:23 and 10:31-33, if possible in different versions). Then read the following story:

Tom is sitting in his hospital bed waiting for the visit of the nurse who will review his oxygen connection. As a doctor, it was my turn to take a brief medical history. Tom had smoked all his life and used to say, "It's my only vice." He had never decided to change his lifestyle even though his wife and family had appealed to him. Now it was too late. He had advanced lung cancer and would be dependent on an oxygen connection for the rest of his life.

Unfortunately, millions of people still die in the world due to smoking. About 1.1 billion people, one in every three adults, are smokers, according to the World Health Organization. Slightly more men smoke than women, and many of them are young people between 25 and 35 years. A few decades ago, Robert F. Kennedy said: "Every year cigarettes kill more Americans than the First World War, the Korean and Vietnam wars together. Every year, cigarettes kill five times more people than traffic accidents."

I. Introductory Aspects About Smoking

A. What's in a Cigarette?

Cigarettes look deceptively simple, consisting of paper tubes containing chopped up tobacco leaf, usually with a filter at the mouth end. In fact, they are highly engineered products, designed to deliver a steady dose of nicotine. Cigarettes contain nicotine, tar and water.

B. What is the Effect of Smoking a Cigarette?

Nicotine is a stimulant that wakes up neurons and stimulates certain cells in the spine. It relaxes the muscles of the body and depresses the reflexes. Another feature is that it's well absorbed, and seconds after being inhaled, reaches the brain. These effects of smoking can be felt not only by the smoker, but also by the people who may be in the same room.

C. Why do People Smoke?

The tobacco industry tells us that it's a voluntary pleasure. Is it just a habit like eating more potato chips or popcorn? Is it a way to control nervousness or stress? Is it a way to lose weight? Or is it the use of a drug accepted by society and the markets? We have to say that these statements are true, but some are more valid than others and apply to different individuals. When you ask a person why they smoke, usually there's no clear answer. They don't know why.

Observation tells us that there are many factors related to why people smoke, for example, following the example of other smokers, having unmet needs, and peer pressure. Everything starts with smoking the first cigarette. Then it becomes a habit, and then a dependency. Not all stimulants create dependency, but cigarettes do. Can pleasure justify the use and abuse of tobacco?

D. Are Teens at Risk to Smoke?

The answer to this question is yes. Remember that in adolescence, young people are searching for an identity, sexual roles are clarified, they want independence, they are learning how to cope with authority and are searching for a purpose in life.

It's a period of growth and discovery. It's also when peer pressure is more evident than ever; to be accepted is to be in the circle. The unfortunate thing is seeing the consequences that this push for freedom and acceptance is having on adolescents.

E. Why We All are Passive Smokers?

A passive smoker is a nonsmoker who is exposed to tobacco smoke in environments inhabited or occupied by smokers. Adults, the elderly, women and children, etc. are all exposed to cigarette smoke when we're in places where there are smokers. Despite the maximum attempt to ban smoking in public places, this still has not been fully achieved. Despite the information that exists, even today there are children who fall into the category of passive smoking, especially if any of the family members smoke at home.

F. What Are the Effects on Health?

There is a clear relationship between smoking and health effects. The more exposure, duration and intensity of the habit, the more serious will be the negative effects. A smoker is 10 times more likely to die of lung cancer, and is almost three times more likely to have heart disease, than a nonsmoker. The risk of dying from heart attack is two to three times higher in male smokers. Other risk factors are present for women who smoke. If a woman smokes more than 35 cigarettes per day, and takes contraceptive pills for family planning, she has an even higher risk of cardiovascular problems. Consuming multiple stimulants such as coffee and cigarettes can affect the digestive system. Combinations such as tobacco and alcohol are factors which may lead to cancer of the larynx.

II. Biblical Approach to the Subject

Interestingly, in 1 Corinthians 6:12 referring to sexual sins, the Apostle expresses: "'I have the right to do anything,' you say—but not everything is beneficial. 'I have the right to do anything'—but I won't be mastered by anything." The Message contemporary English version translates this verse: "Just because something is technically legal doesn't mean that it's spiritually appropriate. If I went around doing whatever I thought I could get by with, I'd be a slave to my whims."

It seems that some of the members of the church in Corinth were mistakenly using the phrase "everything is permissible." They thought that because Christ had forgiven their sins, they could live as they pleased. In addition, many religions of that time felt that it was important to take care of the soul and not the body.

Paul made the following clarification; the fact that Jesus forgave them their sins didn't give them the right to do things that were wrong. The apostle made it clear that although everything is permitted, nothing that doesn't come from God should be master of our lives. Whatever is harmful is sin and must be avoided. This applies perfectly to cigarette consumption.

Later in his letter, Paul states that while we're all free to act, we should know that not everything is beneficial in our lives. Before doing anything, we must examine not only how good or bad it is for our health, which is a very important point, but also what helps us grow in our Christian lives. It may be that something is not harmful to health, but the question is, how does it help us to grow as Christians?

In 1 Corinthians 10:23-24, the apostle says: "I have the right to do anything," you say—but not everything is beneficial. "I have the right to do anything"—but not everything is constructive. No one should seek their own good, but the good of others." The Message puts it this way "Looking at it one way, you could say, 'Anything goes. Because of God's immense generosity and grace, we don't have to dissect and scrutinize every action to see if it will pass muster.' But the point is not to just get by. We want to live well, but our foremost efforts should be to help others live well."

God gives us the ability to decide and make good or bad decisions. He also gives us the title of stewards. We're stewards of our body. That means He will ask us account everything we do with the body He gave us.

God is great and His love, power and perfection created man perfect. All the organs and body systems, even each cell, are related to another in perfect harmony. When this balance is broken, that is when diseases and health complications arise with their respective consequences. Still, God's grace is infinite and enough to sustain and restore this harmony and give us a second chance.

The apostle's words in 1 Corinthians 3:16-17 are decisive. "Don't you know that you yourselves are God's temple and that God's Spirit dwells in your midst? If anyone destroys God's temple, God will destroy that person; for God's temple is sacred, and you together are that temple." Our body is sacred; it's the temple where the Holy Spirit dwells. With the same zeal with which we take care of our church building, where we come together as a people to worship the Lord, we should take care of our physical body.

Conclusion

Health is a holistic concept; therefore, smoking is an addiction that affects our physical, mental and spiritual health.

Resources

Additional Information

Some Data About Smoking

Tobacco use is the leading cause of preventable illness and death in the United States. It causes many different cancers as well as chronic lung diseases such as emphysema and bronchitis, heart disease, pregnancy-related problems, and many other serious health problems.

More than 16 million people already have at least one disease from smoking.

More than 20 million Americans have died because of smoking since 1964, including approximately 2.5 million deaths due to exposure to secondhand smoke.

8.6 million people live with a serious illness caused by smoking.

On average, smokers die 13 to 14 years earlier than nonsmokers.

Nearly 9 out of 10 lung cancers are caused by smoking. Smokers today are much more likely to develop lung cancer than smokers were in 1964.

Nearly 8 out of 10 Chronic Obstructive Pulmonary Disease deaths are a result of smoking. Currently, there's no cure.

Women smokers are up to 40 times more likely to develop Chronic Obstructive Pulmonary Disease than women who have never smoked.

Smoking increases a person's risk of getting tuberculosis and dying from it.

More than 11% of high school students in the United States have asthma, and studies suggest that youth who smoke are more likely to develop asthma.

Smoking slows down lung growth in children and teens.

Lung cancer is the leading cause of cancer death among both men and women in the United States, and 90% of lung cancer deaths among men and approximately 80% of lung cancer deaths among women are due to smoking.

(https://betobaccofree.hhs.gov/about-tobacco/facts-figures/)

How to Quit Smoking

Most smokers today know that smoking is bad for their health and harmful to people around them. They know they should quit but they also know it's going to be hard. Smoking tobacco is both a physical addiction and a psychological habit. The nicotine from cigarettes provides a temporary—and addictive—high. Eliminating that regular fix of nicotine will cause the body to experience physical withdrawal symptoms and cravings. Because of nicotine's "feel good" effect on the brain, they may also have become accustomed to smoking as a way of coping with stress, depression, anxiety, or even boredom. There are many programs in society that offer help to people to quit smoking. The church needs to help people in the congregation find freedom from this habit.

Definition of Terms

Passive smoking is when someone breathes someone else's cigarette smoke. Passive or secondhand smoking can increase the risk of cancer and other health problems. It's also particularly harmful for children. This also applies to small enclosed places, such as cars. Smoke may still be present in large amounts even after the person has stopped smoking.

Additional Activities

Activity: Sorting Out The Problems

Materials: Papers 2 x 2 inches (5 x 5 cm).

Time: Maximum 10 minutes.

Objective: To see that we're totally integrated human beings.

Development: On each piece of paper, write one of the following words: earthquake, flood, theft, drugs, alcohol, AIDS, tuberculosis, depression, poverty, pollution, deteriorating family relations, stress, lack of motivation, lack of employment, "junk" food, alcohol consumption, smoking, smoking marijuana, lack of family planning, inadequate ventilation in housing, sonic disturbances due to loud noises, diabetes, cardiovascular disease.

Then form small groups and give each group an equal number of the prepared papers. Then ask them to classify the papers in three categories: physical, mental and spiritual.

Each team should make groupings according to the area affected. Students will find that some of the issues overlap and cover more than one category. Let them discuss in the group and then try to reach a final agreement. You could also write the words 'physical', 'mental' and 'spiritual' on the board and each group can suggest situations or diseases under the category they think it affects. At the end, the class can discuss the answers.

Could drugs come into our homes?

Alberto E. Ainscough (Argentina)

Memory Verse: " And the prayer offered in faith will make the sick person well; the Lord will raise them up. If they have sinned, they will be forgiven" James 5:15.

Lesson Goal: To make the students aware of the danger of drugs and mobilize action to rescue addicts.

Introduction

The drug problem is one of the worst scourges inherited from the previous millennium. It doesn't respect people, families, societies, cities, or nations. It defeats governments, the police, justice and armies. With all the money created by the illegal drug trade, we could end hunger in the world.

Allow the students to express and share some of the evils of the society where they live caused by the illegal drug business. Ask them the question; Could drugs come into your home? If so how?

I. Causes That Lead To Drug Addiction

They are many and varied causes that make someone start to use drugs, but the most important and common is their lack of inner wellbeing. Generally, a person begins to take drugs because they feel unsatisfied with their lives.

Maybe other people such as their families have asked too much of them and they feel they cannot reach this standard, or maybe they are trying to please others. They may feel dissatisfied with themselves, or in the case of adolescents, they may sense that the family doesn't give them adequate attention.

Drugs offer them false satisfaction; it's like putting makeup on their personality, covering real issues up. It's like dressing-up ... nothing really changes. Instead, the difficulties only increase. Added to the lack of self-worth, they feel a profound void or emptiness each time they take drugs. They begin to feel persecuted, guilty of the weakness that led them down the path of drugs, and they start living a life which takes them on a downward spiral of constant and growing dissatisfaction.

II. Abandoning Addiction

There are many who want to leave their addiction on their own without treatment, but very few succeed. In recent days, I met an addict who confessed that he had corrected many things in his life, such as selling small amounts of drugs, but he had not been able to give up using cocaine, even though he has been trying for years. Many people who try to quit drug use fail because they aim too high to fast in trying to achieve long-term freedom.

There's a biological component that explains the difficulty of maintaining abstinence without treatment. To this we must add the pressure of work, family problems, the environment, or objects and odors associated with the use of drugs that can act in conjunction with biological factors causing relapses.

Research has shown that drug use produces significant long-term changes in brain function. These persist for a long time, even after the person has stopped drug use.

Addicts can come from any stratum of society. The severity of addiction is not the same in all people. It depends on the person, the type of drug, the time consumed and the problems that led to addiction. A person's faith in God and having help is a very important point in the recovery. There are people who, when they know the Lord and accepted him as their Savior, their dependence on the drug disappeared. But on the other hand, there are people who have made their decision for Christ and then had to be hospitalized for proper treatment.

The goal of treatment is not only to stop using drugs, but should be for the individual to work productively within the family, work and community. If their relationships improve in the different areas affected, we can say that the treatment is effective.

In general, treatment is as successful as for other chronic diseases such as asthma, diabetes or hypertension. We recommend that the treatment is carried out in a specialized, multidisciplinary and Christian center, to ensure their spiritual life as well.

Individual results depend on the scope and nature of the problems present in the patient's beginning treatment. When you want to help someone, you have to try to deal with the factors that led to addiction.

III. Our Attitude As Christians

Paul, in his letter to Titus (2:11-12) says, "God's readiness to give and forgive is now public. Salvation's available for everyone! We're being shown how to turn our backs on a godless, indulgent life, and how to take on a God-filled, God-honoring life" (MSG). This passage reveals the great love of God that can help us change from a life that is morally very bad to a life that pleases Him. Isaiah 1:16b-17a says: "…stop doing wrong. Learn to do right;"

First of all, there must be the decision to leave or completely abandon the bad, seek what is good, do good and follow after it. All of us must renounce everything that distances us from God, and not want anything bad about the world; rather we must live in obedience and faithfulness to God.

Daniel shows us how to take firm decisions. He was a young man who found himself in the middle of adverse situations and decided to make a difference and be faithful to God (Daniel 1:8). The person who is under the control of drugs must accept that it's wrong, and must accept that they need God in their life. They need to understand that the first step is to seek help. For the addict and his family, the church can be very supportive. With the weapons of prayer and neighborly love, the church can do wonders.

In Luke 10:25-37, we find a good example of what it means to love our neighbor. In this passage, we can see a practical out-working of compassion (vv.33-34) until complete restoration (v.35). As Christians, we need to act like the Samaritan in the parable who cared for the injured man until he was completely well again.

When we help a person who has drug problems, we must accompany them patiently until their recovery is complete. The other weapon we have as a church is prayer. Our weapons are more powerful than any drug. Satan with all his hosts cannot beat a church that loves and joins in prayer. In James 5:15 we read: "And the prayer offered in faith will make the sick person well; the Lord will raise them up. If they have sinned, they'll be forgiven."

The drug addict is a sick person who has sinned, who has fallen down, and the Lord can forgive, save and lift him up. To accomplish the task, God needs a team of dedicated men and women willing to help and support the addict and his family. The task is not easy or short, but as the psalmist says: "With God we'll gain the victory and he will trample down our enemies" Psalm 108:13.

IV. How To Prevent Drugs From Coming Into Our Homes?

No family is exempt from the possibility that their children might start using drugs. To avoid this, we must start talking to them about their dreams and goals early. We must get to know them, and not demand more of them than what they can do. Paul says: "Fathers, don't exasperate your children" (Ephesians 6:4a). We must always lead them to prayer and reading the Bible, "... instead, bring them up in the training and instruction of the Lord" (Ephesians 6:4b). It's said that Susanna Wesley spent an hour a week to talk with each of her eighteen children about spiritual things.

Listen to your children's concerns, projects, and doubts. Get to know their friends. Talk with them about their school achievement and the dangers they face. Take time to play with them. Try to be their friend. Attend the house of the Lord with them. Don't just send them to Sunday School, go with them. Set an example.

Alcoholism, smoking, drug addiction and responsible sexuality are issues that we need to talk about with our children. In preadolescence, we need to take special care about playmates and school friends. Unfortunately, drug dealers try to get children started at young ages. Most addicts start using drugs in adolescence, so that is the time to work especially hard to have a very close relationship with your children.

If you have an addict son or daughter, don't conceal or deny it. Start using the powerful weapon of the united prayer of the church. The Lord wants to save your child, and the church wants him back. Don't turn your child against you with forceful or aggressive accusations. Don't make moral judgments about young people and drugs. Don't abandon your child after the first relapse, insist and keep on insisting. It's worthwhile.

Conclusion

The fight against drug addiction is not just about your family, or about some Christian or government organizations, it affects the whole of society.

As the body of Christ, we know we can defeat this satanic weapon that destroys many lives. We must not remain indifferent.

Resources

Additional Information

Pastoral Advice

If you suspect that a family member or acquaintance is using drugs, you should:

- Avoid aggressive or exaggerated reactions. Behavioral changes are not necessarily related to drugs. In adolescence, it's normal to see changes in behavior. Care must be taken to assess the situation well and not act impulsively.

- Learn about drugs and how they act in the body.

- Maintain a close relationship with the person; try to know their friends and the places they frequent.

- Try to get to know their problems; don't underestimate the importance of the problem.

- Participate in a discussion about drugs; be open to listen to different opinions. This doesn't mean you have to agree. Go deeper into the subject.

If you suspect that a family member or acquaintance is using drugs, do not:

- Make forceful or aggressive accusations.

- Make moral judgments about young people and drugs.

- Don't abandon your child or friend in the first relapse.

- Don't go into denial: - "My son cannot be ..."

If you are sure that a family member or acquaintance is taking drugs:

- Ensure that you have the necessary facts/proof to discuss the situation.

- Show them that you are on their side; but not on the side of drugs.

- Be affectionate.

- Make the person aware that you are on his side but don't approve of what he does.

- Be aware of the severity of the problem, how long it has lasted and the circumstances that drove the person to become and addict.

- Support the person to receive the best care.

- Consult with professionals on the subject.

- Pray and encourage the church to give loving support

Definition of Terms

Marijuana: Technically it's classified as a minor hallucinogen. In the short term and in low doses, it produces a feeling of wellbeing and tranquility with euphoria. Negatively there will be ocular congestion and difficulty for complex mental processes, as well as temporal and sensory disturbances and other problems.

Cocaine: The effects depend on the degree of purity. The absorption of cocaine is very fast and the effects occur within minutes. There's a sense of general stimulation, but with tachycardia, i.e., increased heart rate; increased blood pressure, sweating, and increased sense of anxiety. Afterwards there may be vomiting, diarrhea, insomnia, burning eyes. The final feeling is of anxiety, decreased attention span and motor difficulties.

Ecstasy and other synthetic drugs: these are distributed in the form of pills, capsules or powders that are ingested orally. The tablets usually have attractive shapes and colors. Most of the users are between 18 and 24 years old. They are social drugs, consumed mostly by immature people who have to get together for use, for example, for a party. Consumption increase during holiday periods. People take Ecstasy to be alert and avoid sleep, and it's often accompanied with energy drinks.

Additional Activity

Investigation

Divide the class into two groups the week before and assign them to bring a report on the most common drugs and their effects. In each case, they should inquire about the origin of the drug, the form of consumption, and its effects on the body. There will be a lot of information on the Internet.

Are You Worried? Tomorrow Will Be Another Day!

Marcela Aguirre (Argentina)

Lesson 34

Memory Verse: "The righteous person may have many troubles, but the Lord delivers him from them all;" Psalm 34:19.

Lesson Goal: That the students should understand what anxiety is, and how we as Christians should handle it.

Introduction

Divide the class into groups of four or five people. Give them four minutes to build a structure a meter high, using newspaper, cardboard boxes and tape, etc. When they have finished, discuss with them about the feelings caused by their activity.

We live in a society where there are many reasons that cause us to be anxious. There are more and more activities and less rest, more sitting down time and little physical exercise, excessive effort to achieve goals and less satisfaction when we get there. To this must be added financial pressure, materialism, drugs, fear of disease, crime and a small or large ulcer that from time to time reminds us that we must soothe our anxiety.

I. What is Anxiety?

Anxiety is a subjective feeling of restlessness, tension, fear or negative thinking. It's a response of our body to prepare for fight or flight when dealing with a threat or a perceived danger.

When we have to run away from something that threatens us, or fight something we believe attacks us, we need strong and immediate answers. That's when emotions can help us as automatic responses that prepare us for action.

The process reaction to anxiety begins with the perception of an external stimulus (person, event, place or object) experienced as a challenge or threat. This sets in motion a response to fear, under one form or another. Such feelings of insecurity are transformed into physical stimulation of the endocrine glands or of the sympathetic nervous system.

Anxiety is a common emotion, along with fear, anger, sadness and happiness, and has an important function related to survival. Anxiety is healthy if it serves to solve problems. It becomes pathological when it reaches levels that affect normal life, becoming an obstacle to our behavior. Among the anxiety disorders are: phobias; panic disorder; obsessive compulsive disorder; posttraumatic stress disorder, and generalized anxiety disorders where sufferers have a diffuse sense of anxiety or fear and desire to flee. Often the person who suffers from this cannot clearly identify the hazard or cause of this feeling. It's the result of problems of various types, and more especially the way the person internalizes and thinks about their problems. People with generalized anxiety disorder are prone to:

- Worry to no avail.
- Dramatize things.
- Relive past unpleasant moments.
- Have a pessimistic view of life.

People who react by being anxious are subject to a high level of stress, which is begun by a feedback mechanism: anxiety creates stress and stress generates more anxiety. The symptoms are very diverse, the most common of which are: tachycardia, shortness of breath, trembling limbs, feeling of loss of control or knowledge, sweating, muscle stiffness or weakness, insomnia, and difficulty communicating.

This anxiety can become a panic disorder in which the person believes he will faint or suffer a mishap. It's common for people with this disorder to visit hospitals frequently, and feel better after being treated.

II. What Does The Bible Say?

Read Matthew 6:19-21, 22-23, 24, 25-34. Then discuss about the two alternatives which Jesus offers in each passage. We must lay up treasures on earth or in heaven (Matthew 6:19-21); live in light or darkness (Matthew 6:22-23); serve God or riches (Matthew 6:24), and our own ways or the kingdom of God (Matthew 6:25-34). Then call attention to the importance of the words: "Therefore I tell you..." (Matthew 6:25). This phrase is a call of Jesus to reflection rather than action. He invites us to calmly look at the options that are before us; corruptible and incorruptible, light and darkness, God and riches (Matthew 6:19-24). He tells us not to be anxious but to seek first the Kingdom of God.

Jesus took it for granted that all human beings should seek a purpose, because we need something to live for, something that mobilizes us to action. Planning for tomorrow is time well spent, but striving for tomorrow is time wasted. To plan is to think ahead, making goals, selecting dates to do things and trusting God's direction. When done well, the anxiousness decreases. Whoever gets too anxious is assaulted by fear and finds it difficult to trust God. They have let their plans interfere with their relationship with the Lord.

The word "worry" means "being pulled by different sides and in different directions." Merimna, the Greek word for anxiety, gives us the idea of splitting into different parts. It implies being anxious before we start out on our daily tasks.

Jesus doesn't deny the body's needs; rather He encourages us to meet them. But He emphasizes that to be absorbed by these needs implies unnecessary worry. Jesus invites us to look at the birds and flowers and see how God takes care of them.

He doesn't prohibit provision ... the Bible praises the ant. The birds provide for their future by building their nests, and many migrate to warmer climates before winter. There's nothing in this passage that prevents Christians from making plans for the future or taking sensible steps for their own safety. What Jesus forbids is anxious thoughts. This obsessive concern is incompatible with:

1. The Christian faith (Matthew 6:25-30); believers are not exempt from experiencing conflicts (Psalm 34:19a), but God promises protection (Psalm 34:19b). God knows the situations that concern us (Matthew 6:34b).

2. With common sense (Matthew 6:34); Worry and anxiety is about what is going to happen tomorrow or later on, but we must experience life today. We cannot enjoy today because we're worried about some event that MAY occur in the future. Therefore, worry is a waste of time, ideas and energy. We must make plans for future eventualities, but we shouldn't worry about it.

Jesus says that an attitude of absolute devotion to God leads to freedom from anxiety, demonstrating that anxiety is not necessary (vv.26, 28-30) nor fruitful (v.27), or a good testimony for the Christian (vv. 31-32).

III. Practical Suggestions

An effective means to reduce anxiety is to stop, and then remove the chain of thoughts that led up to being worried. It's good to replace unpleasant thoughts with pleasant images, accompanied by a good dose of physical activity.

A daily dose of enthusiasm is a powerful antidote to anxiety. Originally, the word enthusiasm came from the Greek "en theos", meaning "in God". We can say that enthusiasm is a powerful force that comes from God, which makes the one experiencing it full of energy, leaving no room for negative thoughts and feelings.

A sense of humor is not only a nice gift that improves interpersonal relationships, but also disables anxiety. According to some medical theories, the release of endorphins that laughter produces has beneficial health effects. One study showed that some stress-related indicators decreased during moments of laughter, which supports the theory that humor relieves stress. Some of the benefits of laughter are:

- Reduces the presence of cholesterol in the blood to the same extent as aerobic exercise.
- Promotes digestion by increasing the contractions of all abdominal muscles.
- Facilitates bowel movements due to the "massage" that it produces on the viscera.
- Helps to calm down anger.
- Contributes to a change of mental attitude which helps with the reduction of diseases.
- It increases the heart rate and pulse.
- It helps reduce blood glucose levels.
- It frees us from fear and distress.

To have a correct perspective of a painting, one needs to stand back and observe the picture from a distance. The same is true of life. We need to have a better perspective. This doesn't mean hiding or running away. We need to have an adequate view of ourselves and what happens. Jesus often withdrew (Matthew 14:23, Luke 5:16). Don't carry on your shoulders more responsibilities than you need to. We shouldn't be subject to the circumstances, but the Lord, who controls the circumstances.

A wise man cried out to God: "Lord, give me the strength to change the things I can change, patience to accept the things I cannot change, and the wisdom to distinguish the difference."

Conclusion

Prepare to face difficulties; they are inevitable realities. But we have His promise that He will deliver His followers. God promises to be with us and free us, but He doesn't always take the problems away!

Resources

Additional Information

Stress can come from any situation or thought that makes you feel frustrated or angry. This varies from person to person.

Anxiety is a feeling of apprehension or fear. The source of this uneasiness is not always known or recognized, which can add to the distress you feel.

Stress is a normal part of life of every person. At low levels, this is good because it motivates and can help people become more productive. However, too much stress is harmful. Persistent stress often leads to anxiety and unhealthy behaviors, such as eating too much or consuming alcohol or drugs.

Definition of Terms

Generalized Anxiety Disorder (GAD) is characterized by persistent, excessive, and unrealistic worry about everyday things. People with the disorder may experience excessive anxiety and worry, often expecting the worst even when there's no apparent reason for concern. They anticipate disaster and may be overly concerned about money, health, family, work, or other issues.

Post-Traumatic Stress Disorder (PTSD) is a disorder that develops in some people who have experienced a shocking, scary, or dangerous event.

Obsessive Compulsive Disorder (OCD) is characterized by unreasonable thoughts and fears (obsessions) that lead people to do repetitive behaviors (compulsions). It's also possible to have only obsessions or only compulsions and still have OCD. For people with obsessive-compulsive disorders, behavioral patterns interfere with their daily lives, making life difficult.

Additional Activity

Invite the students to share their own experiences of fear (past and present) and spend some time praying together.

Slaves of Alcoholic Drinks?

René Rivas Fernández (Guatemala)

> **Memory Verse:** "It is for freedom that Christ has set us free. Stand firm, then, and do not let yourselves be burdened again by a yoke of slavery." Galatians 5:1
>
> **Lesson Goal:** That the students understand that alcohol affects our physical body and enslaves our spirit; we can only deliver the Lord.

Introduction

Advertisements affect how we think and feel. They are not just selling the product itself. Companies that produce alcohol spend a lot of time and money creating images where alcohol drinking seems to be attractive and normal. The message they give is that alcohol will give us a better life, because in the images we're shown joy, youth, dynamism, elegance, power and success, among others. What the ads never focus on is the damage that alcohol drinking can do in the health and behavior of people, affecting their welfare, their family, their environment and society in general.

Ask the students to comment about the ads they have seen or heard and show some examples, perhaps the day's newspaper or a magazine. Ask the class if they have had either personal or family experiences about how alcohol has affected the family negatively.

I. Why Do People Drink?

In a forum on alcoholism, a young girl wrote: "Every time I drink alcohol, at first I feel euphoric and talkative, but then I don't know how to stop and I just keep talking nonsense, nonsense. The next day my head and whole body hurts as if a steamroller has passed over me. I feel terrible about myself and enter into a state of depression."

Faced with the problem of alcohol, we need to ask the following questions: Why do people drink? If it's already scientifically proven that alcohol is bad for one's health, why do societies still accept it?

We do need to take into account that there are many predisposing determining factors which can lead to a state of alcohol dependence which can be classified into biological, social and psychological factors.

1. From the physiological standpoint, it appears that some individuals have a marked deficiency of basic nutritional elements, and alcohol consumption increases the level of these essential vitamins.

2. From the social point of view, there are two situations: some countries or communities drink more heavily; secondly friends, parties and other social encounters can encourage excessive consumption of alcohol.

3. From the psychological point of view, some people with personality problems such as antisocial behavior, depression, low self-esteem, stress and anxiety, as well as imitation, curiosity or negative patterns of family, can lead to alcohol abuse.

II. Damage Caused By Alcohol

The damage caused by alcohol in the person who drinks are of all kinds, ranging from immediate as well as those which occur over time.

The immediate damage is due to absorption in the stomach, which goes directly into the blood, reaching the brain and nervous system in a few minutes. This immediately causes symptoms including euphoria, disinhibition, ("confidence" for people with low self-esteem), insecurity, often yielding to the challenges of peers, dizziness with a feeling of "wellness", nausea and vomiting (when they have exceeded tolerance levels for each person). After drinking two or three glasses, the motor centers of the brain are affected and movement is affected.

Frequently drinking alcohol excessively can also cause damage that can be seen in the long term; developing diseases such as cirrhosis, gastritis, indigestion, stomach ulcer, hormonal disorders and sexual impotence. If a person drinks consistently for more than three or four weeks, alcohol cannot be metabolized by the liver and it goes to the brain causing seizures, delusions and permanent damage.

Systematic alcohol intake decreases hunger and interferes with the absorption of important nutrients such as vitamins A, B, C, E and K, as well as protein, so that the alcoholic tends to suffer from malnutrition and vitamin deficiency.

In the case of women, alcohol consumption during pregnancy can cause problems in the developing fetus, resulting in fetal alcohol syndrome.

Some other problems are:

1. Many heavy drinkers suffer the consequences of alcohol. They tend to become lonely and don't like to be told to change their behavior. Each time they are more and more isolated and may enter a phase of permanent depression. Often the only solution that looks right is suicide. Dementia, anxiety and psychotic episodes usually with little rational judgments about reality, obsessive thinking with possibility of delusions and hallucinations may occur.

2. In addition, alcohol can be a social problem. The alcoholic is a person who doesn't perform well at work so is in danger of losing his job, becoming part of the large group of homeless nameless alcoholics. Other people especially reject them as being annoying or dirty and who cannot hold a reasonable conversation. Many alcoholics end up committing crimes and end up in jail. Young alcoholics stop attending their studies or end up being expelled from school.

3. Alcoholics generally have poor family relationships. They may abandon the obligations of the house. They are usually aggressive with relatives or family members. They are often distrustful, very jealous with their partner and violent to their own wives and children, who are often ignored. (Many cases of deaths from violence so common in today's society occur under the influence of alcohol). Alcohol is one of the main reasons for marriage breakup.

4. Finally, the problem that alcohol poses to road traffic should also be mentioned. Many road accidents are caused by alcohol in the blood. This is sadly true during weekends when many young people have accidents, after having been drinking at nightclubs throughout the night. It's thought that up to 50% of accidents are caused by this problem.

III. Freedom in Jesus

Currently there are many people in the world who have become slaves of liquor and suffer its disastrous effects, but Jesus Christ can make us completely free (Galatians 5:1). Like the Galatians, we need to affirm our faith in Jesus Christ who offers freedom to believers. Jesus died on the cross to give freedom to all who believe (John 3:16), and this includes freedom from dependence on drugs such as alcohol.

Getting drunk is seen in the Bible as sin, and is a result of the fallen nature of man (Galatians 5:21). The madness of this vice is shown in Scripture on several occasions. The Bible also emphasizes the evils resulting from this sin, and shows the ruin that drunkenness produces. God warns us of the dangers of this sin and its consequences. Christ has a purpose for the life of people, and if they drink alcohol and submit to it, how will they be able to do the will of God? Alcohol never helped anybody out of their difficult situations. The Bible warns of the dangers that exist for those who consume alcoholic drinks (Proverbs 31:4-5).

God warns against alcohol and says there's a risk that a persona can be dominated by it (Proverbs 23:29-35). The Word of God commands us to move away from darkness and clothe ourselves in the armor of light (Romans 13:12-14). In Ephesians 5:18-20, the apostle Paul calls us to seek the in filling of the Holy Spirit. Drunkenness leads to foolish ravings, while the fullness of the Spirit imparts wisdom. Drunkenness leads to excesses, whereas the fullness of the Spirit helps an individual to be self-controlled. Drunkenness leads to the dark world of Satan's influences, while the fullness of the Spirit will lead us to holiness.

The mature Christian won't be drunk with wine, which only fills the body; the Holy Spirit fills our spirit. Drunkenness leads to dissolution, but the fullness of the Spirit makes us talk, sing, give thanks, express psalms and submit to one another.

Conclusion

Alcohol causes irreparable physical, emotional and psychological damage. Alcohol is a drug that enslaves and leads the alcoholic gradually on a path of personal, family and social destruction.

Jesus Christ died to make us free from all yokes of bondage. Paul calls us to live in that freedom (Galatians 5:1), and with the help of the Spirit of God, we can do it (Ephesians 5:18).

Resources

Additional Information

What Causes Alcoholism?

Although scientists cannot pinpoint specific reasons why alcoholism develops, they have identified several contributing factors. Genetic predisposition, environment, and mental health are the leading risk factors for developing this disease. These factors explain why members of a family with similar life experiences may respond to alcohol consumption in different ways. Even in families where alcohol abuse and addiction are prevalent, different members may respond very differently to treatment and face unique challenges in recovery http://www.timberlineknolls.com/alcohol-addiction/signs-effects/

Definitions of Terms

Alcoholism: "A term of long-standing use and variable meaning, generally taken to refer to chronic continual drinking or periodic consumption of alcohol which is characterized by impaired control over drinking, frequent episodes of intoxication, and preoccupation with alcohol and the use of alcohol despite adverse consequences" (World Health Organization).

Delirium Tremens (DT) is a severe form of alcohol withdrawal. Heavy drinkers are at risk of developing it. When it does occur, it's treated as a medical emergency.

Alcoholics Anonymous (AA) "is an international fellowship of men and women who have had a drinking problem. It's nonprofessional, self-supporting, multiracial, apolitical, and available almost everywhere. There are no age or education requirements. Membership is open to anyone who wants to do something about his or her drinking problem" http://www.aa.org/pages/en_US/what-is-aa

Additional Activities

Group Activity

Divide the class into two or three groups. After reading Ephesians 5:18-21, have one group make a list of what happens in drunkenness (the life of the slave of alcohol).

Have the second group make a list of what happens in the life which is full of the Spirit of God.

At the end, make a comparative table and write the conclusions of the groups.

Possible answers

Slaves to drink	Being full of the Spirit
Dissolution	Unity
Life away from God	Life of worship
Bad relationships	Good relationships
Ungratefulness	Grateful
Rebelling against each other	Mutual submission

Out Of Class Projects

Discuss with the class the possibility of doing a least one of these projects in the community:

1. Communicate with the services of Alcoholics Anonymous in the community and see how the church can collaborate with them.

2. Organize a film/discussion about alcoholism, and invite people from the community to participate.

3. As a Sunday School class, organize lectures on the subject of alcoholism and present them in schools and colleges in the community.

4. Invite drunken people from the community to share a meal with people from the church and share the love of God with them.

Let's Talk About It!

Erika Ríos Hasenauer (USA)

Memory Verse: "I have the right to do anything"—but I will not be mastered by anything." 1 Corinthians 6:12b.

Lesson Goal: To inform the students about different sexually transmitted diseases and challenge them to live lives which are responsible to God, their neighbor and themselves.

Introduction

Humanity suffers through many difficulties. Sexually Transmitted Diseases (STDs), also known as Sexually Transmitted Infections (STIs) or venereal diseases, bring much suffering. STDs are grouped together because they have the same route of transmission through the intimate contact that occurs almost exclusively during sex. Lives of promiscuous sex contributes to the spread of STDs to many people, which results in a serious problem of public health.

I. Overview of STDs

- They are transmitted by intimate contact (which occurs almost exclusively during sex).

- STDs are one of the consequences of inappropriate use of God-given sexuality. These are transmitted during vaginal, anal and oral sex, and sometimes by touching the sexual organs. Some of these infections can also be transmitted through contact with infected blood.

- STDs are serious; they go beyond itching or abnormal vaginal secretions. However, most common ones don't go beyond these temporary symptoms, and fortunately there are treatments. However, some STDs cause serious long-term problems in the body, such as the case of HIV/AIDS, Hepatitis B and Syphilis.

- The number of infected persons remains high in most of the world, despite scientific advances.

- The WHO (World Health Organization) estimates that more than 1 million sexually transmitted infections (STIs) are acquired every day worldwide (2016).

- There are currently 30 types of STDs, of which 26 attack mostly women, and four to both sexes.

- Traditionally there are five medically important infections: Chlamydia, Gonorrhea, Hepatitis B, Syphilis and HIV/AIDS.

II. More about STDs

A. How Can A Person Become Infected?

Situations that may lead a person to have these infections are varied:

- Abuse: People can get STDs after being raped by a person who has the disease.

- Infidelity: It may be that one of the spouses has had, or currently is having, sex outside of marriage with an infected person, and they infect their partner.

- Negligence: This happens with health workers and others who are often in contact with infected blood or bodies and are not careful.

B. Prevention Is Better Than The Cure

The best weapon to prevent STDs is to practice responsible sexuality. Taking responsible decisions is in our hands. With a lifestyle of abstinence before marriage and fidelity after marriage, it's possible to avoid these problems and consequences. Contrary to what many people believe, with God's help this way of life is entirely possible. However, for those who have taken risks and have gone beyond the limits set by God about sexuality, there's still hope. They need to seek the Lord, repent wholeheartedly, and follow the provisions given to us in His Word.

C. What to do When Someone is Infected?

If you know or suspect someone who may have a STD, there are practical ways to help.

- They need to see a doctor. Most public health departments have specialized clinics for such infections. Usually Family Planning Clinics have information available.

- They must initiate timely and urgent treatment. Not all sexually transmitted infections have the same impact. Most can be cured if detected and treated early.

- As a Christian brother or sister, accompany the person in the process. There will be other issues that need to be dealt with, such as emotional wounds and their relationship with God. Guide them to seek the Lord and receive His forgiveness in order to heal their spirit.

III. Does the Bible Have Anything to Say About This?

Genesis 1:27 says: "So God created mankind in his own image, in the image of God he created them; male and female he created them." In this passage, we see that God created us men and women. He made us sexual responsible beings. From the day of creation, he divided the two different types of people; man and woman with their particular characteristics, and at the end He saw that it was good, and very good (Genesis 1:31).

On the other hand, Genesis 2:24 refers to the following: "That is why a man leaves his father and mother and is united to his wife, and they become one flesh." It's God's command that man and woman join together. It's interesting to note that he didn't make marriage between two women or two men but between the man and the women who was made to be his ideal partner. But it's also God's command to make marriage a priority relationship, even over parents and our closest friends. In marriage, these two become one and share emotionally, physically, and economically.

In the Corinthian church, some men of the Christian community were going to prostitutes, arguing that they were entitled to do so. They thought they were spiritually superior and expressed that it didn't matter what they did with the body. For this reason Paul said: "I have the right to do anything," you say—but not everything is beneficial. "I have the right to do anything"—but I won't be mastered by anything" (1 Corinthians 6:12). From verse 12 to 14, Paul argues with them and confronts the false understanding they had regarding the use of the body. Paul urges them to flee the relationships that are not lawful, as sexual immorality (1 Corinthians 6:8).

Sexual relations are by no means bad, because they are of God's creation. Because as we saw, God created us and said that everything was good. The problem is when we act outside the context that God established (1 Corinthians 7:4-5). In a marriage, the couple should have sex freely unless they decide to abstain by mutual agreement. And Paul warned that these periods should be kept short to avoid temptations.

However, we need to ask what should we do if someone in God's family is suffering from guilt, shame or a cycle of continuous sin and temptations? In these cases, they should seek appropriate counseling. God seeks restoration for people so that they can be an integral body, soul and spirit. This complete healing is possible and is given by God. He is the only doctor able to touch areas that no other doctor can touch; He can heal where medicine has no effect; he can heal the wounds which medicine cannot touch. God is an expert in difficult and impossible situations. Meanwhile the person must recognize that they have sinned and offended God. They need His forgiveness and mercy to overcome the past and face future temptations.

Conclusion

Living under the law of God and the direction of the Holy Spirit is the antidote to counteract any negative effects of past decisions and a fallen world. The person who fears God will be victorious if they live under the guidance and help of His Spirit.

Resources

Additional Information

Definition of Terms

Gonorrhea is caused by the bacterium *Neisseria gonorrhoeae* and can spread through any kind of sexual activity. It can be contracted by contact with the mouth, vagina, penis or anus.

Syphilis is a highly contagious disease caused by a bacterium. It's contracted chiefly by infection during sexual intercourse, but can also be a congenital infection that infects a developing fetus.

Chlamydia is a common STD that can infect both men and women. It can cause serious, permanent damage to a woman's reproductive system, making it difficult or impossible for her to get pregnant later on. Chlamydia can also cause a potentially fatal ectopic pregnancy (pregnancy that occurs outside the womb).

Hepatitis B is a virus. It is spread when blood, semen, or other infected body fluid enter the body of a person who is not infected. People can become infected with the virus during activities such as birth (spread from an infected mother to her baby during birth) or by having sex with an infected partner.

HIV/AIDS is spread only in certain body fluids from a person infected with HIV. These fluids are blood, semen, pre-seminal fluids, rectal fluids, vaginal fluids, and breast milk. In most areas, HIV is spread mainly by having sex or sharing injection drug apparatus, such as needles, with someone who has HIV.

Additional Activities

Discussion groups "A"

Divide the class into groups and give them the list of the following words: STDs, marriage, syphilis, sex, HIV/AIDS, fidelity, adultery, ITSs, sin. They should discuss and give a definition of each. Then they can make larger groups and share the answers to reach a single definition for each word. Or, you can write on the board the definitions the groups are giving.

Discussion groups "B"

Ask them to divide into groups and answer the following questions through discussion:

- What do you know about sexually transmitted diseases (STDs)?

- What do you think the Bible says?

When finished, allow all groups to express themselves and make a list on the board of the conclusions.

Practical Work (outside of class)

Divide the class into groups and assign each a practical project to carry out:

1. Investigate in the community which clinics are working with STDs and if there's any way that the church can cooperate with them.

2. Look for contact information and professionals working in the area of sexually transmitted diseases and organize talks at schools, colleges or other community locations.

3. Together with the relevant leaders, organize a presentation on the topic for church youth.

Is Euthanasia Good or Bad?

Wendy Ayala (Guatemala)

> **Memory Verse:** "There is a time for everything, and a season for every activity under the heavens: a time to be born and a time to die," Ecclesiastes 3:1-2a.
>
> **Lesson Goal:** To understand the sacred value of life, and remember that God, as the Creator and absolute owner, has the right to decide when life should end.

Introduction

The word "euthanasia" comes from Greek origin and means initially "good death" without pain, fullness of consciousness. Since the sixteenth century, it has acquired the following meaning: acceleration or causing the death of a sick person by another person, in order to end intolerable and unnecessary suffering.

Many think that when doctors or loved ones take the life of someone who is terminally ill, they are doing a good thing; especially so when there's terrible suffering involved. Let's see what the Bible says.

I. Euthanasia and the Bible

In the Bible, we do have a case of euthanasia. In 2 Samuel 1:9-16, we're told the story of an Amalekite soldier who killed King Saul, because the King himself had ordered him to do it. Saul was dying and didn't want to die at the hands of their enemies, and so he ordered the soldier to kill him. But when this soldier appeared before David, David was angry because he had dared to kill the Lord's anointed, and David ordered his men to kill this soldier.

In reading this story, we could think that David was unfair, since the soldier obeyed the king's orders. However, we must remember that in those times, life was respected, because it was given by God, and especially when it was the life of Saul who had been anointed to be king. Why was David so upset against this soldier and had him killed?

The author of Ecclesiastes tells us that everything under heaven has its time. He begins by saying that there's a time to be born and a time to die. Here we can see that he knew that everything in life has its time and we must respect this.

In many ways, we want to convince ourselves that Euthanasia is something good, something that helps people and must be done to stop the pain and suffering. However, we know that only God has the right to decide when to end life. In this sense, we must be careful and not let ourselves get carried away by the feelings for the person who is suffering. We need to understand that we must deliver them into the hands of God and ask His will, because if God says "not yet," we must say, "yes Lord," instead of arguing with the Creator and Sovereign of life. Christians must also reject the attempt of the modern movement to promote euthanasia as the "right to die." This attempt of secular society to establish this "right" is wrong for two reasons:

1. Allowing someone the right to die is tantamount to promoting suicide, which the Bible condemns. We're forbidden to kill, and that includes the killing of oneself. In addition, Christians are commanded to love others as they love themselves (Matthew 22:39; Ephesians 5:29). The concept of self-love is implied in this commandment. Suicide is hardly an example of self-love. Perhaps we could call it self-hatred. Suicide is selfish. It usually implies escaping from pain and problems, often leaving family and friends deeply hurt that they couldn't help deal with them.

2. The so-called "right to die" denies God the sovereign opportunity to work in a destroyed life and bring glory to His name. When Joni Erickson Tada realized she would have to spend the rest of her life as a quadriplegic, she asked in despair: "Why can't they just

leave me to die?" When her friend Diana, trying to comfort her, said, "The past is dead, Joni; you're alive," Joni replied, "Am I? This is not life." But through the grace of God, Joni's despair gave way to her firm conviction that even her accident was permitted by God and her life could bring glory to Him. Now she shares with the world her firm conviction that "suffering prepares us for heaven."

God has a purpose for everything. We must just give thanks and accept the will of God. God in His Word also tells us that we won't be tempted beyond what we can bear (1 Corinthians 10:13). The Lord is faithful, and wants the best for His children, but often we don't know why certain things happen. The Lord won't leave us. Remember that the enemy is like a roaring lion looking for someone to devour, so let's not be easy bait, because he came to kill, steal and destroy, but Christ came that we might have life and life in abundance (John 10:10).

II. Suffering Is Part Of Life

Physical death is a natural event and it's not the end. Sometimes God allows a person to suffer for a long time before they die; other times not. No one enjoys suffering, but this doesn't justify ending life. Often God's purposes are accomplished through the suffering of a person. "When times are good, be happy; but when times are bad, consider this: God has made the one as well as the other. Therefore, no one can discover anything about their future" (Ecclesiastes 7:14). Romans 5:3 teaches that tribulations produce patience. God cares about those who cry out for death to end their suffering. God in His wisdom and perfection knows what is best, even the time of each person's death.

At the same time, the Bible doesn't command us to prolong the life of a person. If a person has been kept alive only by machines, it's not immoral to turn off the machines and allow the person to die. If a person has been in a vegetative state for an extended period of time, it wouldn't be an offense to God to turn off the machines. If God wants to keep the person alive, He's perfectly capable of doing so without the help of tubes and machines.

Conclusion

Remember that any decisions we make, the first thing is to go is to God. He knows what is best and certainly will reveal his will to us. We must fully trust God and He will act (Psalm 37:5).

Resources

Additional information

Joni Erickson Tada was born in 1949 in Baltimore, Maryland, the youngest of four daughters. As a teenager, Tada enjoyed riding horses, hiking, tennis, and swimming. On July 30, 1967, she dove into Chesapeake Bay after misjudging the shallowness of the water. She suffered a fracture between the fourth and fifth cervical levels and became a quadriplegic, paralyzed from the shoulders down. During her two years of rehabilitation, according to her autobiography, she experienced anger, depression, suicidal thoughts, and religious doubts. However, Tada learned to paint with a brush between her teeth, and began selling her artwork. She can also write this way. To date, she has written over forty books, recorded several musical albums, starred in an autobiographical movie of her life, and is an advocate for disabled people. She married Ken Tada in 1982. They live in Calabasas, California. In 2010, she announced that she had been diagnosed with breast cancer. She emerged successfully from cancer surgery and is hopeful of a positive prognosis. (You can show this short testimony of Joni's life https://www.youtube.com/watch?v=VVXJ8GyLgt0).

Manual of the Church of the Nazarene

31.5. Euthanasia (Including Physician Assisted Suicide).

We believe that euthanasia (intentionally ending the life of a terminally ill person, or one who has a debilitating and incurable disease that is not immediately life-threatening, for the purpose of ending suffering) is incompatible with the Christian faith. This applies when euthanasia is requested or consented to by the terminally ill person (voluntary euthanasia) and when the terminally ill person is not mentally competent to give consent (involuntary euthanasia). We believe that the historic rejection of euthanasia by the Christian church is confirmed by Christian convictions that derive from the Bible and that are central to the Church's confession of faith in Jesus Christ as Lord. Euthanasia violates Christian confidence in God as the sovereign Lord of life by claiming sovereignty for oneself; it violates our role as stewards before God; it contributes to an erosion of the value the Bible places on human life and community; it attaches too much importance to the cessation of suffering; and it reflects a human arrogance before a graciously sovereign God. We urge our people to oppose all efforts to legalize euthanasia.

31.6. Allowing to Die. When human death is imminent, we believe that either withdrawing or not originating artificial life-support systems is permissible within the range of Christian faith and practice. This position applies to persons who are in a persistent vegetative state and to those for whom the application of extraordinary means for prolonging life provide no reasonable hope for a return to health. We believe that when death is imminent, nothing in the Christian faith requires that the process of dying be artificially postponed. As Christians, we trust in God's faithfulness and have the hope of eternal life. This makes it possible for Christians to accept death as an expression of faith in Christ who overcame death on our behalf and robbed it of its victory (2013-2017, pp. 55-56).

Definition of Terms

Euthanasia: "the act or practice of causing or permitting the death of hopelessly sick or injured individuals ... in a relatively painless way for reasons of mercy—also called mercy killing" (Webster's Dictionary).

Additional Activities

The teacher can read to the students any of the following cases, and then open a discussion time.

Case Study "A"

Mark, 17, good student, with a close and happy family was riding his bicycle a few blocks from his house, when there was a shootout and a stray bullet hit his body. Immediately they took him to the hospital where he underwent emergency surgery. Afterwards, the doctors said that Mark would be kept under observation. His liver, kidneys and intestines were damaged and he would have to breathe with the help of a machine. After several months, Mark's condition didn't improve. This gave rise to the next question: Will Mark need to be on the artificial respiration machine forever? If they turn it off, would he die immediately? What would you do? Now let's change the character. This is someone you love: your best friend, a parent or a brother, what would you do?

Case Study "B"

Emily is an elderly woman who is very sick. Medicines cannot ease the pain she suffers. She can hardly eat; she is totally deaf and is almost blind. Every day that passes, her suffering increases. Realizing that there can be no improvement, should she stop taking her medicines and be allowed to die naturally?

At the end of the discussion sum up the answers and measure them against God's standards.

Stewards of Our Bodies

Erika Hasenauer (USA)

Memory Verse: "…you were bought at a price. Therefore honor God with your bodies." 1 Corinthians 6:20

Lesson Goal: To learn that we're responsible to God about how we care for our bodies, including being very careful to lead a healthy life.

Introduction

You can start with the activity: "advertising and body care."

Different studies say that overall health has improved in the last 50 years, more than in the rest of the history of mankind. Experts announced that by 2025, life expectancy will improve to a world average of 73 years, and deaths in children under five will be reduced by half.

However, the reality is that today in the countries of Africa and Latin America, as well as in many other countries around the world, children still die from malnutrition. Pandemics such as HIV/AIDS continue to devastate rich and poor countries. Currently 24 million children continue to be born each year with low birth weight, half a million are born with HIV and more than 10 million die before they are five years old. By 2000 they wanted to eradicate polio, but this has not happened. It's estimated that other diseases, such as diabetes, will double by 2025; diseases such as colorectal cancer and lung cancer will increase while stomach, cervical and liver cancers will decrease.

These prognostics are often discouraging and even hard to believe. But we need to realize that change begins with ourselves. As Christians, we declare God as our Lord and Master; we must change bad habits in our lifestyle. Our body is the temple of the Holy Spirit and as such, we must treat it with special care.

I. What Does The Bible Say About Our Bodies?

Ask people in the class to look up the Bible texts indicated. When they have finished, ask for their conclusions and guide the summary of each point.

Gen. 1:1-25, Gen. 1:26-3, Gen. 2:7; 21-23, Matt. 10:28, 2 Cor. 4:16; Rom. 8:10; 2 Cor. 5:1-10; Rom. 8:23, Phil. 3:20-21, Matt. 14:36; Luke 7:7; John 5:6, 1 Cor. 6:20, 1 Thess. 5:16-24.

- God is the author of life (Genesis 1:1-25). God made us in His image and gave us a mandate to be stewards of everything that was created by Him (Genesis 1:26-31).

- Our physical bodies were created by God (Genesis 2:7; 21-23) and there's no part of our bodies which we should think or assume to be bad.

- The body will end up in heaven or hell (Matthew 10:28).

- The present body is mortal (2 Corinthians 4:16; Romans 8:10); but Christians know by faith that he/she will receive in the resurrection a new body that is not earthly but comes from God (2 Corinthians 5:1-10). God has promised to redeem our bodies (Romans 8:23). Our bodies will be transformed like the one Christ had after his resurrection (Philippians 3:20-21).

- God is the best doctor (Matthew 14:36; Luke 7:7; John 5:6). God cares for our total well-being.

- We belong to God (1 Corinthians 6:20). This includes our body. We don't belong to ourselves, we belong to God. He is our real owner; we must take care of what He has given us.

- God promises his continued fidelity (Deuteronomy 7:9; Isaiah 49:7), but mankind is responsible for breaking and disturbing the perfect balance in which God created us.

- God cares about our well-being in all areas: physical, emotional and spiritual (1 Thessalonians 5:16-24).

We understand that God, as our redeemer and owner, cares about our overall health, and therefore we should be concerned too. If a part of our being is affected, the rest will suffer too. For this reason, we must be good stewards, and as far as we can, care for ourselves responsibly.

II. Being Good Stewards

If we're stewards of the body that God has given us, we must take care, be observant and manage it well. Taking care of our body as part of our being is an important and priority task. The following are some basics ideas about good health, disease and preventive medicine.

- Health is the state of being free from illness or injury.

- Disease is a disorder of structure or function in a human, animal, or plant, especially one that produces specific signs or symptoms or that affects a specific location, and is not simply a direct result of physical injury.

- Preventive Medicine is the specialty of medical practice that focuses on the health of individuals, communities, and defined populations. Its goal is to protect, promote, and maintain health and well-being and to prevent disease, disability, and death.

The causes that lead us to have problems in our health could be:

- Human biology can cause genetic problems or inherited diseases.

- Environment, whether it's physical, chemical, biological, psychosocial or sociocultural, can contaminate us, causing diseases.

- Bad lifestyles, such as the use of drugs, physical inactivity, incomplete or poor diet, stress, violence, and poor utilization of health services.

Of the three reasons mentioned, there's one that we can control directly, our lifestyle. By different factors (social group, work, study, media), we're motivated to develop lifestyle habits that may affect our health in the short or long term. So we must be careful about common harmful habits that appear to be normal. For examples: a sedentary lifestyle, eating junk food or food with high caloric or fat content, drinking soft drinks, not controlling our stress, not consuming the water required by the body, not sleeping enough, not going for preventative medical tests, not wanting to visit the doctor when indicated, and taking medicines following the advice of family or friends instead of doctors.

Without doubt, all people want to have good health, as well as to please God by caring for our bodies. The good news is that we can do it. Being a good steward of our body is to value our bodies as a special place where God dwells.

Ask the class: Think a moment and answer. What bad habits do you have in your current lifestyle?

III. Let's Do It!

You can read the illustration: "A True Story Of Gradual Suicide."

Prevention is one of the keywords to be good stewards of our bodies. Waiting for things to happen is not good practice for us as good stewards. Doing things right every day making the right decisions is what will lead us to minimize problems and strengthen us to face the inevitable things. As we saw earlier, in terms of health, there are causes that cannot be avoided, but there are others that can, and those are the ones we should concentrate on.

Here are some practical suggestions to care for our bodies:

- Celebrate Life! Enjoy yourself for the blessings received from God, and especially the life He gives. This is enough reason for us to take care of ourselves.

- Visit the doctor annually and get the recommended lab tests done.

- Go to the dentist regularly. Every six months is recommended.

- Maintain good personal hygiene and keep the house clean. Remember that germs aren't seen and are the main transmitters of diseases.

- Ensure a balanced diet by informing yourself and learning to eat everything your body needs, not just what you like.

- Eat safely. The food sold on the street is usually very tasty and economical, but in many cases, heavily contaminated. Avoid eating in places outside your home unless you are sure that the place you go to eat follows the rules of hygiene and good food handling.

- Do physical exercise. Be consistent and don't be discouraged. Start small and build up. Exercising can be pleasurable and not a burden on your list of responsibilities.

- Learn to say 'no.' Avoid taking on too many commitments. Convince yourself that you cannot do everything and that everything shouldn't depend on you.

- Sleep well. Sleep requirement varies from one person to another; this can change according to the stage of life. However, getting enough sleep each day will be a perfect tonic as it will provide the necessary energy to continue the next day.

- Smile more! A good attitude towards life will reduce the risk of disease, make for a relaxed family, create a better work environment, and will help you to clarify your thoughts and to manage stress better.

- Live in the present. Be content with "little" before achieving "a lot."

Invite people from the class to develop their own lists of new aims for better care of their health.

Conclusion

Remember that we're God's creation. He himself made our physical bodies, and his Word shows us how important and good the body is. Let's honor God by being good stewards of the bodies that God has given us. Let's make it happen in our daily lives!

Resources

Additional Information

Medical science claims that there are certain diseases that are preventable and can be detected early. It's up to us. Some examples of harmful health habits to avoid are: smoking, which is linked to lung cancer and cancer of the digestive tract; alcoholism, which is associated with liver cancer and cirrhosis; drugs associated with multiple consequences.

Here are some examples of prevention.

- Cervical cancer: by performing the Pap tests every year for women over age 30 who are sexually active.

- Breast cancer: through constant self-examination and consultation with the doctor to detect any abnormality. After 40 years of age it's advisable to have an annual mammogram.

- Prostate Cancer: It's recommended that men over 40 years have an examination each year.

- Sexually transmitted diseases: practicing a lifestyle according to the law of God, having sex only within marriage.

Illustration

A True Story Of Gradual Suicide

Edward was a special friend as well as colleague. He was an enthusiastic and caring person, and as a pediatrician, he wanted to serve the community. He was a successful doctor, trained and dedicated to his patients, the community, the church and his family. He knew he had a heart problem, but did nothing to lose weight and improve his fitness. Then it happened. On a cold and rainy day, while cleaning the drains in his home, my friend at the age of 53 died, leaving behind his beloved wife, wonderful children and a community in need.

The death certificate of my friend said, "coronary artery disease in an advanced stage." However, quite rightly I could have said: "Suicide." Yes, suicide … gradual suicide. It was not deliberate. He didn't choose a place to do it or leave a note explaining the reason. Rather, he chose a mortal life style (Hull, Jerry and Larry, Holiness and Health, Kansas City, USA: CNP, 2002, pp 143-144.).

Definition of Terms

"*Health* is a state of complete physical, mental and social well-being, and not merely the absence of disease or infirmity" (World Health Organization)

•"*Disease* is a definite pathological process having a characteristic set of signs and symptoms. It may affect the whole body or any of its parts, and its etiology, pathology, and prognosis may be known or unknown" (Dictionary of Medicine).

Additional Activity

Advertising And Body Care:

Bring to the class several magazines and newspapers that emphasize the importance that society gives to health care. Divide the class into groups of three or four people. Give one or more publications to each group. After a few minutes of searching for information, they can discuss what they found using the following questions:

- Is all this emphasis on having a perfect body a good thing?

- How are we affected by stereotypes?

- Is it the same to feel good as to feel alright?

- Do diets, pills and devices that are advertised to lose weight quickly and effortlessly actually work? Are these things good or bad?

- Is beauty the same as health?

Taking Care of Our Bodies (Review)

Lesson 39

Patricia Picavea (Guatemala)

> **Memory Verse:** "If anyone destroys God's temple, God will destroy that person; for God's temple is sacred, and you together are that temple." 1 Corinthians 3:17
>
> **Lesson Goal:** To affirm the knowledge about the importance of looking after our bodies that we have studied this quarter.

Introduction

Plato believed that the body is a shell that oppresses the soul of mankind. He believed that the soul was good, while the body was evil. According to Plato the body was a prison that held the soul which needed to be released from the body. But the biblical view is that our bodies are good because God created them. Paul teaches that our bodies are the temple of the Holy Spirit, and as such, need to be looked after: "If anyone destroys God's temple, God will destroy that person; for God's temple is sacred, and you together are that temple" (1 Corinthians 3:17).

We are stewards of the body that God gave us. We cannot do things lightly without thinking of the consequences. The apostle Paul says that we should take care of the temple of God in everything we do: "I have the right to do anything," (1 Corinthians 6:12a). All things are allowed, I have the right to do whatever I want. Not everything is helpful or beneficial. Not everything is a blessing. Christian freedom must be in submission to the principle of spiritual well-being.

The second principle that should govern our actions is self-control. The apostle Paul says: "... I have the right to do anything" - but I won't be mastered by anything" (v.12b). To be dominated by 'freedom' is slavery disguised as freedom. There's no greater slavery than be a slave to freedom, and no greater freedom than to be free from the bondage of 'freedom.'

I. We Must Be Careful About What We Eat

Hypertension, high cholesterol and triglycerides in the blood, diabetes (elevations of blood sugar), anorexia, bulimia and other diseases or disorders that result from having a poor diet or lack of it are all health problems, and if they aren't treated they become serious and can trigger other major diseases such as heart problems and strokes. It's very important to note that only weight gain (being overweight or obese) usually leads to one or more of the aforementioned problems. On the other hand, the lack of energy without medical supervision produces anorexia and causes problems in the heart, liver, kidneys, slowing down body functions, lowering blood pressure, as well as pulse and breathing rates. Lack of energy leads people to feel dizzy and have short attention spans. It also causes anemia through the lack of red blood cells, hair loss, brittle nails, and in extreme cases, leads to a severe malnutrition that causes death. Bulimia causes constant stomach pain. As a result of vomiting, teeth can deteriorate due to the constant presence of acid vomit in the mouth.

In assessing life, we must keep in mind that in Genesis 1:31 we're told that when God created man and woman, He saw that they were very good. He also created the plants, seeds, fruits and animals for food (Genesis 1:29-30); He gave us all that we need to maintain good health. If we're good stewards of the body that God has given us, we must take care of it. Taking care of our body as part of who we are is an important and priority task.

II. Let's Be Aware Of Diseases

A. Sexually Transmitted Diseases

The best weapon to prevent STDs is to practice responsible sexuality. It's up to us to make responsible decisions. With a lifestyle of abstinence before marriage and fidelity after marriage, it's possible to avoid many problems and consequences of this kind. Contrary to what many people believe, with God´s help, this lifestyle is entirely possible.

However, for those who have taken risks and have gone beyond the limits set by God about sexuality, there's still hope. They need to repent, seek the Lord's forgiveness, and follow Him wholeheartedly in accordance with the provisions of His Word.

Sexual relations are by no means bad, because they are God's creation. Because as we saw, God created us and saw it was a very good. The problem is when we don't act in the context that God has established (I Corinthians 7:4-5). In marriage, there must be mutual surrender to full spousal responsibility unless there's a decision to abstain by mutual agreement; although Paul recommended that this shouldn't be for long periods to keep away from the devil's temptations.

B. Diseases Derived From Difficult Situations

Anxiety is a common emotion along with fear, anger, sadness, and happiness, and each has an important function related to survival. Anxiety is healthy if it serves to solve problems. It becomes pathological when it reaches levels that affect normal life, becoming an obstacle to our behavior.

People who react anxiously are subject to a high level of stress. One thing feeds into another: anxiety creates stress and stress generates more anxiety. The symptoms are very diverse, the most common of which are: tachycardia, shortness of breath, trembling limbs, feeling of loss of control or knowledge, sweating, muscle stiffness or weakness, insomnia and difficulty in communicating.

Jesus said, "Therefore I tell you, don't worry about your life" (Matthew 6:25a). Jesus calls us to reflection rather than always just immediate action. He invites us to look calmly at the options that are before us; both those that are corruptible and incorruptible, light and darkness, God and riches (Matthew 6:19-24). Only when we have chosen the good options will our lives be balanced without excessive anxiety.

Stress: Stress is a normal response of the body in which the person feels anxious and tense in situations of danger. Too much stress is harmful when we feel threatened by our circumstances, either because we cannot face them, or we interpret the situation which stresses us as a threat. Stress is caused by the body's instinct to protect itself. If a person is not able to deal with it, stress will be their worst enemy and can lead to death.

Any emotional response, situation or thought (whether positive or negative) that makes you feel frustrated, angry or anxious can cause stress. Remember that Jesus said: "So don't worry, saying, 'What shall we eat?' or 'What shall we drink?' or 'What shall we wear?' For the pagans run after all these things, and your heavenly Father knows that you need them" (Matthew 6:31-32). Beware of things that torment us! It's good to take the time to write things down and analyze them, as this will help us see things more clearly and from the right perspective.

III. Let's Beware Of Addictions

A. Smoking

There's a clear link between smoking and bad health. The more exposure, duration and intensity of the habit, the higher negative effects will be. A smoker is 10 times more likely to die of lung cancer, and is almost three times more likely to have heart disease than a nonsmoker. The risk of dying from a heart attack is two to three times higher in male smokers. We're stewards of our body. That means He will ask us to account for everything we do with the body He gave us.

God is great and His love, power and perfection, has created man perfect. All organs and body systems, even each cell is related to another in perfect harmony. When this balance is broken, that is when diseases and health complications arise, bringing with them their respective consequences. Still, God's grace is infinite and enough to sustain and restore this harmony and give us a second chance.

The apostle's words in I Corinthians 3:16-17 are decisive. "Don't you know that you yourselves are God's temple and that God's Spirit dwells in your midst? If anyone destroys God's temple, God will destroy that person; for God's temple is sacred, and you together are that temple." Our bodies are sacred; they are where the Holy Spirit dwells. With the same zeal with which we take care of the sanctuary, where we come together as a people to worship the Lord, we should take care of our bodies.

B. Drugs

There are many and varied causes that make someone start using drugs, but the most common one is their inner lack of well-being or self-esteem. Generally, a person begins drinking as a result of the inability to feel good about their life. If you have a child or family member who is addicted, don't conceal or deny it. Use the powerful weapon that is the united prayer of the church. The Lord wants to save your child and the church wants him back. Don't go against your child or family with forceful or aggressive accusations. Don't make moral judgments about youth and drugs. Don't abandon the addict on their first relapse, insist and insist again, it's worthwhile carrying on, crying out to God for His grace and mercy and not losing heart.

C. Alcohol

The damage caused by alcohol in the person who drinks is of all kinds, and these occur immediately as well as over time. The immediate damage is due to the quick absorption that occurs from the stomach and goes directly to the bloodstream, reaching the brain and nervous system in a few minutes. The immediate effects include euphoria, disinhibition, insecurity (they often yield to peer pressure), dizziness with a feeling of 'happiness,' nausea and vomiting (when they have exceeded tolerance levels). After drinking two or three glasses, the motor centers of the brain are affected and gait can become awkward.

Drunkenness is seen in the Bible as a sin and as a result of the fallen nature of man (Galatians 5:21). The madness of this vice is shown in Scripture on several occasions. The Bible also emphasizes the evils resulting from this sin and the ruin that drunkenness produces. God warns us of the dangers of this sin and its consequences (Proverbs 23:29-35).

Conclusion

All excesses are bad and may gradually lead us down a path of personal, family and social destruction. Jesus Christ died and makes us free from all the chains of bondage. Paul calls us to live in freedom (Galatians 5:1), and we can do this with the help of the Spirit of God (Ephesians 5:18).

Resources

Additional Information

Food

Food is an important element for good health. We need to take into account the quality of food, the amount of food, and eating habits. Fruits and vegetables contain vitamins, minerals, carbohydrates and fiber. These substances are necessary to keep the body functioning during all stages of life. For this reason, it's recommended to eat two fruits and two kinds of vegetables daily. Vitamin pills cannot replace a full balanced diet that contains all the vitamins and minerals required.

All this quarter we have seen different things that harm our body that God gave us to use and enjoy every day. This body is the temple of our God where His Spirit dwells. God gives us everything necessary to take care of our bodies and have a healthy life. In Genesis 1, he tells us that God himself took time to create natural food and when He finished He saw that it was good. Enjoy it!

Additional Activity

Testimony

Invite some Christian who has had some addictions or eating problems or problems with anxiety and have overcome them. Ask them to share what they suffered and how they managed to get ahead.

Journey's With
A Purpose

Trust & Obey, For There's No Other Way
Called to Free the Slaves
A Journey To Freedom
The Journey Back Home
Journey with a Surprising Outcome
A Journey to Restore
The Refugees' Flight to Egypt
Jesus Travels to the Desert
In the Middle of the Storm
Guided Tour Which Led to Blessing
Jesus Meets Saul on the Road to Damascus
An Excellent Traveling Companion
Traveling With A Purpose

Trust and Obey, For There's No Other Way!

Marco Rocha (Argentina)

Memory Verse: "I will bless those who bless you, and whoever curses you I will curse; and all peoples on earth will be blessed through you." Genesis 12:3

Lesson Goal: To learn that in order to enjoy the blessings of God, we need to have faith in His Word and obey him.

Introduction

Start the class by showing photographs or magazine clippings with pictures of the end of a sporting event and the medal ceremony. Then ask students to draw up a list of five prerequisites that athletes believe they need to reach the goal and get the top prizes offered by the race. Once completed, explain to the class: 'today we'll learn about Abraham's call, and the prerequisites for achieving God's blessings.'

Abraham was one of the most outstanding men of Old Testament times. He was the son of Terah, grandson of Shem, the son of Noah. At first, his name was Abram, which means 'exalted father.' Later God gave him the name Abraham (Genesis 17:5), meaning 'father of a multitude.' God commanded him to take a journey to an unknown land. The response to the divine call of Abraham has captured the imagination of many seekers of God. On his journey through faith, Abraham suffered many difficulties, but persevered in doing God's will.

I. To Achieve Blessings, We Need To Have Faith In God's Word.

Genesis 11:27-30 tells us that Abraham lived with his family in Ur of the Chaldeans. This was an important cultural center in southern Iraq. Subsequently, Terah, the father of Abram, left Ur with Abram, Sarai (Abram's wife) and Lot to go to the land of Canaan. On their way, they stayed for some time in Haran, in eastern Syria.

Genesis 12:1-3 tells us that God called Abraham, who proved his faith, obedience and service.

A. The Call Was Accompanied By Demands (12:1)

1. Abraham had to leave his economic and political security. He had to leave his own land. This meant going to an unknown place, risking everything he owned, because he didn't know what he was going to find.

2. Abraham had to leave his family and friends. He had to leave his father, relatives, acquaintances and friends. This meant leaving those he held most dear, and as well as the safety and comfort that they represented. Moreover, in their patriarchal system, Abraham, as Terah's eldest son, gave up his privileged rightful place in society.

God told Abraham to abandon his family and rights and accept the unknown. Through this call, God challenged Abram to believe, surrender his will, to be convinced that although he couldn't see what God was asking, it was for real, and to put aside his own personal dreams and accept God's plan for his life.

If we were to carry out a survey, we would be surprised by the large number of people who say they 'believe' or 'have faith' in God. But many of them don't know what God's will is for their lives, or simply turn a blind eye to what they dislike or bothers them in the Bible. Today, believers have God's will revealed in the Bible. To approach Him and His blessings, we need to believe in His Word, recognizing that through it, He will show us his will.

Often, as in the case of Abraham, believing in God often involves us in facing uncertain directions, so we need to look at the example of this man of God, and like him, accept the promises of God. Do you believe all that God has revealed in His Word? Try for a moment to put yourself in the place of Abraham. What would be your reaction if God challenged you to move from where you are to an unknown country?

II. Faith In His Word Involves Obedience

Read Genesis 12:4-5 and ask the students to help you draw on the board a list of feelings that must have passed through Abraham's heart when he was packing up his things to leave for an unknown destination, in obedience to God's voice.

A. When God Called Abraham, (Vv.4-8) He Lived Under The Following Conditions:

1. His family came from Ur of the Chaldeans, where idolatry was practiced, because with the passage of time, the nations descended from Noah had turned their backs on the knowledge of God.

2. His wife Sarah was barren (Genesis 11:30), which was a great tragedy in the ancient world. She had no hope of having children. Lot was Abraham's orphaned nephew, whom he seems to have adopted. He accompanied Abraham and become his heir if Sarah couldn't conceive a child.

3. His economic situation was favorable in Haran as we can see by the amount of goods and servants he had accumulated.

These conditions could have made Abraham doubt this call, but he set out on his journey in obedience. Abraham accepted God's call with all its risks, apparently without raising questions. After accepting the call of God, Abram had to put his faith to work, and that meant preparing for departure.

Hebrews 11:8 says: "By faith Abraham, when called to go to a place he would later receive as his inheritance, obeyed and went, even though he didn't know where he was going." Abraham's response was based on faith, that is, he unconditionally trusted the God who had called him. In his response to God's revelation, he believed God and was patient. "The Lord appeared to Abram and said, 'To your offspring I will give this land.' So, he built an altar there to the Lord, who had appeared to him." (Genesis 12:7). Abraham had a personal relationship with God. Amidst a culture of idolatry and paganism, he worshiped the only true God publicly and exclusively.

III. Obedience Is The Way To Put Our Faith Into Action

Have your students read James 2:14-24 and then name some brief examples of how to put faith into action through obedience. From this passage, we learn that to enjoy the blessings of God, it's not enough to only believe, but we have to obey him. Perhaps we're challenged like Abraham to leave bad habits or traditions that don't edify us, to believe that He can make possible what is impossible in our eyes, or to leave situations of comfort and go to the unknown. We shouldn't let anything stop us from completely obeying God's voice, and He will fulfill His will in us.

A. Obedience Brings Blessing

Write on the board the promise of Genesis 12:2-3. Read together the text and mark what things would be blessed if Abram believed and obeyed God's voice. In Genesis 12:2-3, we find the purpose of the journey that Abraham had to make. God made the following promises if Abram obeyed his call (v. 2):

1. Blessing of material prosperity: God would make Abram a great nation, which included having many descendants, possessions and geographical territory.

2. Blessing of personal recognition: "I will bless you and make your name great." God would bless and exalt the name of Abram. It would remembered and respected with the passing of the years by God and the people: (Exodus 2:24; 4:5, 6:3; Leviticus 26:42; Deuteronomy 1:8; 1 Kings 18:36; 1 Chronicles 16:16, etc.).

3. Blessing of spiritual prosperity for others: "... and you'll be a blessing" "... and all peoples on earth will be blessed through you" (12:3b; 18:18, 22:18, 26:4, 28:14). This verse reveals God's missionary purpose and points to Jesus, the Messiah).

We must understand that the consequence of faith is to have God's blessing in our lives. Although Abraham didn't see with his own eyes the entirety of the scope of these blessings, today we can know through the Bible that his offspring became the chosen people ... especially the Messiah, Jesus Christ, the Saviour of the World. Likewise, we must believe that the blessing of God for our lives is available if we have genuine faith, trusting in God despite all adverse circumstances that might occur.

As the athlete who, when approaching the goal sees no competitors nearby, starts enjoying the award of reaching the finish line, so we can start enjoying today God's blessing if we believe in his promises, hoping for the final reward that awaits us after the race.

Conclusion

Allow your students to respond freely: What could be the conclusion of what was learned today? One conclusion could be 'just as in the case of Abraham, when God calls us He also has a purpose. In order to have God's blessings, we must have faith and obey.

Resources

Additional Information

With the call of Abraham (Genesis 12:1-3), the Bible begins a new chapter in the history of human sin and redemption. Abraham, 'the father of the faithful,' marks a watershed in Old Testament thought. The true God repeatedly was known as 'the God of Abraham' or, in conjunction with his son and grandson, 'the God of Abraham, Isaac and Jacob.' God's call to Abraham was a call to faith; to leave his ancestral home, and go to the land that God would show him, promising blessings for him and through him, blessings 'for all the families of the earth' (v. 3) (Explorando la Santidad Cristiana, CNP. p. 39 (Tr. from Spanish).

Definition of Terms

Faith: the word is used in four different ways in the Bible

1. A personal belief, mental acceptance & acknowledgement of God's existence (Heb. 11:1, 6; 2 Cor. 4:18; Jn. 20:27-29, etc.).

2. A conduct or work inspired by compete surrender: "we show our faith by our works." (James 2:14-26; Rom 1:5; 15:18:16:26; Heb. 11:8-12 "Abraham's faith," etc.)

3. A trusting or trustworthiness (Mt 24:45; 25:21, 23; Lk 19:17 "faithful servant"; Rom 3:3 the faithfulness of God, etc.).

4. The system of doctrine and morality peculiar to Christianity: Eph. 4:23 until we all attain to the unity of the faith; 1 Tim. 1:13 'reprove then that they may be sound in the faith' (http://www.bible.ca/s-faith-defined-basics.htm).

Obedience: a succinct definition of biblical obedience is 'to hear God's Word and act accordingly.' Although obedience is also used in the secular sense, the central meaning derives from the relationship with God. He makes known his will through his voice or written word. Obedience to God is total surrender to his will, and therefore obedience and faith are closely related (Genesis 15:6; 22:18; Romans 10:17).

Additional Activities

1. *Brainstorming* (3 minutes)

Objective: To find out how your students understand the concept of faith. Write their suggestions on the board. This can be used to introduce the first point. Some answers could be 'believe,' 'trust,' and 'fidelity' (among others). Finally look at the biblical definition in Hebrews 11:1.

2. *Believe In Order To Arrive* (4 minutes)

Materials: a scarf to blindfold and different obstacles (chairs, desks, etc.).

Objective: To help the students understand the need to trust God and obey his voice to reach the final goal, even if we don't see things very clearly.

Divide the class into two groups and ask them to choose two representatives per group. One will be blindfolded and the other one will guide the 'blind 'one by the hand through an obstacle course. The team who wins will be the one whose team members reach the finish first.

Called to Free the Slaves

Lesson 41

Samuel Pérez (Puerto Rico)

Memory Verse: "The Lord said, "I have indeed seen the misery of my people in Egypt. I have heard them crying out because of their slave drivers, and I am concerned about their suffering." Exodus 3:7

Lesson Goal: To recognize and affirm that God is not indifferent to our historical reality. He continually intervenes in the process of our history, especially in circumstances of injustice, oppression and abuse of power.

Introduction

The Exodus, as the departure of the Hebrews from Egypt, is considered to be the fundamental fact of the formation of the people of Israel. The Israelites were slaves to the Egyptians, who oppressed them for several centuries. Then they cried out and God heard their cry (Exodus 2:24). God decided to deliver them from the hand of the Egyptians and bring them out of that land. To do this, God called Moses.

I. The Context

God uses diverse circumstances and events when he wants to call someone to do a specific task. Moses was about 80 years old when God revealed Himself to him. He was looking after his father-in-law's sheep and goats when God called him to carry out a challenging and complex task. God didn't call him when he lived in the palace enjoying relating to palace officials, nor when he was being prepared in the school of the Egyptians. He called him in the desert when his circumstances had changed drastically.

Living in Midian, Moses had come to know the Sinai desert very well. At this point, the preparation was over. Now God took the initiative, and even though Moses didn't necessarily seek God, God sought Him. One day Moses "was tending the flock of Jethro his father-in-law, the priest of Midian, and he led the flock to the far side of the wilderness and came to Horeb, the mountain of God" (Exodus 3:1). It was at this spot that his life was going to change completely.

In the Judeo-Christian tradition, the 'mountain' suggests the place of God's self-revelation. God took the initiative to reveal himself in a special way and to communicate to Moses His plan and purpose, in which Moses was to play a key role (vv. 2-3).

II. Divine Revelation and Human Response

A. The Theophany

God revealed himself to Moses in the figure of the Angel of the Lord (Exodus 3:2). This mode of appearance is known as a 'theophany.' This event shocked and caught the attention of Moses. God used the burning bush to attract his attention. Fire is a symbol of the presence and power of God (Genesis 15:17; Exodus 19:18; Deuteronomy 4:24; Acts 2:3; Hebrews 12:29).

B. Human Response

Exodus 3:2b says, "Moses saw that though the bush was on fire, it didn't burn up." Moses was sensitive to his environment. How many of us now are able observe what is going on around us? Moses passed from sensitivity to availability. It's not enough to be sensitive; we need to be available to meet the needs of the society in which we live and respond to God's call. But, being available represents taking risks. We need to move from theory to practice, from discouragement to hope. It means leaving the comfort zone and taking risks.

III. Calling, Commission and Divine Purpose

A. Divine Calling

Given the availability of Moses, 'Yahweh,' the 'I am who I am' (Exodus 3:14a), the incomparable, called Moses. The Lord Himself called him in the middle of the burning bush: "God called to him from within the bush, 'Moses! Moses!' And Moses said, 'Here I am'" (Exodus 3:4). God begins with an order, "'do not come any closer.' God said 'Take off your sandals, for the place where you are standing is holy ground'" (v.5). The order was in accordance with the customs Moses knew from his experience of watching the Egyptian priests who took their shoes or sandals off to go into their temples. This act meant much more than mere reverence or respect; it consisted of a personal confession of contamination and indignity in the presence of great holiness. When we speak of the Holy Land, we're talking about the presence of God in that place. Moses needed to be aware that he was in the presence of God. As Moses approached the bush, God ended his shepherd life and sent him out to be the liberator of his people. Holiness is a necessary and vital quality if we're going to answer God's call. The holiness of God committed his people to the life of holiness (Leviticus 19:1-2).

God is not identified as a new god. Rather He presents himself as the God of the Covenant (Exodus 3:6). The same God that their ancestors recognized, worshiped and served. God had not forgotten the promises made to the patriarchs. Moses needed to know without a doubt who was calling him, even though at that point he didn't know what his mission was going to be. Moses recognized his humanity when he covered his face, fearing to experience the holiness of God.

A. Commission and Divine Purpose

In Exodus 3:8-11, God told Moses the nature and purpose of his calling and commission. We observe three key elements in these verses.

1. God revealed his firm and determined decision to deliver his suffering people from the hand of the Egyptians (verse 8).

2. God chose Moses to be the human instrument to liberate the people (v.10).

3. Moses resisted taking on such a big and difficult responsibility (v.11).

It was time that God would deliver the people. The verbs used indicate that it was the turning point. "The Lord said, 'I have indeed seen the misery of my people in Egypt. I have heard them crying out because of their slave drivers, and I am concerned about their suffering. So I have come down to rescue them'... 'So now, go. I am sending you'" (vv.7-10). The cry of the children of Israel had come to the Lord, and He had seen the oppression of the Egyptians (verse 9). "Then the Lord said to Moses, 'So now, go. I am sending you to Pharaoh to bring my people the Israelites out of Egypt'" (v.10). The commission to Moses was to 'liberate' Israel from the power and political injustices of slavery in Egypt, and bring them to Canaan.

Canaan was called a land flowing with milk and honey (v.8 and Numbers 13:27). Centuries before, the patriarchs, as foreigners, had put their tents there as guests and passers-by. Soon they would own the land of Israel as the Lord had promised. God said that he would take them to "the home of the Canaanites, Hittites, Amorites, Perizzites, Hivites and Jebusites" (v. 8b).

IV. Moses' Objections and Replies

At first, Moses objected to the divine call. He saw his own inability and the impossibility of the task (Exodus 3:11). Often today people raise similar objections when God calls them. Moses incredulously replied, who am I? Who are you? They won't believe me. Send someone else.

A. The Sense Of Personal Insecurity

"Who am I that I should go to Pharaoh and bring the Israelites out of Egypt?" (Exodus 3:11) Moses reminded God that he was a fugitive of Egyptian justice. Despite his sense of inadequacy, who could have been better prepared? He knew the Egyptian language, culture, beliefs and even their leaders. He was an adopted grandson of Pharaoh. He knew his way around the palace without an official guide. Furthermore, he knew intimately the desert and villages in the area, and had taken a special course of theology from Jethro, the priest of God.

Although he was unaware of it, God had prepared Moses well. But he had one more thing to learn: God is sovereign, and He, not Moses, would deliver the people from Egyptian power. God didn't need a powerful self-seeking man, but was looking for a sensitive and obedient instrument.

The Lord's answer is one of the most significant texts of all Scripture, and a promise that gives encouragement to all those called by him: "And God said, "I will be with you. And this will be the sign to you that it's I who have sent you: When you have brought the people out of Egypt, you'll worship God on this mountain'" (v.12). The sign was the presence of God with him: "I will be with you." The first half of the verse contains the promise; the second half is a statement that they'll serve God on Mount Horeb (Sinai) after the exodus. The future confirmed Moses in his task; he would lead the people out of Egypt, and bring them to the holy mountain of God. God would not stay in Horeb. The divine presence would accompany Moses all the way. The next test would be in the future, when the people encounter God at the foot of Mt. Sinai.

B. Credibility

Moses was concerned about his credibility; he feared that the people would not believe (Exodus 4:1). For this reason, God gave him different signs (vv. 3-7).

C. The Problem Of Communication

Moses attempted to justify himself, saying he had never been 'eloquent' and was 'slow of speech and slow of tongue' (Exodus 4:10). But yet, we see that he had no difficulty in presenting the reasons why he shouldn't do the work and made excuses and gave reasons why the Lord should not send him. He was slow to say 'yes' to the call and was quick to say 'no.' It seems that the problem was not so much about being unable to talk as much as the lack of personal conviction. God didn't argue with him. Simply he said: "Now go; I will help you speak and will teach you what to say" (Exodus 4:12). Still, Moses asked God to send someone else. Then God was angry with Moses, and told him that his brother Aaron would go with him and he could talk for him (vv. 14-16).

V. What Does This Story Teach Us Today?

God uses leaders who must have the following qualities:

- Being willing to do God's will.
- Being sensitive, vulnerable and obedient to God's voice.
- Despite feeling insecure, they must trust that the Lord's presence will always accompany them.

Men and women who serve the Lord best aren't those who have the most talents to offer, but those who are willing in humility to let the Lord use them. When the Lord calls someone to serve Him, His presence will accompany the call and help to accomplish the task. A statement of futility to serve God can simply be an excuse not to engage in the work of God.

Conclusion

Our God continues to call men and women to be agents of His mission, to bring freedom and complete salvation. Let's not hesitate in accepting the Lord's call to serve him because His presence assures victory.

Resources

Additional Information

Angel means 'messenger,' and can refer to a human or a heavenly being. Before the time of Moses, God's revelation came mainly through angels.

The exodus, or the departure of the Hebrews from Egypt, is considered the fundamental fact of the formation of the people of Israel especially during the journey from Egypt to the Promised Land. Exodus is the prototype of every salvific act of God. God is not alienated from the historical reality of His people. God breaks into the history of nations and He reveals himself to those He calls.

Definition of Terms

Theophany (from Ancient Greek theophaneia) refers to the appearance of a deity to a human.

Additional Activities

Contextual Dramatization

You can do a little drama of God's call to Moses, only bring it up to date. Change Moses' name. You can use different technological resources you have available, projector, sound, etc.

Interview

You can invite the pastor and interview him/her about how he/she received their call from God and how they identified God's purpose in their life.

A Journey To Freedom

Jorge Fernández (Uruguay)

Memory Verse: "Then Deborah said to Barak, "Go! This is the day the Lord has given Sisera into your hands. Has not the Lord gone ahead of you?" Judges 4:14a.

Lesson Goal: To learn that God is our traveling companion, and that despite difficult situations, he will lead us to victory.

Introduction

While Joshua (Moses' successor) and those of the older generation were alive, the Israelites served God. But when that generation died, everything changed (Judges 2:10-12). From Judges 2:12 onwards, we're told of the apostasy of Israel and the work of the judges. The age of the judges was characterized by frequent rebellion against God; the people provoked God's wrath and punishment. When they were distressed by the oppression of foreign nations, they repented and cried to the Lord. He in His mercy sent judges, who led them to fight their enemies (Judges 2:16, 3:9, 15).

I. God Permits Difficult Situations

The book of Judges records a series of dominations by foreign powers, followed by liberations of the people of Israel. The normal sequence was: rebellion – servitude – anxiety – prayer – and finally liberation. Judges 4:1-9 tells us that the Israelites were oppressed for 20 years because Jabin, king of the Canaanites, had invaded them. Once again, they had abandoned the Lord, doing evil in His eyes (Judges 4:1-2). These were difficult times in different aspects:

A. Economically, they were impoverished and politically, and they had lost their freedom for many years. They felt that God was no longer blessing them. Life was hard. It's very difficult to have hope for the future in these situations; also, Sisera, Jabin's general, was powerful. He "had nine hundred chariots fitted with iron and had cruelly oppressed the Israelites for twenty years..." (Judges 4:3).

B. At that time, there was a lady leading the nation called Deborah (Judges 4:4). Today this doesn't seem so strange, but in the midst of a society where the men led and ladies took a secondary role, the presence of a woman ruling the nation is noteworthy.

C. The people were paralyzed by a generalized state of despondency that didn't allow them to take on challenges.

The Israelites were cruelly oppressed by Jabin and again "they cried to the Lord for help" (Judges 4:3). At no time had God abandoned them, and in the midst of this situation he sent a solution. To lead this process of change, God chose a woman named Deborah, a prophetess, the wife of Lapidoth, to lead Israel at that time.

What about us? We need to ask the following questions: have we abandoned the ways of the Lord? Are we prepared to receive the consequences in our lives of forsaking the ways of the Lord? Are we willing to fight against difficult situations and try to find a way through by turning to God in genuine repentance?

II. Preparations for the Journey to Freedom

In the most difficult moment of oppression, Deborah sent for Barak son of Abinoam, who lived in Kedesh in Naphtali, to give him a message from God (Judges 4:6-7). Here we can learn some things: a) we too are called to fulfill a mission, b) we're also given a strategy and c) and we're shown the final result.

God promised to deliver Sisera into Barak's hands in the Kishon River (v. 7). To fight, Sisera would have to cross the plain through which the Kishon River, the second largest river of Palestine, flowed into the sea. All Barak had to do was believe God and do what God commanded. One of our greatest difficulties as human beings is to believe in God and depend on Him. This has been true from the beginning and continues today. Not only must we be able to believe in Jesus as our personal Savior, we must also believe and depend on God each step of the way.

In this story, we see that God had mercy on Barak, and spoke with him personally through Deborah. Barak was persuaded to believe that God would use him to free his people, but he needed to trust and act according to the will of God.

III. The Journey and The Final Victory

Barak agreed to obey God's command as long as Deborah would accompany him (Judges 4:8). She accepted, assuring him however that this would mean no glory for him, since the Lord would deliver Sisera into the hand of a woman (Judges 4:9). Deborah went with him, and her presence gave both Barak and his army the assurance of God's blessing and the promise of freedom for the people. Her presence reminded them that it was God who was leading them into battle.

Debora's work was always to exhort, encourage and support so that the final victory would be achieved. "So Deborah went with Barak to Kedesh. There Barak summoned Zebulun and Naphtali, and ten thousand men went up under his command. Deborah also went up with him" (Judges 4:9b-10).

In Judges 4:10, we find two important lessons if we want to have God's victory in our lives: 1) we must obey faithfully the commands that God gives us, obeying in the way that God commands, not as we want to; and 2) God's intervention this time was not based on individual efforts but on teamwork; where everyone had a different responsibility to fulfill and everything worked towards the same end result.

A nomad called Heber the Kenite with his wife Jael pitched their tent by the great tree near some water (4:11). Later on in the story, Jael played an important role (Judges 4:17-22). When Sisera learned that Barak had gone to Mount Tabor, he gathered his nine hundred chariots and his army

from Harosheth Haggoyim (v.13) and came to the banks of the river Kishon. "Then Deborah said to Barak, "Go! This is the day the Lord has given Sisera into your hands. Has not the Lord gone ahead of you?" So Barak went down Mount Tabor, with ten thousand men following him" (Judges 4:14). There was a great military victory "At Barak's advance, the Lord routed Sisera and all his chariots and army by the sword, and Sisera got down from his chariot and fled on foot" (v.15).

In Deborah's song in chapter 5, we learn that there was a helping hand from nature. "The River Kishon swept them away, the age-old river, the river Kishon. March on, my soul; be strong!" (5:21). This verse indicates that the battle was the Lord's from beginning to end. The River Kishon grew suddenly, turning the valley into a quagmire in which the chariots of the Canaanites got stuck. The result was the total defeat of the forces of Sisera and their complete destruction. Sisera abandoned his chariot and fled on foot, reaching the tent of Jael, Heber's wife. When Jael saw him come running, he called to her to let him hide in the tent. When he fell asleep, Jael killed him with a tent peg and a hammer (Judges 4:17-21). So the prophecy came true; Sicera fell at the hands of a woman. When Barak arrived, chasing his enemy, Jael called to him: "I will show you the man you're looking for" (v.22a).

The victory was complete "On that day, God subdued Jabin king of Canaan before the Israelites. And the hand of the Israelites pressed harder and harder against Jabin king of Canaan until they destroyed him" (vv. 23-24). These two chapters from the book of Judges show us the consequences of rebellion against God, but also His mercy and victory when we cry out to Him in repentance.

Conclusion

God will lead us to victory as long as we're obedient to His Word, fulfilling God's purposes. We're not called to have the occasional victories, but God wants us always to be victorious in Him.

Resources

Additional Information

Definition of Terms

Judges: The judges were temporary and special deliverers, sent by God to deliver the Israelites from their oppressors; not supreme magistrates, succeeding to the authority of Moses and Joshua. Their power only extended over portions of the country, and some of them were contemporaneous. Their first work was that of deliverers and leaders in war; they then administered justice to the people, and their authority filled in the gap left by having no regular government. Even while the administration of Samuel gave something like a settled government to the south, there was scope for the irregular exploits of Samson on the borders of the Philistines; and Samuel at last established his authority as judge and prophet, but still as the servant of Jehovah, only to see it so abused by his sons as to exhaust the patience of the people, who at length demanded a king, after the pattern of the surrounding nations (http://biblehub.com/topical/j/judges.htm).

The purposes of the Book of Judges are (1) to bridge in some manner the historical gap between the death of Joshua and the inauguration of the monarchy, (2) to show the moral and political degradation of a people who neglected their religious heritage and compromised their faith with the surrounding paganism, (3) to show the need of the people for the unity and leadership by a strong central government in the person of a king (https://www.biblicaltraining.org/library/book-judges).

Additional Activity

"Help! I'm In Trouble"

(No more than 9 minutes)

Have available some extra pieces of paper and pencils

Objective: God will always provide a way out of difficult situations, but we must be willing to do what He asks, even if it seems difficult.

Development: Ask students to each write on a piece of paper what strategies they use when facing a difficult situation, and identify the obstacles that may prevent them from doing God's will. Ask if anyone wants to share with others what you have written.

The Journey Back Home

Carlos Cordero (Venezuela)

> **Memory Verse:** "May the Lord repay you for what you have done. May you be richly rewarded by the Lord, the God of Israel, under whose wings you have come to take refuge." Ruth 2:12
>
> **Lesson Goal:** To discover that even in the midst of making various decisions, one can act with mercy and do the right thing.

Introduction

Read Ruth 1:1-22 in a modern version. Make sure that everyone is acquainted with the characters mentioned in the passage as well as the situation they find themselves in. The book of Ruth contains the beautiful story of a foreign woman from the land of Moab who came from paganism and idolatry to a true knowledge of the God of Israel. Her name was included in the family tree of David, and also in the genealogy of Jesus, the savior of the world (Ruth 4:13-21; Matthew 1:5; Luke 3:32). She decided to leave her land and her gods and accompany her widowed mother-in-law, choosing to follow the faith of Israel (Ruth 1:16-17).

The experience of Elimelek and Naomi is part of the reality of many people and families today in different parts of the world who, trying to overcome their adverse situations, leave their countries in search of a better economic or social situation. Ask the class if any of them have experienced this or know of someone who has. How did they feel about leaving their family, acquaintances and culture?

I. Israel Was In A Moment Of Crisis

"In the days when the judges ruled, there was a famine in the land" (Ruth 1:1). In order to escape the crisis, Elimelek and Naomi, both Ephrathites of Bethlehem, emigrated with their two sons, Mahlon and Kilion to the neighboring land of Moab. At that time, there was peace between Israel and Moab. There are many people today escaping from famine and disease. Emigration is challenging and brings with it radical changes.

God had promised to bless His people. It seems that Elimelek had forgotten that promise and thought he should find something better elsewhere. So, he decided to leave his country and go elsewhere in search of better horizons for his family. It was not easy to move, but the important thing was that the whole family went together to seek out new horizons. We see here a good example of family unity. Often in our world many families are fragmented, some staying in the homeland while other family members leave to try to find some "economic benefits." These separations often deteriorate the family relationships. When changes are inevitable, what should families keep in mind? What is the most important thing for a family that needs to go to another country or city?

Some issues to consider are: personal values, family values, family unity and social customs. We must keep these in mind in a world where the trend is constant and rapid change; family disintegration is all too common and values are relativized. Postmodernism is a constant threat to the family, which can be destroyed while seeking safety. Discuss the values that predominate in families today.

II. Unexpected and Painful Results

This family went to Moab and there initiated a new life. The sons grew up and got married. Mahlon married a Moabite woman named Ruth and Kilion another Moabite called Orpah. "Now Elimelek, Naomi's husband, died, and she was left with her two sons...After they had lived there about ten years, both Mahlon and Kilion also died, and Naomi was left without her two sons and her husband" (Ruth 1:3-5). The experience of the loss of her husband and two sons marked Naomi's life, her expression says it bluntly: "I went away full, but the Lord has brought me back empty.

Why call me Naomi? The Lord has afflicted me; the Almighty has brought misfortune upon me" (Ruth 1:21).

Discuss with the class experiences of families where there have been unexpected and painful experiences. Naomi understood how difficult it would be for her and her daughters to live in a foreign country, so she decided to return to her hometown, Bethlehem and begged them to return their homes. Everything had gone wrong for Naomi. She had lost her husband and children and the desire to live and fight. Her decision to go back home was to go back and die in her own land. She wanted her daughters-in-law to be happy, to get married again. She didn't want to drag them off to Bethlehem with her, so she told them to go back to their mothers' home and she would go back to her own home alone (Ruth 1:8).

III. Adopting a New Life

A. In Misfortune, Grace Abounds

Orpah decided to leave and go her way, but Ruth chose to go with her to Judah. It's interesting to read Ruth's famous statement at the request of her mother to go back home: "Don't urge me to leave you or to turn back from you. Where you go, I will go, and where you stay I will stay. Your people will be my people and your God my God. Where you die, I will die, and there I will be buried. May the Lord deal with me, be it ever so severely, if even death separates you and me" (Ruth 1:16-17). Her unwavering decision to stay at Naomi's side is one of the most memorable examples of devotion and love that can be found throughout the Bible.

For Naomi, though she didn't understand it at first, God used Ruth to express His faithfulness. She would not have to be alone because Ruth promised to be with her for the rest of her life. Naomi had suffered a lot. She even wanted to change her name from Naomi (pleasant) to Mara (bitter) (Ruth 1:20). Even amidst sadness and loss, although we may lose objectivity, God doesn't abandon us.

Things changed for Naomi and Ruth so much so that: "The women said to Naomi: "Praise be to the Lord, who this day has not left you without a guardian-redeemer. May he become famous throughout Israel! He will renew your life and sustain you in your old age. For your daughter-in-law, who loves you and who is better to you than seven sons, has given him birth" (Ruth 4:14-15).

Get the class to think of some similar situations that might occur today; such as the child who stays with his ailing father and sacrifices even marriage plans, or the brother or sister who sacrificed their projects in order to help their siblings.

B. God Will Use People And Situations In Adversity

On the return trip, Naomi would no longer be alone, and in the future she would regain her reason to live. No matter how rough the crisis, God always expresses and gives us His blessing. Although Naomi wanted to die, God provided a woman of redeeming human qualities who was able to restore her. Both Naomi and Ruth took risks since Judah was going to be a strange country for Ruth. We can imagine that to engage in this journey toward a new world and a new culture was not easy for Ruth, but her love for her mother-in-law was so great that she was willing to leave her culture, family and religion.

When the journey back had been accomplished, Ruth was able to marry Boaz, a near relative of Naomi. This trip back changed their lives forever and gave them a purpose in God's saving plan. Ruth was a balm to Naomi, an instrument of blessing helping her mother-in-law to regain her self-esteem and the desire to live. Ruth´s baby became king David's grandfather, and Ruth is mentioned in Matthew's genealogy of Jesus. The book of Ruth ends with a lovely scene of Naomi with her grandson on her lap: "Then Naomi took the child in her arms and cared for him. The women living there said, "Naomi has a son!" And they named him Obed. He was the father of Jesse, the father of David" (Ruth 4:16).

Discuss with the class situations or people that God has used to bring blessing in difficult times.

Conclusion

Ruth, full of love, chose to go back with Naomi. They took the journey back and ended up being part messianic lineage.

Additional Information

Ruth and Boaz: "It was spring in Bethlehem during the barley harvest, when Naomi and Ruth returned. Looking for work, Ruth went to glean in the lands of a rich Ephrathite named Boaz, a relative of the family of Elimelek. Boaz showed Ruth great deference, allowing her to eat among them, which was forbidden ... Ruth was a Moabite (Deuteronomy 23:3). He soon fell in love with her. Naomi supported the intentions of Boaz, arranged a marriage under levirate law (Deuteronomy 25:9-10; Ruth 4:7-8). This made it possible for Boaz to redeem the inheritance of Naomi's family and paved the way for his marriage to Ruth" (Explorando el Antiguo Testamento USA, CNP p.150, tr. from Spanish).

Definition of Terms

Levirate Law: "An injunction that if a married man died without children, it was the duty of a brother or other near relative to marry the widow, and the son of the union would be reckoned to be the son of the first husband (Deut. 25:5–10). The law didn't forbid a man to be married twice (Deut. 21:15–17), but it was possible for a brother or kinsman to relinquish his right to marry a widow by taking off his shoe and giving it to a neighbor (Ruth 4:7). Levirate law seems to be presupposed in the dialogue of Matt. 22:23–30 between Jesus and the Sadducees—religious conservatives, who didn't believe the comparatively recent doctrine of resurrection but did acknowledge the authority of the Pentateuch. Jesus argues that life after death is of a different order from that of the present, and the Levirate law doesn't apply to the case cited by the Sadducees. Jesus quotes Exod. 3:6" (http://www.oxfordbiblicalstudies. com/article/opr/t94/e11189).

Additional Activity

Dramatization

Divide the class into groups and ask them to dramatize the story using present day context, expressing the positive and negative aspects of the families' decisions.

Journey With A Surprising Outcome

Zeida Perales Lynch (Argentina)

Lesson 44

Memory Verse: ". . .while he(David) and all Israel were bringing up the ark of the Lord with shouts and the sound of trumpets." 2 Samuel 6:15

Lesson Goal: To challenge the students to obey God and decide to seek divine guidance in every aspect of their lives.

Introduction

Have the students read Exodus 25:10-22 and indicate the Ark's measurements (112.5 cm long with 67.5 cm wide and high, 44.30 inches long by 26.57 inches wide and high). Prepare a drawing of the Ark of the Covenant. Present it to the students and take time to discuss the importance that the Ark was to the people of Israel. (It represented God's presence among them, it was also known as the Ark of the Testimony). Inside the Ark could be found Aaron's rod that budded, the tablets of the covenant, and a golden urn holding manna (Hebrews 9:4).

In order that students can understand the passage being studied, they should review together some previous incidents. Form groups and assign the following Bible passages to each, then ask them to report briefly what happened to the ark.

1. Judges 20:27. During their journey through the wilderness until they settled in Canaan, the Ark had always been with them.

2. 1 Samuel 4:1-11. Israel disobeyed God continually. At one point, they wanted to use the Ark as a talisman to defend themselves from their enemies. In their hearts, there was no true worship of God. For that reason, God allowed the Ark to be taken away by the Philistines.

3. 1 Samuel 7:1-2. When the Ark reached Philistine territory, God showed his power by sending them pests and diseases. The Philistines decided to return the Ark to Israel. After preparing gifts, they hitched the Ark to oxen, and it went to Kiriath Jearim to Abinadab's house. It stayed there for 20 years.

I. David and the Ark

Read with students the passage from 2 Samuel 5:17-25 and then take the following questions you have previously written on cards and have students take one of them. Then ask them to read the question and give the correct answer, starting with question one. Possible answers are in parentheses.

1. Who wanted to make war on David (17-18)? (The Philistines who had stolen the Ark)

2. What was the attitude of David (19)? (To find God's direction for the fight)

3. What was the outcome of the fight (20-21)? (David won the battle)

4. What was the new response of the Philistines (22)? (To continue fighting)

5. What was David's new attitude (23-24)? (To seek God's guidance again)

6. What was the result (24-25)? (The Lord fought for them and David smote the Philistines).

When David inquired of the Lord (19, 23) and followed his instructions (20, 25), God gave him victory over the Philistines. Therefore, it's vital to consult God before making a decision.

2 Samuel 6:1-11 reports that David attempted to bring the Ark to Jerusalem. David made the decision to go with his people to the house of Abinadab (v. 2), to take the Ark of God and bring it to Jerusalem. The new king wanted Jerusalem to be not only the military and political capital but also the religious center of the nation. He decided, therefore, to take the Ark of the Lord, the most sacred symbol that Israel had representing the presence of God, from Baalah (Kiriath Jearim)

to the new capital; David's desire was good. The Ark should be in Jerusalem. That would help the people be closer to God. In 2 Samuel 6:1-5, we can read the preparations they made to carry the Ark.

There were many people, about 30 thousand. They put the ark of God on a new cart (v.3), and two people drove the cart: Uzzah and Ahio, sons of Abinadab (v.3). David and many others were praising God with songs and dances (v.5). Talk to students about the behavior of David. David was grateful to the Lord and wanted to bring the Ark to the capital of his kingdom. There David was very excited, possibly because of his victory over the Philistines.

II. God and the Ark

Remember that the Ark represented the presence of God among the people of Israel. God had given very specific laws regarding how they should lead the Ark and who should do it. One of the requirements was that no one could touch or look inside the Ark (Exodus 25:14-15; Numbers 4:15.20, 7:9).

When David and the whole company came to the threshing floor of Nakon, Uzzah reached out and held the ark because the oxen stumbled. God immediately fulfilled what he had said, and Uzzah was killed in the presence of all (2 Samuel 6:7-8).

Talk to your students about this situation. Ask them what they think about this action of God. At first glance it may seem an unfair action by God, but God is true; He delivers what He promises whether it's reward or punishment. God could have taken care of the Ark even if the oxen had stumbled. His commandment regarding the Ark was that no one should touch it. David didn't consult with God about this journey (2 Samuel 6:1-2). God showed that He was still the God who brought them out of Egypt, and they should remember all that he had told them in the desert. God's demand is for us to be obedient to his mandate. God doesn't want us to worship in our way, but in His way, and this is in spirit and truth.

David felt great sadness at the death of Uzzah. Then he was afraid and said in the second part of verse 9: "How can the ark of the Lord ever come to me?" 'The fear of the Lord' is a common phrase in the Old Testament. It's used to define reverence and deep sense of awe at the bright light of the infinite holiness of God. As a result, David abandoned his plan to bring the Ark to Jerusalem. He decided to send it to the home of Obed-Edom the Gittite, where it remained for three months.

III. A Blessed Journey

2 Samuel 6:12-16a tells us that David brought the Ark to Jerusalem. While the Ark was in the house of Obed-Edom, God had blessed his family. When David heard this, he decided to bring the Ark of the Covenant to Jerusalem. "...So David went to bring up the Ark of God from the house of Obed-Edom to the City of David with rejoicing" (6:12). Verse 13 says: "When those who were carrying the Ark of the Lord had taken six steps" indicating that the Ark was being carried as God had commanded on the shoulders of the priests (Numbers 7:9b).

During the journey to Jerusalem, David offered sacrifices and danced before the Lord because of the joy he felt (13-14). "David was dancing before the Lord with all his might, while he and all Israel were bringing up the Ark of the Lord with shouts and the sound of trumpets" (14-15). Finally, the Ark of the LORD came to the city of David (v.16). This time the trip was blessed by God and there was no cause for sadness, because they had obeyed what God had commanded.

Ask the students what they think we can learn from this story. How are our relationships with God? Are we trying to do things in our own way or are we seeking His advice before making decisions?

Conclusion

We often start to do something like a journey or a project without first talking to God. When He shows us our mistake, we must humble ourselves and wait for His time. When it's the right time, we must obey the specific instructions He gives us in His Word.

Resources

Additional Information

Definition of the Ark of the Covenant

"The Ark of the Covenant was a sacred chest built by the Israelites, under exact specifications given to them by God. It included a pledge by God that he would dwell among his people and give them guidance from the mercy seat on the top of the Ark. Made of acacia wood, the Ark was covered inside and out with pure gold and measured two and a half cubits long by a cubit and a half wide by a cubit and a half high (45" x 27" x 27"). Near its four feet were gold rings, through which wooden poles, also covered with gold, were inserted, for carrying the Ark.

Special care was taken on the lid: solid gold with two hammered gold cherubim, or angels, on it, facing each other, with their wings overshadowing the lid. God told Moses: "There, above the cover between the two cherubim that are over the ark of the Testimony, I will meet with you and give you all my commands for the Israelites." (Exodus 25:22, NIV) God told Moses to place the tablets of the Ten Commandments inside the Ark.

During the Jews' wanderings in the desert, the Ark was kept in the tabernacle tent and was carried by priests of the Levite tribe as the people moved from place to place. It was the most important piece of furniture in the wilderness tabernacle. When the Jews entered Canaan, the Ark was usually kept in a tent, until Solomon built his temple in Jerusalem and installed the Ark there with a solemn ceremony. Once a year, the high priest made atonement for the people of Israel by sprinkling the mercy seat on top of the Ark with the blood of sacrificed bulls and goats. The term "mercy seat" is associated with the Hebrew word for "atonement." The lid of the Ark was called a seat because the Lord was enthroned there between the two cherubim.

The Ark was an important foreshadowing of Jesus Christ as the sole place of atonement for sins. As the Ark was the only place Old Testament believers could go (through the high priest) to have their sins forgiven, so Christ is now the only way to salvation and the kingdom of heaven (http://christianity.about.com/od/glossary/qt/JZ-Ark-Of-The-Covenant.htm).

Definition of Terms

The Idea of Covenant. The term "covenant" is of Latin origin (*con venire*), meaning "a coming together." It presupposes two or more parties who come together to make a contract, agreeing on promises, stipulations, privileges, and responsibilities (http://www.biblestudytools.com/dictionary/covenant/).

Additional Activity

A Race In The Classroom

(Maximum 10 minutes)

Objective: To teach that following orders is important and that we must do them without changing anything.

Have ready some small papers with the following commands written on them: (1) Recite a text of the New Testament just to the teacher; (2) Recite a text of the Old Testament out loud so that everyone can hear; (3) Write the vowels on the blackboard starting with the last one in the Alphabet and writing them from right to left; (4) Sit down in your place, fold your arms be silent.

Development: Form two groups or more depending on the class. Then setup 4 areas or stations and place a person in each one with one of the slips of paper with the written orders. Then explain that each group must pass through each of the stations as listed and do exactly what is asked.

Those responsible for the stations must be strict and give a score of 1 to 10 depending on how accurate they carry out the order asked.

Wait for the last order to be carried out and add up the points for each team to know which is the winning team. Those that didn't win can explain their failures.

Explain that the purpose was not to win but see who followed the instructions best.

Finally explain that it's often difficult to obey the instructions given to us, but if we don't comply we may fall into unknown dangers. We must consult God and accomplish what He asks of us.

A Journey To Restore

Macedonio Daza Chambi (Bolivia)

Memory Verse: "Your people will rebuild the ancient ruins and will raise up the age-old foundations; you will be called Repairer of Broken Walls, Restorer of Streets with Dwellings." Isaiah 58:12

Lesson Goal: To understand that God can use us to be restorers.

Introduction

For many years, God through His prophets admonished the people of Judah for their idolatry; but they chose stubbornly to disobey. Many times God called them to repent, but they wouldn't listen to His voice, despite the warnings of God's warning that Judah and Jerusalem would be destroyed and the people deported to Babylon (Jeremiah 1:14.4:5 -31.25:1-14). 2 Chronicles 36:5-21 tells the story of the desolation of Judah and Jerusalem at the hands of the Babylonians who killed the young people, looted and burned down the house of God, broke down the walls of Jerusalem, burned all the palaces and took captive to Babylon those who escaped the sword. However, along with the warning, God gave them the promise that He would deliver them from their captivity in Babylon after 70 years, and that the city would be rebuilt and restored (Jeremiah 33:4-9). God kept his word. In Ezra 1:1-7, we see that God allowed the return of the remnant of Judah to Jerusalem, and later the restoration process began. Zerubbabel, Ezra and Nehemiah were the three great leaders of the restoration.

Today we'll learn about Nehemiah, whose journey was to restore and rebuild, and whose example can teach us to learn to restore lives and communities. Ask two people to read Nehemiah 2:1-10 with some dramatic emphasis. One of them read can represent Nehemiah, the other the king. After the reading, ask the class to name some characteristics of Nehemiah, and write on the board the fundamental ideas expressed. Then ask the class: What does it mean to restore? Restore means to recover, repair, renovate or relocate a thing to the state in which it was before.

I. The Characteristics Of The Restorer

Nehemiah's name means "comforted by Yahweh." He belonged to a Jewish family that had been deported to Babylon. In the beginning of the story of his book, he worked as the cupbearer of the king of Persia. Nehemiah was a godly Jew, who upon learning of the situation in which the Jews, who had survived the captivity as well as the ruinous situation of Jerusalem (Nehemiah 1:1-12), prayed to God for forgiveness for his people and decided on a restoration plan. We see that Nehemiah:

A. Was Informed Of The Needs Of His People And This Affected His Mood:

1. He was sad (2:1-2).
2. The sorrow of his heart was obvious to other people

B. Was A Person Of Prayer (1:11.2:4).

C. Had A Project to Rebuild the City Walls (2:5) and Had Well-Defined Objectives:

1. Get permission for the work
2. Get resources
3. Make the trip
4. Rebuild the walls of Jerusalem

D. He Seized The Opportunities (2:6A).

1. The queen was with the king. If it had only been the king, he could have rejected him; but since the queen was present, the situation changed. Women are often more sensitive to human needs.
2. He obtained permits to travel freely to reach Judah.

3. He received letters for the forester to obtain some wood.

4. He had a schedule (2:6b).

5. He had a budget; he knew what he needed (2:8); he took advantage of the possible and available resources.

6. He set out on his journey to restore (2:9).

7. He faced opposition and was victorious (2:10).

8. He used teamwork and was a good organizer.

II. He Depended Completely On God

Nehemiah showed his complete dependence on God in a moment where, because of his position, he could have only sought help from others.

A. Nehemiah Was Totally Dependent On God

Once he learned of the needs and problems faced by his compatriots, he prayed to God; then, when he had to express his restoration project to the king, we find him praying again; he prayed for God's direction. Having made his request to the king, he acknowledged that all that he had obtained was through the "good hand of God" (2:8). He didn't attribute his success to his own ability or job position that he had.

B. Results Of His Dependence On God

We can see that his dependence on God helped him in the mission that lay ahead. He obtained from the king: i) permission to be absent from work to travel to Judah to restore the walls of Jerusalem; ii) letters of safe conduct so that he could travel freely and; iii) timber.

"This man of noble spirit," says Adam Clarke, "attributes it all to God." "God favored me," he seems to say, "and influenced the king's heart to do what I wanted." He acknowledged God in it all. He didn't attribute his success to favorable circumstances, nor the opportunity to present his petition, or to the good-natured monarch, or all these things together. Secondary causes don't explain the result. He attributed his success to its true source, God and God alone should have all the glory" (in Beacon Bible Commentary, tr. from Spanish).

III. Application for Today

A. Our God Is Restorer Par Excellence

In the Old Testament after the fall of man, God had a plan of redemption. When His chosen people failed, God sought ways to rescue them. God wants our restoration as well. In the restoration process, the Divine plan has not been a matter of theory or abstraction. God has had to operate continuously even at the price of becoming man and giving His own life. Evangelism cannot be limited to transactions or changes at an abstract level. The Good News brought by Jesus Christ must always have an actual impact on this world.

B. We're Called To Restore

First, like Nehemiah, we must consecrate our lives to God. Ask the students how we can maintain our ongoing relationship with God? Write the responses of students on the board.

We must always be aware of what is happening in the community where we live, and learn to perceive the needs. What can we do to be more aware of what is happening around us? We need to observe, dialogue with different people (police, teachers, and neighbors), listen, read the newspapers, etc.

When we're informed about the needs of the people around us, we'll realize that there are many ruined lives. We must put ourselves in the place of others, following Jesus' example of coming to this world because he loves us. The needs of our neighbor should touch our hearts; we need to be concerned about them; we have a responsibility to influence our generation.

Conclusion

If we put our lives in God's hands, he will help us to be good restorers.

Resources

Additional Information

"Nehemiah personifies a beautiful combination of personal piety and public action. He prayed, and then went to Jerusalem and carried out an urban community development program. He listened to the community and heard they needed a wall. Now the impoverished remnant of Israel didn't only need a wall. They needed to know how to build a wall, and needed instruction and economic development. So, Nehemiah organized the community and put each person to work on a small section of the wall. Since this approach to the process progressed very slowly, Nehemiah toured the place and organized the whole community to build the wall using everyone; everyone got involved. Community organization involves not only the faithful, pious believers. Community organizers also work with non-believers and people of other faiths. Nehemiah operated as a good community organizer. He came, listened to the community and got everyone involved in building that wall" (Raymond Bakke).

The church in all its activities should reflect the heart of God: his passion for the restoration of all things and strategy to speak and act in accordance with the specific context of each situation. The model or highest expression of this was the incarnation of God in history. Therefore, the church cannot limit the proclamation of the Kingdom to mere verbal expressions, but must act alongside those whom they are seeking to bring to the Kingdom. Most situations of injustice, suffering and pain are the result of human activities and structures. Neutrality or passivity is tantamount to complicity or alignment with such structures. If we want to enjoy the privilege of participating in God's mission, it's essential to integrate what we say with what we do, being sensitive to the context of each person and situation in the quest for the restoration of all things! (Miguel De Angulo y Luz Stella Losada, La Restauración de Todas las Cosas).

Definition of Terms

Cupbearer was an officer of high rank with Egyptian, Persian and Assyrian as well as Jewish kings (1 Kings 10:5). It was his duty to fill the kings cup and present it to him personally (Nehemiah 1:11).

Nisan: according to the Jewish calendar, Nisan was the seventh month of the civil and first of the religious year, usually coinciding with parts of March and April.

Additional Activities

1. A Puzzle To Illustrate The Lesson

Show the students a picture of a person, then with scissors cut it into pieces in different shapes, making it into a puzzle. Keep the pieces in the bag without losing any of them. At the appropriate time, give two students the 'puzzle' to restore the picture. Provide a sheet of paper the size of the picture so they can glue the pieces when the puzzle has been solved. Give them a time limit. When they have finished, ask them: What procedure did they follow? Discuss this and then help them to think about the fact that God wants us to be active in helping broken people to be restored through His love.

2. Building Up One Another

(No more than 5 minutes)

Objective: To teach that our comments can also build or destroy.

Get the students to sit in a circle and invite them to say something really nice and positive to the person on their right. For example: 'You're very friendly and have potential to be good servant of God,' 'you're very patient,' 'you can be a good counselor,' etc.

Once everyone has shared with their neighbor, you can ask them how they would feel if the comment had been a negative one. It's possible to destroy people by being negative. As Christians, we must highlight the positive aspects of our brothers and sisters to lift them up and build up their self-esteem.

The Refugees' Flight to Egypt

Lesson 46

Joel Castro (Spain)

Memory Verse: "So he got up, took the child and his mother during the night and left for Egypt ..." Matthew 2:14.

Lesson Goal: To understand that God's desire is to lead in every decision of our lives, and thus protect us from many evils and dangers as we fulfill the divine purpose.

Introduction

We begin now to consider some biblical journeys from the New Testament. Today´s story is about Joseph the carpenter, Jesus' father. He had a lot in common with Joseph of the Old Testament.

1. Both are named in the first book of each Testament (Genesis and Matthew).

2. Both settled in Egypt (Genesis 39; Matthew 2:14).

3. Both had a father named Jacob (Genesis 35:24; Matthew 1:16).

The meaning of the name 'Joseph' in Hebrew is 'God will provide' or 'God will add.' Joseph, the carpenter, was the husband of a dedicated servant of God, and then was the earthly father of our Savior Jesus. The grace of God was on his life. Joseph's life, according to the Gospels, is marked by three journeys he made: from Nazareth to Bethlehem (Luke 2:1-7); from Bethlehem to Egypt (Matthew 2:13-18); and the last from Egypt to Nazareth (Matthew 2:19-23). In these three trips Joseph was directed by God through an angel.

In this lesson, we'll discuss the second journey and see God's answers to the following concerns: Why did the angel of God order him to move? Why did he go to Egypt? What were the results of his journey?

I. Joseph Is Directed By The Voice Of God

It's important to note the degree of spiritual consecration of Joseph. God not only sought a humble, sensitive and consecrated woman like Mary for starting His redemptive work; Joseph was also a responsible and just person. There aren't many records of Joseph's life, but we do know that he was sensitive to God's will. We can see this in what he did.

A. He Was A Just Man

When Joseph learned of Mary's pregnancy, his reaction was not to defame and denounce her publicly, but to do it secretly so as to avoid her having to suffer the punishment demanded by the law of Moses (Deuteronomy 22:23-24). On the one hand, he didn't want harm to Mary (he loved his neighbor); and on the other hand, he wanted to have a blameless life (love for God). God saw the humble and wholehearted Joseph and helped him understand that the baby that Mary was expecting was conceived of the Holy Spirit. Therefore, Joseph obeyed God and took Mary as his wife. Joseph's decision was not easy, but he always put his trust in God.

B. He Was A Brave Man

Matthew tells us that wise men had come from the East to worship the 'King of the Jews' that had been born, and Herod wanted to kill him (Matthew 2:1-12). Therefore, the order God gave to Joseph in a dream was: "Get up, and take the child and his mother and escape to Egypt" (Matthew 2:13). Joseph was a just and upright man, able to discern the voice of God speaking to him at night, even in the midst of his dreams. He woke up and bravely helped his family pack their things and leave as quickly as they could to save their lives (v.14). Joseph knew who the child was since the angel in the previous dream had announced that Jesus would be the Savior of his people. So, Joseph obeyed the command of God and traveled to Egypt.

The devil is very astute; knowing who Jesus was (Mark 1:24b), he tried to kill him while he was still an infant. However, God in His perfect search found a man who fulfilled the role perfectly as the earthly father of the Son of God.

C. He Was A Righteous Man (Matt. 1:19)

Joseph was a man of his word. In him there was no duplicity. His decisions were made with a lot of commitment to do what he knew he had to. Today, God is looking for men and women who, like Joseph, obey Him with responsibility and fidelity. How committed to Christ are we today? Our commitment must be to serve, worship and devote our lives to be used by Him.

The book of Proverbs describes the blessings of the righteous: "Teach the righteous and they'll add to their learning" (9:9); "The Lord doesn't let the righteous go hungry" (10:3); "Blessings crown the head of the righteous" (10:6); From the mouth of the righteous comes the fruit of wisdom" (10:31); "The righteous person is rescued from trouble" (11:8); "The righteous lead blameless lives; blessed are their children after them" (20:7). Joseph as a righteous man was delivered from his enemies and God blessed him on his journey. protecting Joseph and his family.

II. Joseph Was Obedient

Obedience is a virtue that brings good results, and Joseph's life was marked by his obedience to God in everything.

A. He Got Up... (V.14)

The Bible says in Romans 10:17: "Faith comes from hearing the message, and the message is heard through the word about Christ." Faith is put into action when we hear the voice of God through His Word. Just as Abraham, after hearing God's voice, traveled by faith with his family to the Promised Land. Joseph, hearing the voice of God, went to the place where God promised to protect his family.

Surely God protected and cared for them all the way. He had even provided for them though the gift of gold given by the Magi. Joseph had confidence in what God said, and knew that even though they were refugees in a foreign land, God had promised to look after them in this long journey.

Here are some promises that can help us along our personal journeys. As the students read the verses, ask them what it is that God promises in each verse.

Exodus 33:14: He promises his presence and rest.

Isaiah 43:2: He promises to look after us in adversity.

Isaiah 43:5: He promises his company.

Deuteronomy 31:8: He promises his constant care and provision.

Genesis 28:15: He promises to keep us from all evil and to fulfill His purposes in our lives.

God promises us his comprehensive care and his company; but above all, as we see throughout the Bible, He won't abandon us.

B. And Went To Egypt (2:14B)

Many theologians claim that Egypt is synonymous for returning to sin, but this time the flight of Joseph and his family to Egypt was just a safe geographic background. Why did they go to Egypt? It was not as far as Babylon or Persia. There were many Jews there, which meant they could quickly belong to a community (Jeremiah 43:7; 44:1; Acts 2:10). In Egypt, they would be outside the Herod's jurisdiction.

Actually, the trip to Egypt was very hard. They would have had to walk some 250 miles. The journey could well have taken them one or two weeks, and they would have had to cross the desert at the top of the Sinai Peninsula.

C. They Stayed In Egypt Until The Death Of Herod (2:15).

We don't know how long they were there. We do know that this period when they were in Egypt as political refugees saved their lives. Jesus' life was saved so that we can be saved through him. Among the plans of God, everything is perfectly in order.

III. God Has A Purpose For Our Lives

God is a God of purpose. At we take each step in life, He wants to give us advice about how to go forward. In light of the experience of Joseph, we learn that God wants to direct our lives:

A. He Wants To Take Care Of Our Family

Joseph, Mary and Jesus were a very special family. God, through the blood of Christ has made us very special, and He wants us all to be well. There are many testimonies of families who have trusted in God when they have had to immigrate to other countries, and He has guided them and helped them to obtain His blessings in every area of their lives, even though they were living in a different culture.

B. He Wants To Keep Us From Dangers

He stopped Herod from killing the infant Jesus (Matthew 2:13, 16-18). It was very sad that the children of Bethlehem were killed so cruelly (Matthew 2:16-17 cf. Jeremiah 31:15).

Today, there are many modern 'Herods' threatening children. Some children are stolen and sold for adoption, or their bodies used for organ transplants, for child pornography, drug dealing, or child exploitation. They often are in danger at the hands of psychological and physical abusers. Ask the students to comment about this danger that modern children are faced with. Discuss general possible dangers that all family members may face regardless of age.

God protected Joseph's family and He also wants to protect each of us from many dangers.

The psalmist tells us: "The angel of the Lord encamps around those who fear him, and he delivers them" (Psalm 34:7).

Our lives are full of journeys: long trips, short trips, business trips, pleasure trips, complicated trips, routine trips, new trips, special trips, etc. However, if each of these journeys is guided by the Spirit of God, however difficult it might be, it will reap great blessings for our lives and for our families, and most importantly the work of God can be fulfilled.

Conclusion

The Bible tells us the sacrifices that Joseph and his family had to make during their flight and sojourn into Egypt. Although it was not easy, God provided for them and protected them. They were able to fulfill the divine purpose.

Resources

Additional Information

Definition of Terms

Righteous: Morally upright; without guilt or sin; someone who has irreproachable conduct and maintains a good testimony before others.

Herod the Great was the villain in the Christmas story, a wicked king who saw the baby Jesus as a threat and wanted to murder him. Although he ruled over the Jews in Israel in the time before Christ, Herod the Great was not completely Jewish. He was born in 73 B.C. to an Idumean man named Antipater and a woman named Cyprus, who was the daughter of an Arab sheik.

King Herod was a schemer who took advantage of Roman political unrest to claw his way to the top. During a civil war in the Empire, Herod won the favor of Octavian, who later became the Roman emperor Augustus Caesar. Once he was king, Herod launched an ambitious building program, both in Jerusalem and the spectacular port city of Caesarea, named after the emperor. He restored the magnificent Jerusalem temple, which was later destroyed by the Romans following a rebellion in A.D. 70

(http://christianity.about.com/od/newtestamentpeople/a/JZ-Herod-The-Great.htm).

Additional Activity

1. Show the class or draw on the board a map showing Bethlehem, Jerusalem, and Egypt. Point out the distances and the difficult terrain.

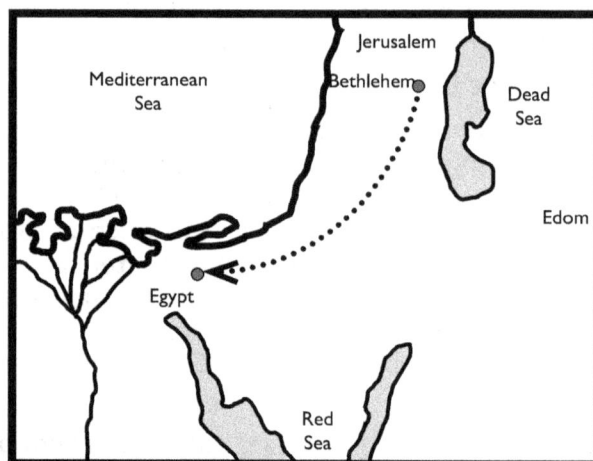

2. Write promises about God's protection on pieces of colored paper and give the students one each. Have them read their promise out loud to the class at the end of your class time.

Promises mentioned in point II A of the lesson (Exodus 33:14; Isaiah 43:2; Isaiah 43:5; Deuteronomy 31:8; Genesis 28:15). Here are some more: Deuteronomy 20:4; 31:6; 33:29; Judges 6:12; 1 Samuel 12:22; Psalms 3:3; 17:8; 46:1; 34:7; 27:1; 9:9-10; 1 Peter 5:7; Isaiah 41:10, 13.

Jesus Travels to the Desert

Lesson 47

Ernesto Bathermy (Dominican Republic)

Memory Verse: "Then Jesus was led by the Spirit into the wilderness to be tempted by the devil" Matthew 4:1

Lesson Goal: To understand that God moves us to do certain things because He has a purpose for our lives.

Introduction

As we study the Bible we can see that when God does anything or sends his servants to perform certain actions, He always has a purpose that He wants to accomplish. And not only does He have a purpose, but He has a holy purpose. For this reason, when God sends us somewhere or shows us something we should do, we must obey without hesitation. In the Old Testament, God told Abraham to leave his land, his kindred and his father's house to go to the land He would give him; and although Abraham didn't know where he was going, God's purpose was to lead him to be the first father of Israel, and from Israel the Messiah, the Savior of the world, would be born.

The evangelist Philip is another good example to help us understand the importance of being guided by God and His Spirit. In Acts 8:26-38, we're told that an angel of the Lord told Philip to go by the desert road without further explanation. He obeyed and his obedience resulted in the Ethiopian eunuch becoming a Christian. Today's lesson will help us see how Jesus obeyed the Holy Spirit by going to the desert, and what was the result of that obedience.

Please read Matthew 4:1-11; Mark 1:12-13 and Luke 4:1-13 in different versions of the Bible for a better understanding of the passage of study. Ask the class to read and make comparisons of these passages and answer the following questions:

Who led Jesus into the wilderness? For what purpose was he led into the wilderness? By who was he tempted? Let them give their opinions.

I. Jesus, the Son of God

Have students read Matthew 3:16-17 and 4:1, and invite them to give their opinions on how being led by the Holy Spirit and the declaration of the Father would have affected the life and ministry of Jesus. Matthew 4:1 begins with the word 'then.' This is very significant because it marks the relationship between Matthew 3:17 and 4:1. Matthew 3:16-17 says, "As soon as Jesus was baptized, he went up out of the water. At that moment heaven was opened, and he saw the Spirit of God descending like a dove and alighting on him. And a voice from heaven said, "This is my Son, whom I love; with him I am well pleased." It's important to note that John was baptizing in the Jordan and Jesus came to be baptized like many other people. However, two things were difference between Jesus and the rest of the people. The first is that the Spirit descended upon Him like a dove, and the second, the statement of the Father. What a wonderful experience! God's desire is that each of your children is to be filled with the Holy Spirit.

A. The Descent Of The Spirit Upon Jesus

The fact that the Holy Spirit came down upon Jesus was clear evidence that He was the Son of God, the promised Messiah. This made Jesus a target for the attack of the enemy. Satan is always opposed to the salvation of mankind. Surely Satan would not sit idly by hearing John's declaration: "Look, the Lamb of God, who takes away the sin of the world!" (John 1:29). His baptism was the starting off point of his ministry.

B. The Statement Of The Father

God spoke out "This is my Son, whom I love; with him I am well pleased" (Matthew 3:16-17; Mark 1:10-11; Luke 3:21-22). This statement declares Jesus as the Messiah. It's important that every Christian is sure of his/her identity as a child of God. This will help us at all times, but especially when we go through times of temptation. Knowing that we're children of God and are filled with the Holy Spirit gives us courage when faced with the temptations of the enemy. That infilling of the Holy Spirit (Luke 4:1) and the declaration of the Father completely marked Jesus' life and ministry.

II. Jesus and His Journey to the Desert

A. What is a Desert?

Ask students to describe the features of a desert. The Bible often speaks of wilderness both literally and figuratively. Literally a desert is a dry place, with not much to eat or water to drink; lonely and in the presence of beasts. Moreover, the Bible speaks of desert figuratively to refer to the difficulties that Christian often must face. Christians sometimes go through situations of drought, famine and spiritual loneliness that come to resemble the difficult times experienced by the people of Israel in the wilderness.

B. The Purpose of Jesus' Journey

Ask students what was the purpose of Jesus' journey into the wilderness. In Matthew 4:1, we're told that "Then Jesus was led by the Spirit into the wilderness to be tempted by the devil." The purpose of being led into the wilderness was to be tempted. Sometimes it's difficult to understand the fact that Jesus was led by the Holy Spirit into the wilderness to be tempted by the devil, but when we read the story of Job (Job 1:6-22), then it becomes more understandable. Have you wondered at some point why God allows you to go through some difficult situations? God has a purpose for which He allows things to happen in our lives.

Why was Jesus tempted? The Epistle to the Hebrews goes further than any other part of Scripture to answer this question. We read about Christ: "For this reason he had to be made like them, fully human in every way, in order that he might become a merciful and faithful high priest in service to God, and that he might make atonement for the sins of the people. Because he himself suffered when he was tempted, he is able to help those who are being tempted" (Hebrews 2:17-18). The last part declares a revealing truth: Jesus suffered while being tempted. It was not a comedy. It was a hard and tough battle. The temptations of Jesus were as real to him as ours are for us, and just as agonizing.

Ask two or three students to define the word 'to try' or 'to tempt'; then explain that the Greek word for tempting is peirazó. It can also be translated as 'try' or 'test.' The biblical concept of temptation doesn't always imply an incitement to sin, but in most cases it refers to the idea of testing the character of a person. So Jesus was led into the wilderness to be tested. Although the intention of the devil was to make him fall, God's purpose was another: to test the strength of his character. We must accept that in our Christian life we'll be tempted, and this will allow God to test the firmness of our character and our maturity in our faith.

III. Results Overcome Temptation

During the temptations in the wilderness, Jesus answered the devil with the Word of God and defeated him. At every temptation he replied, 'It's written ...' citing Deuteronomy 8:3, 6:16 and 6:13 respectively. Matthew 4:11 concludes: "Then the devil left him, and angels came and attended him." Jesus won the victory over temptation.

We saw that the Father's purpose was to test the character of his beloved Son, before He could begin his earthly ministry. Then, after his baptism and having overcome temptation, Jesus was ready to begin his public ministry. Through baptism, he confirmed his decision to take upon himself the sin of the world. He showed that he was worthy, because he triumphed over the devil in the desert. Where Adam, our representative, failed, Jesus was victorious. So now nothing prevented him from performing the assigned task that he voluntarily assumed. Jesus returned to Galilee and lived in Capernaum. Matthew tells us "From that time on Jesus began to preach, "Repent, for the kingdom of heaven has come near" (4:17).

Ask the class: Has God been talking to you in recent months, weeks or days about doing something or going somewhere for Him? What was your answer? Did you say yes to the Lord? Are you struggling with a decision that can affect your relationship with God?

Remind them that when God commands us to go to a place or perform some task, however difficult it may be, it will always be the best for us; and that nothing that keeps us from God or offends him can be good for our life.

Conclusion

Jesus went to the desert in an attitude of obedience, under the guidance of the Holy Spirit, and overcame the temptations. We must resist Satan with the presence of the Holy Spirit in our lives, and use "the sword of the Spirit, which is the Word of God" (Ephesians 6:17) following Jesus' example.

Have you been letting God fulfill His purpose in your life? Reflect on your decisions in recent days. If not, what do you think you should do for God to fulfill His purpose in your life?

Resources

Additional Information

"Corresponding to the Hebrew bahan is the Greek dokimazo. It's used of the testing of buildings (1 Cor. 3:13) and precious metals (1 Peter 1:7), as well as of Christian character (Rom 5:4; James 1:2-3). But by far the most common term in the New Testament is peirazo. This verb expresses the idea of trying in the sense of attempting (Acts 9:26; 26:21), but the overwhelming majority of uses denote the testing of persons (Gal 6:1; Heb 11:17).

Christian believers are encouraged to test themselves (2 Cor 13:5). Sometimes the precise objective is stated: to ensure fitness for the Lord's Supper (1 Cor 11:28) or to distinguish authentic prophetic utterances from unauthentic ones (1 Thess 5:21; 1John 4:1). Second Corinthians 13:5 shows that testing can have a negative outcome even though that is not its intended purpose.

In general, testing and temptation are facts within God's world and constitute some of the tools through which he is bringing to fulfillment his redemptive purpose. Both trials (as revealing and stimulating character and progress) and temptations (understood as allurements to evil) may minister to the divine purpose, provided the outcome is positive (James 1:12). But there's this important distinction: since temptation embodies incitement to evil, it cannot be God's doing (James 1:13). Hence the tendency of the biblical writers is to say that while God sustains his people during testing (Rom 5:3; Rev 3:10), he delivers them from temptation (1 Cor 10:13; 2 Peter 2:9). What is true in the private experiences of individuals is also true in the history of salvation in which the testing of Abraham (Gen 22:1), Israel (Psalm 66:8-12), or Christ (Heb 2:17-18) contributed to the furtherance of God's saving purpose

(http://www.biblestudytools.com/dictionary/temptation-test/).

Additional Activity

"Let's Put It On Paper"

(No more than 8 minutes)

Objective: To make sure that the students understand the term temptation and clarify the concept.

Have some pencils, paper, crayons or colored pencils and tape ready.

Divide the class into two or three groups with not more than five people in each one. Give each group a sheet of paper, pencil and crayons or colored pencils and give them two minutes to express in the form of a drawing what they understand about temptation. Only drawings … no words allowed.

Once they have finished, ask each group in turn to come and stick their art work on the board. The other groups have to try to interpret the drawing of each group. If they don´t explain it correctly, the team who made it should interpret it.

Finally by consensus, make a clear definition of the meaning of temptation.

In the Middle of the Storm

Leonel de León (USA)

Lesson
48

Memory Verse: "But Jesus immediately said to them: 'Take courage! It is I. Don't be afraid'." Matthew 14:27

Lesson Goal: To understand that God always has control of our lives and everything that happens will always have a purpose.

Introduction

Just before the account of what we're going to study today, Jesus fed the five thousand people (Matthew 14:13-21, John 6:1-14). Jesus showed compassion by healing the sick and giving them enough to eat by multiplying five loaves and two fishes. Not surprisingly the people said, "Surely this is the Prophet who is to come into the world" (John 6:14b). After this miracle, Jesus sent his disciples across the Sea of Galilee to Capernaum. During that journey, they learned how to trust Jesus in the midst of the storm.

I. Confronting the Storm

The disciples had just had an extraordinary experience, seeing Jesus multiply the loaves and fishes. This was an act of faith and power. Now they were about to learn another lesson. They were going to need faith and power to be able to accomplish the purpose for which the Lord had called them.

Jesus wanted to be alone to pray "After he had dismissed them, he went up on a mountainside by himself to pray" (Matthew 14:23). The disciples were rowing against the wind and the waves were boisterous. John says "By now it was dark, and Jesus had not yet joined them. A strong wind was blowing and the waters grew rough" (6:16).

When the disciples had rowed about three or four miles, they saw something strange. Someone was coming to them walking on the water, approaching the boat. They were frightened. They may well have been half way across the lake. The disciples had two things to contend with: the sea was very rough and many boats sunk in storms on the Galilean sea, and they were seeing something strange.

What had Jesus been praying for up there on the mountain? Perhaps he was praying that his future leaders would not be sidetracked by

what they had just witnessed. Also according to Matthew, he had just heard about John the Baptist's cruel death (14:12).

The disciples had been beaten by the waves for several hours and were still far from their destination. Matthew tells us "Shortly before dawn Jesus went out to them, walking on the lake" (v. 25). The reaction of the disciples in such a situation was not long in coming. "When the disciples saw him walking on the lake, they were terrified. 'It's a ghost,' they said, and cried out in fear" (v. 26).

Let's look at what was happening. A few hours before, they had witnessed the Lord's power in multiplying the loaves and fishes. Jesus had ordered them to meet him on the other side of the lake. They went obediently because Jesus had sent them. So if everything was under the master's control, why were they terrified?

Fear is sometimes more powerful than faith. Rightly, the Word of God always commands us not to be afraid, but to be brave and to resist. It's understandable then that fear is an obstacle to understanding the Lord. But amid fears we can learn to depend more on Him who loves us and gave himself for us.

II. Jesus' Answer

Jesus knew what they were experiencing at that moment and heard their cry. Immediately, Jesus said to them, "Take courage! It's I. Don't be afraid" (Matthew 14:27). This reply contains three powerful phrases that we can still hear from God and apply to our lives.

A. "Take Courage"

When hopes are weakened due to conflict, then we can hear a beautiful voice saying 'be strong.' When Jesus tells us to be strong and take courage, we can rise above our problems. The presence of the Lord with us will make us brave. Jesus identifies himself with his creatures. He loves us and can accompany us in the storms of life which will come along the way. He is the most precious, holy and loving person who ever lived.

B. "It's I"

It's hard for us to imagine what the disciples were thinking. Matthew suggests that they thought they were seeing a ghost (14:26). When Jesus said "It's I" they knew it was Jesus. People don't walk on water. But Jesus is God. When Moses asked God his name at the burning bush, God said his name was "I am" (Exodus 3). Jesus, the son of God, chose his disciples and guided them step by step, and had given them many proofs of his power and love. The Creator of the universe, the Lord of the storms, the Lord of sea, tells his disciples today "Fear not."

C. "Fear Not"

The presence of the Lord made them secure. Jesus orders them to take courage. They needed to discover that He is their teacher and Lord. Then he assures them that it really is himself and finally he tells them not to fear. In other words, he was telling them that he was in control of the situation; nothing terrible could happen to them while he was with them. They had to discover that he was their Lord, recognize that he was God and trust that he knew what they needed. The disciples were comforted by this short order and their fear changed instantly into joy.

III. The Answer To His Disciple

A. Peter's Faith

Take a moment with the students to carefully read Matthew 28-29. Note that Peter was still not sure that the person they had in front of them was Jesus. Peter, the rather impulsive disciple, conditioned his faith "Lord, if it's you," Peter replied, "tell me to come to you on the water" (v. 28). Jesus replied "come." Peter already knew the power of the Lord, so he asked something he knew no one else could do. The interesting thing was that Peter didn't know that he would have to walk on water to obey this command. Faith is powerful. Jesus confronted many times the disbelief of his disciples.

We always need the teacher's voice to strengthen our faith and trust. But words are not enough. There must be action, courage and determination to meet the challenge. Peter had to leave his area of safety and comfort, had to defy the laws of nature, and to defy his own instinct of survival. There were many factors that were in play for Peter to act. But Peter knew that

if the Master had called him to come, he should believe. Jesus still says "come" to the weary and afflicted. This is a "Come" full of challenge and hope. Obedience is full of surprises.

Peter got out of the boat and literally walked on the water. Until then, Peter was really obeying the call of the Master, and once again he realized that in the name of God everything is possible. "But when he saw the wind, he was afraid" (v.30a). This was the first step to breaking his faith. God never told us that to be brave we'll not be afraid. There any many passages in the Bible that encourage us to be strong and brave. We need to act in spite of fear. Fear with faith makes heroes.

Verse 30 tells us that Peter "beginning to sink, cried out, "Lord, save me!" Was Peter a coward? Or did he have no faith? Peter was brave to face the challenge of walking on water, and fully trusting in Jesus. Ask the students why they think that he started to sink? Talk about our need of constantly depending on God.

Maybe Peter started to think about himself, about his ability (or lack thereof). He seems to have forgotten that the one who ordered him to walk was his teacher. Peter needed to rely all the time on the power of his Master. Verse 31 says, "Immediately Jesus reached out his hand and caught him. 'You of little faith,' he said, 'why did you doubt?'" Discuss with the class the common doubts we have. We need to remember that the Lord will fulfill what he has promised.

B. Our Faith Today

Obedience to God includes experiences that will polish our character and grow our faith. To obey the Lord is to put our lives into His hands, the hands of the divine potter who will shape us. The Lord will always use circumstances to shape our character. While in prison, Paul wrote several letters, reflecting in them about our freedom in Christ. This teaches us a precious principle; Paul talks about freedom in Christ in the midst of being in prison.

Jesus and his disciples did the same; they were free from fear in the midst of circumstances. Peter and Jesus "climbed into the boat, the wind died down" (v. 32). They continued rowing and reached their destination. So they had learned a great lesson: storms are instruments of God to help us to rely on His grace. This experience of the disciples teaches us that when the Lord commands we must obey, no matter how difficult the challenge or dark the road seems to be. He is always in control and knows just when we have learned the lesson.

Jesus had taught a powerful lesson to his disciples! They had seen him multiply the bread and fish, and He had tested their faith in the storm. His disciples not only had seen him do miracles, but had been active participants. The result was that they worshiped him "Then those who were in the boat worshiped him, saying, 'Truly you are the Son of God'" (v. 33).

Conclusion

When we begin to see the dark waves, which could represent today the problems and difficult circumstances we may have to encounter, our faith might fail and we might sink down into despair. For this reason, we must always keep our eyes on Jesus because He is in control.

Resources

Additional Information

Three Lessons From This Story

1. Matthew tells us that "the boat was already a considerable distance from land, buffeted by the waves because the wind was against it. During the fourth watch of the night Jesus went out to them, walking on the lake" (Matthew 14:24–25). Though they were only to travel a short distance, the storm was so violent that despite all their efforts to control their boat, the storm had driven them nearly four miles out into the very midst of the sea. Being the fourth watch of the night (3:00 AM to 6:00 AM), they had been rowing and straining at their oars for approaching nine hours! They were totally exhausted.

2. Mark tells us that when the disciples saw Jesus walking on the lake, they thought He was a ghost. They cried out because they all saw Him and were terrified (Mark 6:48–50). And this brings us to the second significant point of this miracle. Jesus always comes to us in the storms of life. This is reminiscent of the words of God to Isaiah: "When you pass through the waters, I will be with you; and when you pass through the rivers, they'll not sweep over you" (Isaiah 43:2). The Lord may not come at the time we think He should come, because He knows when we need Him the most. Jesus had waited until the boat was as far from land as possible, when all their hope was gone. In essence, Jesus was testing the disciples' faith, and this meant removing every human prop. Why did Jesus walk on the water? To show His disciples that the very thing they feared, the raging, seething sea was merely a set of steps for Him to come to them. Often, we fear the difficult experiences of life such as illness, loss of loved ones, and financial hardships, only to discover that these experiences can bring Jesus closer to us. But we have to ask, why did they not recognize Jesus? The answer is they were not looking for Him. Had they been waiting by faith, they would have known Him instantly. Instead, they jumped to the false conclusion

that His appearance was that of a ghost. The point is this: fear and faith cannot live in the same heart, for fear frequently blinds the eyes to the presence of the Lord.

3. The third significant point is that Jesus proved Himself to be in command of the elements, something only God can do. He revealed this truth to the disciples who recognized His divinity and responded with a confession of faith in Jesus as God: "The wind died down. Then those who were in the boat worshiped him, saying, 'Truly you are the Son of God'" (Matthew 14:32–33). This was the first time Jesus was called the Son of God by the disciples, a statement that, in fact, built on what they had said earlier about Him in Matthew 8:27: "What kind of man is this? Even the winds and the waves obey him." Here they answer their own question: "Truly you are the Son of God" (http://www.gotquestions.org/walking-on-water.html).

Additional Activities

Drama: Time of Terror

Aim: To emphasize the despair one feels when something is uncertain, doubtful and can cause pain or suffering. If it's an especially frightening event, there will be suspense and a lot of insecurity.

Start the lesson by dramatizing a moment of terror (for example a student can enter the class saying that there are thieves in the church or invent something dramatic and believable or ask someone to present a small drama);

Read Matthew 14:22-33 (put as much expression in the reading as possible)

Then compare the drama with what the disciples experienced at sea when the storm caught them. And in the midst of darkness, without hope, and with fear wrecking their lives, they saw someone walking on the water and cried out in terror, thinking he was a ghost.

Ask students how they would feel in such a situation. You can also ask if anyone has experienced a traumatic experience that they would like to share briefly.

Guided Tour Which Led to Blessing

Lesson 49

Eduardo Velázquez (Argentina)

Memory Verse: "For those who are led by the Spirit of God are the children of God." Romans 8:14

Lesson Goal: To learn that God wants to lead us step by step in his will, and when we do we can be a blessing to others.

Introduction

Ask a volunteer to step outside of the classroom for a few minutes. While he/she is not there, make a path around the classroom with a series of objects along the way as guideposts. Bring the students back and put a blindfold on. Ask the rest of the students one at a time to guide him. At the end of the circuit you can have a plate of biscuits or sweets that the class can share. You can ask the volunteer student how he/she felt as they made their way around the classroom.

Take the time to read Acts 8:26-40 in different versions of the Bible with different students reading the passage each time. This will help to broaden the understanding of the text. Begin the class by referring to the game just played, emphasizing the point that God is showing us every step of his plan for us.

The desire of every sincere believer is to please God and do His will. But sometimes we find ourselves in situations we don't know what to do or which way to go. At other times we have to decide between several alternatives pathways forward, we must make a decision, and we wonder what could be God's will for this situation. In this lesson we can see that God doesn't leave us alone on our pilgrimage in the Christian life, but He is eager to guide us and lead us to His perfect will, just as he did with his servant Philip who was brought to an Ethiopian who was a seeker, and contribute to making him a disciple of Christ.

I. A Blind Journey

Philip was a servant of God who had become a Christian in the early years of the church. In Acts 6:1-6 we see that he was elected as deacon. God was also using him in other ministries as we can see from Acts 8:5-6, "Philip went down to a city in Samaria and proclaimed the Messiah there. When the crowds heard Philip and saw the signs he performed, they all paid close attention to what he said." We're told that Philip was evangelizing in Samaria and many were giving their lives to Christ and were being healed.

It's there that God spoke to Philip to go "to the desert road—that goes down from Jerusalem to Gaza" (8:26). We note that God didn't give details - only that Philip had to go exactly to that place. When he arrived there he found an Ethiopian eunuch sitting in his chariot. "The Spirit told Philip, "Go to that chariot and stay near it" (v. 29). He still didn't know why God was telling him to do this.

The Ethiopian was on his way to his land from Jerusalem, where he had been worshiping, and he was reading the prophet Isaiah. In New Testament times, reading aloud was normal, even if one read to oneself. Disrupting this important official, who was in charge of all the treasury of the queen Kandake, Philip was received with remarkable humility and gentleness. Traveling was often long and annoying, and Philip was not this man´s social equal. However, he was invited to come up and sit with him in order to explain what he was reading. The eunuch was reading Isaiah 53 and was prepared to receive Christ into his life.

Sometimes it happens to us in the Christian life and in our relationship with God that certain stages are completed and we must make decisions to start out again on some new adventure. During times like this it's so important to pray to God to guide us. We must realize that God doesn't always give us the big picture of what we must do; however there are certain guidelines that He gives us little by little to understand his will for us. God told Philip to go to the desert road, and when he got there a new guideline was given. Philip went forward obeying God step by step. This is the great adventure of a life of faith and trust in the Lord, which believers are called to live.

II. A Guided Tour

Phillip didn't begin his journey into the unknown on his own; God sent him to this deserted place. On the one hand we see that God used different agents to lead his servant to the Ethiopian: Acts 8:26 says "Now an angel of the Lord said to Philip, "Go south to the road—the desert road—that goes down from Jerusalem to Gaza." In verse 29 we see that "The Spirit told Philip, "Go to that chariot and stay near it." But Philip also understood the will of God by observing the desire and need of the Ethiopian who was reading with interest and curiosity the Word of God. Philip was on a blind journey, with God as his guide. God always has the complete picture of His plan for us, and although He doesn't give us all the details of it, He takes care of us by giving us guidelines so that we can understand His will.

The eunuch was intrigued about who was being described in Isaiah 53. Thus, Philip had a wonderful advantage as he was able at once to announce the gospel of Jesus. The eunuch suggested his own baptism and asked, "Look, here is water. What can stand in the way of my being baptized?" (8:36). Perhaps at another time he had been denied Jewish proselyte baptism (a normal step in the full conversion to Judaism) and this man had lost hope of being baptized. But we see that when we're guided by God, we can come just at the right time and guide people to be part of the body of Christ.

Jesus said on one occasion: "My sheep listen to my voice; I know them, and they follow me" (John 10:27), so God wants us to follow his direction. We also have a sure guide in his Word, which contains the general plan of God for us. In the Bible, the Lord has laid out a blueprint of how to live a good life. He wants us to enjoy life, and points the way to a good relationship with him and with our fellow men and women. He gives us details about how He wants us to serve him and carry out our personal mission, as well as the overall mission of the church. The apostle Paul states in 2 Timothy 3:16-17 that: "All Scripture is God-breathed and is useful for teaching, rebuking, correcting and training in righteousness, so that the servant of God may be thoroughly equipped for every good work."

In the Bible, we find that God has always guided his servants and his people to do His will. Recall for example Moses and the Israelites wandering in the desert, being guided by a pillar of cloud by day and a pillar of fire by night (Exodus 13:21), or the prophet Elijah when he was aided and directed by an angel of the Lord to continue his way to the mountain of God (1 Kings 19:7-8). And in the New Testament, for example, we find the Holy Spirit leading Paul to Macedonia to preach the Word of God there and establish the church in Philippi (Acts 16:6-10).

III. A Journey That Brought Blessing

Philip finally reached the main reason for his journey, he saw the eunuch give his life to Christ (v. 37). This man received Christ as Savior and Lord. Philip baptized and instructed him in the early stages of his Christian life. We might think that the blessings ended there, but many biblical commentators argue that this stranger took the gospel to his homeland where many others came to give their lives to Christ. Maybe he was the first African Christian.

How beautiful it is to think that when we're willing to obey God and follow His direction for our lives, this will result in immediate blessings. How many other people are blessed due to our obedience even if we may never perceive or come to know about it? Best of all, when we act in faith and obedience, God can use us to bless others. This is especially true when it comes to presenting the message of salvation to those who have not recognized Jesus Christ as Savior and Lord of their lives. We don't need an angel of the Lord or the Holy Spirit to show us that this is the will of God, since it's very clear in the Scriptures. When we obey, how many people can be blessed, maybe one person, a family, a city or, why not, on an entire country?

This was the case of a disciple named Ananias, whose story is told in Acts 9:10-19, who obeyed and followed the direction of the Lord to pray for Saul of Tarsus, an archenemy of early Christianity. Ananias, overcoming his fear, went with courage to obey God, and his obedience resulted in the consecration of one of the most outstanding servants of God, the apostle Paul. If we put ourselves in the place of Ananias, I don't think we would have imagined what God could do through this declared enemy, Saul of Tarsus. Small tasks, carried out in obedience to the Lord, show us that however small they maybe, they can bring many blessings to others.

Conclusion

Get the students to stop and think for a moment. Who led them to Christ? And how many people have been influenced through their testimony (family, friends, neighbors, etc.)? Get them to write some names of people and ask the Lord to use them to bless these folk at every opportunity.

Resources

Additional Information

Here are four things that help us understand this Ethiopian dignitary.

1. His Journey's Purpose

We are told in the 27th verse that he had made the long journey for the purpose of coming to worship the God of Israel. Literally this involved coming to the Temple in Jerusalem to offer a sacrifice. This would have taken several weeks each way. For a man in his position as Minister of the Treasury of Ethiopia, this meant the expense of a long journey for not only himself but for his entire entourage. He was a Cabinet Minister to the Queen, and would never travel alone. Travel would likely be by boat and then overland using chariots. At the outset of this narrative, he is returning to his homeland.

2. His Reception Was Proscribed

He finds that on arrival in Jerusalem, he has several strikes against him. First, he cannot actually enter the Temple. No Eunuch was permitted to enter the Temple. Second, he was a Gentile, and at best could have only entered the Court of the Gentiles, but that too was now unattainable. (Deut. 23:1; Lev.22:25) So he couldn't fulfill his objective; to worship God directly, as he had purposed.

3. His Understanding Was Perplexed

The rules and regulations of the Temple Worship had perplexed him, but he had procured a copy of the holy writings upon which so much of the religion was based. It was a copy of the book of the prophet Isaiah, a book that would have taken a scribe a year to write. There were many detailed rules that were required of a scribe to ensure that the book was perfectly copied from a master copy. It must have cost the Eunuch an enormous sum of money. Having invested a small fortune in this book, he commenced to read it as he traveled homewards. Again, he was perplexed as he read this book of Isaiah. He didn't understand what the prophet was saying. He desperately wished for someone to unravel all this mystery.

4. His Heart And Mind Were Persuaded

God, who knew this man's heart, had already decided to intervene. Now God's man Philip was walking the road to Gaza; and the Spirit of God instructs him to join himself to this chariot. The Eunuch was reading aloud, as all the People of Jewish faith are instructed to do from Isaiah 53. Acts 8:32-33 tells us what Philip heard the man read. This was a prophecy concerning the Judgment and Crucifixion of Jesus. Philip asked the Eunuch if he understood what he was reading, and was invited to explain this writing. "He promptly baptized the Eunuch in the water." Philip realized that God had put him there in that place and time to lead this hungry searching man to know the God of Israel and His Son, Jesus the Anointed One (http://globalchristiancenter.com-the-eunuch-of-ethiopia).

Definition of Terms

Ethiopia in the Bible: The country which the Greeks and Romans described as 'Aethiopia' and the Hebrews as 'Cush' lay to the south of Egypt... Shortly before our Savior's birth a native dynasty of females, holding the official title of Candace (Plin. vi. 35), held sway in Ethiopia, and even resisted the advance of the Roman arms. One of these is the queen mentioned in Acts 8:27. (http://www.bible-history.com/geography/maps/map_nubia.html).

Eunuch: a castrated man, especially one formerly employed by rulers in the Middle East and Asia as a harem guard or palace official (http://www.dictionary.com/browse/eunuch).

Additional Activity

Discussion Groups

Form groups of four or five students and give them 5 minutes to discuss about other ways, other than those that were studied in this lesson, that God uses to guide His children. They may use biblical examples as well as their experiences of knowing and following God's direction. Each group can report back and you can summarize what everyone has shared. This activity also serves to detect and correct any misconceptions on the part of students as to how God directs us.

Jesus Meets Saul on the Road to Damascus

Lesson 50

Osmel Pozo (Cuba)

Memory Verse: "'Who are you, Lord?' Saul asked. 'I am Jesus, whom you are persecuting,' he replied. 'Now get up and go into the city, and you will be told what you must do'." Acts 9:5-6

Lesson Goal: To learn that life is a journey of constant change and that we must be willing to re-orient our lives around the plans and purposes of God.

Introduction

In the Bible we find the stories of many characters who traveled with a purpose, and these trips forever changed their lives. Ask students if they can name a few. For example: Abraham traveled to see the Promised Land and took possession of it; Jacob traveled fleeing from his brother because he had cheated his brother of the first-born rights and inheritance, and also to get a wife from the family of his mother; Moses traveled to liberate God's people from slavery to which they were subjected; Jonah traveled to escape the presence of the Lord and not preach in Nineveh. But one of the most amazing journeys was that of Saul.

I. A Wrong Start

Who was Saul and what was the purpose of his journey? This character was a tireless traveler, nothing stopped him, neither storms nor dangers or threats; nothing made this man give way in his mission.

Saul was a Jew of the tribe of Benjamin (Philippians 3:5), a native of Tarsus, with Roman nationality and fluent in several languages. He belonged to the group of the Pharisees and the Sanhedrin (Acts 26:10). He studied in Jerusalem at the feet of Gamaliel, one of the most prominent Pharisees of his time. His profession was to make tents (Acts 18:30).

The apostle Paul (as he was called after his conversion) commented in Philippians 3:7, "But whatever were gains to me I now consider loss for the sake of Christ." This impressive phrase reveals a change of purpose and life.

Read Acts 9:1-12 with the class. Luke tells how Saul began in the Christian faith, what the purpose of his first journey was and how God changed him. He went to Damascus with his mind set on destroying the Christians, but ended up being one himself.

A. Journey to Damascus

Damascus was a city of Syria on a plateau watered by the Abana and Pharpar rivers (2 Kings 5:12). This region was a vast oasis with converging routes to and from Egypt, Arabia and Baghdad. Saul was a Pharisee belonging to the Sanhedrin, who went to Damascus to carry out a very important task in his view: to persecute Christians, or as they were called at the time 'those of the Way' (Acts 9:2). Following the death of Stephen, a follower of Jesus, Saul had unleashed severe persecutions on the followers of Jesus.

B. Journey With a Wrong Purpose

Acts 9:2 tells us that Paul asked for a letter from the principal leaders of Jerusalem to have authority to persecute the Christians in Damascus, imprisoning them and bringing them to Jerusalem for trial. The Christians at this time were of Jewish origin, since the gospel had not yet been preached to the Gentiles. For this reason the letter was addressed to the synagogues in Damascus. Saul was sure he was doing the right thing, but soon realized that his purpose was not God's purpose. He was on the wrong track. We too need to analyze our lives from time to time. Is what we're doing in line with the divine plan?

II. An Unexpected Encounter

A. The Persecutor Was Found

Saul was about to accomplish his goal. He was near Damascus when what happened was what he least expected; while trying to erase the name of Jesus he was forced to have an appointment with him. It was around noon (Acts 22:6) when a light more intense than the sun surrounded them, and they all fell to the ground (26:14). Then later, the apostle described it as 'the glory of God' (22:11). Who can remain standing before the glorious manifestation of God? All pride, all vanity and all human strength fade before his majestic presence.

B. Reasons And Results Of That Meeting

The text suggests some of the reasons for that meeting:

1. Paul needed to acknowledge the reality of the folly of persecuting God. "He fell to the ground and heard a voice say to him, "Saul, Saul, why do you persecute me?" "Who are you, Lord?" Saul asked. "I am Jesus, whom you are persecuting" (Acts 9:4-5).

2. He needed to know that Christ was not a fallacy as he supposed, "I too was convinced that I ought to do all that was possible to oppose the name of Jesus of Nazareth" (Acts 26:9-11). But Jesus was real and had risen (9:5).

3. He needed to experience Jesus before he could stop making people suffer for their faith (9:16).

Saul gave himself up in total surrender. Jesus said to him: "Now get up and go into the city, and you'll be told what you must do" (9:6). Meeting with Christ will result in a changed attitude and total dedication; every believer must be willing make him Lord of their lives.

III. Paul Had To Wait

A. His Task Did Not Begin Immediately

He was told to get up, go to the city, and that there he would be told what to do. Like the disciples before the day on Pentecost, he had to wait (Acts 1:4-5). Paul's waiting lasted three days, and to top it off, he had a physical limitation, he couldn't see. When Ananias came to Simon's house, where he was staying, he said, "Brother Saul, the Lord Jesus, who appeared to you on the road as you were coming here, has sent me so that you may see again and be filled with the Holy Spirit" (Acts 9:17). The delay had a purpose: Saul was filled with the Holy Spirit and thus, like the apostles, could testify with power from on high

B. While The Answer Comes

What did Saul do while waiting? The text says he fasted and prayed for three days. While this was happening, a disciple of the Lord whose name was Ananias was receiving in a vision the command of God Himself (v.10-14) to visit Saul, and the emphasis of this visit was his prayer life; "for he is praying" (v.11b). Saul knew he had to wait, but decided to do it the best way: seeking the face of the Lord, praying until the obstacle (his blindness) was removed (v.12).

What should we do until we have clear answers? There are many ways to deal with waiting, but the best of them was taken by Saul - to pray.

IV. A New Direction and Call To Travel

A. The Answer Came In Its Own Time

The man who was praying was not wrong, God sent his disciple and through him, healed him, filled him with his Spirit, and gave a new meaning to his life. Acts 22:16 tells us that Ananias told Saul: "And now what are you waiting for? Get up, be baptized and wash your sins away, calling on his name." The response was immediate; God healed him physically and spiritually. There's no sin that God cannot remove. Saul, the persecutor of Jewish Christians who were just a small group in a small nation, received a much more important mission:

1. He had had an encounter with the risen Lord. Paul testifies that Ananias told him "'Brother Saul, receive your sight!' And at that very moment I was able to see him." Then he said: 'The God of our ancestors has chosen you to know his will and to see the Righteous One and to hear words from his mouth" (Acts 22:14).

2. He was to be God´s instrument to reach the gentiles. "But the Lord said to Ananias, 'Go! This man is my chosen instrument to proclaim my name to the Gentiles and their kings and to the people of Israel'" (Acts 9:15).

3. He would be a witness for Jesus and would suffer for him. "Jesus said to him 'You will be my witness to all people of what you have seen and heard.' (Acts 22:15) 'I will show him how much he must suffer for my name'" (Acts 9:16).

B. An Urgent Response To God's Plan

The persecutor became an apostle of Jesus Christ, and he testified before King Agrippa of what Christ had done for him and for mankind (Acts 26:19-20). Saul the persecutor became Paul the apostle. Everything in his life had changed because, as he himself said, narrating his conversion to Agrippa, "I was not disobedient to the heavenly vision." We learn through many passages of scripture that Paul became a tireless preacher of the gospel and visited more cities than all the other apostles combined (2 Corinthians 11:23)

How many of us know what we have to do (Matthew 28:19-20) and have been disobedient to the heavenly vision? Acts 9:20 tells us "At once he began to preach in the synagogues that Jesus is the Son of God." 'At once' indicates Paul's urgency. He began preaching in Damascus, then he went to Jerusalem and finally to the Gentiles. Paul had to make significant changes in his life, and although he had a wrong start, he had a glorious ending. His encounter with Jesus gave a new meaning to his life. In one of his letters to one of his collaborators, the beloved Timothy, he said: "For I am already being poured out like a drink offering, and the time for my departure is near. I have fought the good fight, I have finished the race, I have kept the faith. Now there's in store for me the crown of righteousness, which the Lord, the righteous Judge, will award to me on that day—and not only to me, but also to all who have longed for his appearing" (2 Timothy 4:6-8).

Conclusion

Ask the students to think about their lives. Do they have it all planned out? The Christian life is a journey of constant changes, and we must be willing to re-orient our lives around the plans and purposes of God.

Resources

Additional Information
Definition of Terms

Gentiles: The word Gentile is an English translation of the Hebrew word goyim ("people, nations") and the Greek word ethne ("nations, people groups, people"). The Latin Vulgate translated these words as gentilis, and this word was then carried over into English as "Gentile." The term refers to a person who is not a Jew.

Paul was a Greek-speaking Jew from Asia Minor. His birthplace, Tarsus, was a major city in eastern Cilicia, a region that had been made part of the Roman province of Syria by the time of Paul's adulthood. Two of the main cities of Syria, Damascus and Antioch, played a prominent role in his life and letters. Although the exact date of his birth is unknown, he was active as a missionary in the 40s and 50s of the 1st century A.D.. From this it may be inferred that he was born about the same time as Jesus (c. 4 BC) or a little later. In his childhood and youth, Paul learned how to "work with [his] own hands" (1 Corinthians 4:12). His trade, tent making, which he continued to practice after his conversion to Christianity, helps to explain important aspects of his apostleship. He could travel with a few leather-working tools and set up shop anywhere. He was converted to faith in Jesus Christ about AD 33, and he died, probably in Rome, circa A.D. 62–64.

Of the 27 books in the New Testament, 13 are attributed to Paul, and approximately half of another, Acts of the Apostles, deals with Paul's life and works. Thus, about half of the New Testament stems from Paul and the people whom he influenced. Paul was one of the leaders of the first generation of Christians, often considered to be the second most important person in the history of Christianity (condensed from Britannica.com).

The Sanhedrin was composed of religious leaders of the Jews; it was the body of supreme authority in religious matters in New Testament times.

Additional Activities
Where Do You Want To Go?

At the beginning of the class, get out a world map and divide the class into three groups; each group with a leader. Give five minutes for each group to choose the site of the world where they want to go if given the opportunity.

Then ask them why they want to travel to their chosen part?

Did the biblical characters who made journeys away from their homes always know where they were going or why they were on the road?

An Excellent Traveling Companion

Lesson 51

Moisés Champo (USA)

> **Memory Verse:** "For the Spirit God gave us does not make us timid, but gives us power, love and self-discipline." 2 Timothy 1:7
>
> **Lesson Goal:** To understand that God often sends his messengers to unexpected places for the benefit of his work.

Introduction

Many people have made memorable trips. Ask one or two students to share briefly where they have traveled to and what was their purpose in doing so. In preparing the lesson you can find photos of the places you yourself have traveled to. There are different types and reasons for travelling, such as to explore, to conquer, for fun, to learn about other cultures, business trips, evangelistic trips, mission trips and imaginary journeys. But they all have their characteristics, their risks and their purposes.

Ask students for a moment to close their eyes and imagine a trip to a place they dream about or would like to go to if they had the opportunity. Where did they get to in their dreams?

I. An Ideal Travel Companion

Mark Twain said, "If you want to know a person, travel with him/her." Who was Timothy? Timothy was an excellent travel companion to Paul (Acts 17:14; 18:5; 19:22; 20:4). Some commentators consider that Timothy cared for Paul's health. He was also his secretary since his name is mentioned as co-writer of seven of Paul's letters. Through his multicultural background, both as a Greek and as a Jew, Timothy had an adaptable character, an important resource for communication with other cultural groups. He was a young traveler with a great physical strength to withstand the rigors of travel.

To study Timothy means addressing the challenge of bringing the gospel to many places and many other cultural and linguistic groups. Think of the need to evangelize different groups of people in your community: poor, rich, politicians, people of different ethnicities, etc. Surely in our immediate community there are challenges to meet the evangelistic goal. Ask the students if they are willing and who are the people who are well prepared for this task.

A. Traveling With A Believer

Timothy was a believer. His name Timothy means 'God-fearing.' He was the son of a Greek father and Jewish mother who was also a believer. Timothy was a faithful disciple of Christ. For Paul, it was important to travel with someone who could share his faith; this would help in any eventuality during the entire trip. Timothy was someone who believed in God's protection when they met dangers on the road; a partner who believed in the miracles that God can do to impact the lives of unconverted. Timothy proved to be that excellent companion.

B. Timothy Had A Good Christian Testimony

"The believers at Lystra and Iconium spoke well of him" (Acts 16:2). In the Work of God, you cannot or shouldn't take risks with your reputation. Paul couldn't allow his own reputation to be damaged. The popular proverb says, "Tell me who your friends are and I'll tell you who you are." Paul was careful in his associations, but Timothy gave him the guarantee of a good testimony. The apostle's life was in sight of everyone, so he wanted to eliminate unnecessary risks.

II. Prepared For The Travel

A. Cultural Alertness

Timothy was the son a Jewish mother, Eunice, and Greek father. Timothy had a very important advantage for those times which is increasingly important today, that is, understanding cultures and being informed of what is happening in the world. Today's global society demands it. When we travel we face different cultures. Not only

161

when we're visiting other countries or distant places but also when we talk about different groups within our own cities and countries.

B. Timothy's Education And Skills

Paul needed a traveling companion who could offer a variety of resources to ensure the success of the trip, taking into account that Paul was engrossed in such a broad mission. Something as insignificant to us today as literacy was of great value to Paul. This speaks to the intellectual abilities of Timothy.

You can discuss the importance of education in Christianity. Timothy's good testimony and affability would make him acceptable among those from other cultures. You can discuss the importance of Christian morality in a debauched world.

C. Important Details for the Missionary Journey

Because of the Jews, Paul circumcised Timothy. The case of the circumcision of Timothy has been subject to various interpretations and debate. However, Paul realized its importance as Timothy was the son of a Jewish mother. Surely they would find on their journeys Jews accustomed to the cleansing rituals required by all Jews. Even in this Paul wanted to avoid being a stumbling block. Although there's no direct parallel to circumcision, for us today it is also important to maintain healthy habits that prevent murmurings, such as being baptized, being a member of a local church, giving our tithes, etc. Although these practices could be identified as having only an external value, complying can make the difference between people rejecting or accepting the gospel.

III. Itinerary And Purpose Of The Missionary Journey

A. Timothy Accompanies Paul And Silas

When Paul and Barnabas went their separate ways (Acts 15:36-41), Paul began his second missionary journey and came to Lystra where he met Timothy and took him to replace John Mark (Acts 16:1-3). When Paul struggled in Thessalonica and Berea, Timothy stayed there with Silas while Paul moved to Athens (Acts 17:1, 10, 14). They met up again in Corinth (18:1, 5) and went together to Ephesus, where he was sent with Erastus to Macedonia (19:22). Finally, he appeared among those who accompanied Paul to Asia (20:4) on the trip to Jerusalem (21:17).

B. The Purpose Of His Travels

- Timothy was sent to Thessalonica to confirm believers (1 Thessalonians 3:1-6).

- He was the personal messenger of Paul to Corinth with a delicate mission. Paul affectionately recommended him (1 Corinthians 4:17, 16:10) and exhorted the Corinthians to send him back in peace (16:11).

- He was sent to strengthen the Gentile churches (Philippians 1:1; Colossians 1:1-2; Philemon 1:1). Timothy was one of those who worked hard to build up the Gentile churches. In Philippians 2:19, Paul expressed the desire to send Timothy to them soon so that he could get a direct report on the state of the Philippian church. Paul highlighted the genuine interest that Timothy had for believers (Philippians 2:20-23).

- Paul left Timothy in Ephesus to make sure that certain people didn't try to teach false doctrines any longer (1 Timothy 1:3). Timothy was sent to teach sound doctrine (1 Timothy 4:6-16, 6:14, 20-21).

- When Paul was imprisoned again, Timothy went to Rome, but we don't know the exact date of arrival. We only know that Timothy himself was a prisoner (Hebrews 13:23).

Paul had confidence in Timothy and was able to rely on him. This young man was in God's hands so Paul didn't hesitate to leave the church in his hands and send him to different places.

Conclusion

Comment with the students that we're all participating in a journey of faith, which is both challenging and wonderful. God sent us all on a defined mission: to bring the Gospel to the nations. As God sent him away from his city, are we ready to go too? Do we have the resources? Do we have enough faith to succeed?

Resources

Additional Information

Timothy, Paul's spiritual Son (2 Timothy 2:1), became his companion and assistant (Philippians 2:19-22). He was born in Lystra. His mother, Eunice, was a Jewish Christian and he had a Greek father (Acts 16:1; 2 Timothy 2:5). He became a Christian in Paul's second journey. He witnessed the sufferings of the apostle (2 Timothy 3:11). Paul mentions him as coauthor of several of his letters (1 Thessalonians 1:1) and wrote two personal letters to him (First and Second Timothy). Paul describes him as a servant of God in the gospel, with some prestige among the apostles (1 Thessalonians 2:6, 3:2). The letters of the Paul's captivity have Timothy as his faithful companion and collaborator. The Pastoral Epistles, written by Paul to Timothy, present a more complete picture of his personality. He was very emotional, and a little bit shy (2 Timothy 1:4.7). He needed personal admonitions from Paul. None of Paul's companions was so ardently praised for his loyalty (Philippians 2:21). Timothy was sent to Ephesus where he developed an extensive ministry, he became the chief bishop and it was there that tradition says he was martyred in 97 A.D. It's believed that 2 Timothy was the last book written by Paul in 66 A.D.

Additional Activities

Looking For A Companion To Go On A Mission Trip

Before starting the class, ask students to list the features you would expect from a person who could accompany them on a missionary journey to proclaim the gospel. Write a list on the board with input from students.

Geographic Location

1. Find a map of Paul's journeys (often to be found in the final pages of the Bible). Talk about the distances, places, geographical challenges and logistical difficulties that needed to be overcome.

2. Locate the places where Timothy accompanied him.

3. Find a map of your locality where the church needs to share the gospel.

Traveling With A Purpose

Martha de Bradna (Guatemala)

Memory Verse: "And without faith it is impossible to please God…" Hebrews 11:6a

Lesson Goal: To help students understand that God has a specific purpose for our lives and that He wants us to obey His Word in every step we take.

Introduction

In this quarter we have studied twelve journeys that several biblical characters took; in different dates and contexts, but with similar characteristics in the way they were called and their response to the call. All those journeys had a purpose according to the divine plan and therefore had blessed results.

I. God's Call

A. How Were They Called?

God used diverse circumstances and events to call his servants. To some people, He spoke directly; to others, through dreams; or through angels or through other people.

1. *God Called Some Directly*

- God spoke to Abraham saying, "The Lord had said to Abram, "Go from your country, your people and your father's household to the land I will show you" (Genesis 12:1).

- The Angel of the Lord appeared to Moses in a flame of fire in the middle of a bush. When Moses realized who God was, God said, "So now, go. I am sending you to Pharaoh to bring my people the Israelites out of Egypt" (Exodus 3:10).

- Jesus himself sent the disciples on a journey across the Sea of Galilee (Matthew 14:22)

- Jesus spoke to Paul on the road to Damascus:"Saul, Saul, why do you persecute me?" (Acts 9:4) …"Now get up and go into the city, and you'll be told what you must do" (9:6).

- Jesus was led into the wilderness by the Holy Spirit to be tempted (Matthew 4:1).

2. *God Called Through Angels*

- An angel of the Lord appeared in a dream to Joseph (Mary's husband) and said, "Get up," he said, "take the child and his mother and escape to Egypt. Stay there until I tell you, for Herod is going to search for the child to kill him" (Matthew 2:13).

- An angel of the Lord spoke to Philip, saying, "Go south to the road—the desert road—that goes down from Jerusalem to Gaza" (Acts 8:26).

3. *God Calls Through Other People*

- In the case of Barak, God used Deborah to give him God´s message. Deborah told him "The Lord, the God of Israel, commands you: 'Go, take with you ten thousand men of Naphtali and Zebulun and lead them up to Mount Tabor. I will lead Sisera, the commander of Jabin's army, with his chariots and his troops to the Kishon River and give him into your hands'" (Judges 4:6-7).

- Ruth was probably touched by Naomi's story and was willing to leave her village, her family and her gods to go with Naomi to Bethlehem.

- What happened to David? David wanted to bring the Ark of the Covenant to Jerusalem, the capital of his kingdom. The first time he tried he was not able to do it because he had not followed the instructions given by God, and Uzzah died. So David sent the ark to Obed Edom's home. Three months later, "Now King David was told, "The Lord has blessed the household of Obed-Edom and everything he has, because of the ark of God." So David went to bring up the ark of God from the house of Obed-Edom to the City of David with rejoicing" (2 Samuel 6:12).

- As for Nehemiah, God used people who reported the condition of the remnant of the captivity and the destruction of Jerusalem. Nehemiah prayed for his people and God put in his heart the desire to travel to Judah to restore Jerusalem.

- God called Timothy to the ministry through the apostle Paul, as he chose him as his traveling companion (Acts 16:1-5).

II. The Answers To God´S Call

The common response of these characters was obedience to God's call. Each call of God had specific conditions, but they all reacted in total obedience. Some like Abraham obeyed immediately (Genesis 12:4). Joseph acted as soon as he woke up (Matthew 2:14). Phillip got up and went to the place that the angel had indicated (Acts 8:27). Paul obeyed the voice of Jesus by going to Damascus (Acts 9:20). Ruth said: "Your people will be my people and your God my God" (Ruth 1:16b). And she went with Naomi.

David was determined to bring the Ark from Obed-Edom's home to Jerusalem obeying God's instructions (1 Chronicles 15:2.12-15). Nehemiah also obeyed God's call, he asked for His direction, and with the support of the king of Persia, traveled to Jerusalem. The disciples traveled across the Sea of Galilee, as Jesus commanded them, even though it was night. Timothy accepted God's call to ministry, and following Paul.

Our greatest example of obedience is Jesus. He went to the desert in an attitude of obedience, under the guidance of the Holy Spirit, and overcame the temptation. It was "obedient unto death, even death on a cross" (Philippians 2:8).

Both Moses and Barak obeyed, but not immediately. At first, Moses objected to the divine call. He saw his own inability and the impossibility of the task (Exodus 3:11).

Barak didn't obey when God called him the first time. Deborah had to call him and repeat the command of God. He agreed to go into battle if Deborah went with him (Judges 4:8).

III. The Purposes Of God's Call And The Results

A. The Purposes Of God´S Call

God has always had a specific purpose for each call.

1. Salvation

- Abraham was called to form the nation of Israel, from which the Messiah would be born. This call was meant to test his faith and obedience. Abraham believed God, and it was counted for righteousness (Genesis 15:6).
- Joseph was called to protect and preserve the life of Jesus when Herod wanted to kill him.
- God sent Philip to bring the gospel of salvation to the Ethiopian.
- In the case of Paul, although he traveled to Damascus with the wrong purpose, God intended to save him and choose him as an apostle to the Gentiles.

2. Liberation

- Moses was called to deliver his oppressed people out of the hand of the Egyptians and lead them out of Egypt to the Promised Land.
- God called Barak to deliver Israel from the oppression of Jabin, king of Canaan, which had lasted twenty years.

3. Restoration

- Although Naomi wanted to forget about everything in her suffering, God provided Ruth, a woman of redeeming human qualities and restorer. Her unwavering decision to stay at her side is one of the most memorable samples of devotion and love that can be found throughout the Bible.
- Nehemiah was a man used by God to restore Jerusalem.

4. The Ark of God

- Because the Ark of the Covenant symbolized the presence of God in Israel, David wanted to bring the Ark to Jerusalem.

5. Strengthen Faith

- Jesus commanded his disciples to go across the sea because he wanted to keep them away from people who wanted to make him king (John 6:15; Matthew 14:22). Perhaps it was mainly because Jesus wanted to be alone in communion with his Father, and also for the disciples to learn to recognize Jesus and trust Him in the midst of the storm.

6. Find A Fellow Traveler

- Paul took Timothy and took it with him.

7. Being Tested

- Jesus was led into the wilderness in order to test the firmness of his character before beginning his ministry.

B. The Results Of God´s Call

- Abraham was the patriarch of Israel, through whose line which the Messiah came.

- Joseph delivered Jesus from the death at the hand of Herod. Later, Jesus gave his life for us resulting in the salvation of humanity.
- The result of Philip's journey was the salvation of the Ethiopian.
- The result of Paul's call was totally unexpected and contrary to his personal purpose of going to Damascus. Paul gave himself totally to Jesus, changed his purpose and life, and was the apostle to the Gentiles (Ephesians 3:1-8).
- Moses was the liberator of the people of Israel out of Egypt and he guided them to the Promised Land.
- When Barak obeyed, God brought about the victory of Israel and the destruction of Jabin.
- Ruth knew the true God and became part of the Messianic line. In addition, Naomi was restored.
- Nehemiah rebuilt the walls of Jerusalem and reorganized the Jewish people.
- When David followed God's instructions, he could fulfill its purpose of bringing the ark to Jerusalem.
- The disciples learned to recognize Jesus and trust Him in the midst of the storm. And they worshiped Jesus.
- Timothy became a faithful companion and collaborator of Paul, his personal messenger and coauthor of several Pauline epistles. He was sent to strengthen the Gentile churches, becoming a leading pastor.
- Jesus was tested, overcame temptation and thus was prepared to do his ministry. He succeeded as our representative where Adam had failed.

IV. What Can We Learn?

A. Faith And Obedience

As we have seen, God called different people at different times and places, in different ways and with specific purposes. Through these stories, God presents some important lessons to us.

The way to implement our faith is through obedience. The results of obedience are the blessings of God. To achieve victory is to obey; we need to get up and make the decision to act. Obedience to God is total surrender to his will, and therefore obedience and faith are closely related (Genesis 15:6; 22:18; Romans 10:17).

When in an attitude of obedience, we must let God's Spirit lead us. We can count on His support at all times. We always need the teacher's voice to strengthen our faith and trust. With our faith and obedience, we bless others whom God also wants to reach with his blessing, especially when we share the message of salvation to those who have not recognized Jesus Christ as Savior and Lord of their lives.

B. Putting God First

We must consult God before making a decision, and obey his commands. Before performing a task, we must seek God's direction.

C. God Is In Control

God is always in control of our lives and everything that happens to us always has a divine purpose.

D. Other Valuable Lessons

- When the Lord calls, we must obey, no matter how difficult seems the challenge, or however dark the road seems to be.
- We must overcome the temptation using the Word of God, as Jesus gave us an example.
- Storms are instruments of God to help us rely on His grace.
- Just like Nehemiah, we must also plan, organize, implement and evaluate what God commands us to do.
- We must determine if our dreams and personal projects are part of God's plan for our lives.
- No matter how rough the crisis may be, God will always reach us with His blessing.
- God wants us to depend on Him for every action we take.
- Paul's answer should always be in our mouth; Lord, what do you want me to do? (Acts 9:6)
- We constantly need to analyze our lives, our motives, our purposes in terms of the way we're serving God. We need to know if we're living our lives according to his will.

Conclusion

When God sends his servants to perform certain actions, there's always a purpose. Each call of God has specific conditions, but they all require complete obedience. All Christians are participating in a journey of faith, which is challenging and wonderful; it's a journey with a defined mission - to bring the Gospel to the nations. Are we living in obedience?